THE TEACHER:

OR

MORAL INFLUENCES

EMPLOYED

IN THE INSTRUCTION OF THE YOUNG.

INTENDED CHIEFLY TO ASSIST YOUNG TEACHERS IN ORGANISING
AND CONDUCTING THEIR SCHOOLS:

BY JACOB ABBOTT,

PRINCIPAL OF MOUNT VERNON SCHOOL.

REVISED

BY THE REV. CHARLES MAYO, LL. D.

LATE FELLOW OF ST. JOHN'S COLLEGE, OXFORD.

LONDON:
PUBLISHED BY L. B. SEELEY AND SONS,
AND R. B. SEELEY AND W. BURNSIDE.

1834.

CONTENTS.

Preface. iii

CHAPTER I.
Interest in Teaching. 1

CHAPTER II.
General Arrangements. 24

CHAPTER III.
Instruction. 67

CHAPTER IV.
Moral Discipline. 118

CHAPTER V.
Religious Influence. 170

CHAPTER VI.
The Mount Vernon School. . . . 195

CHAPTER VII.

SCHEMING. 242

CHAPTER VIII.

REPORTS OF CASES. 269

APPENDIX. 320

PREFACE.

Suppose an intelligent parent to have launched his eldest son into active life. After a considerable interval, during which the youth has been thrown into a variety of situations, and mixed with different classes of society, he revisits the scenes of his childhood. Time has produced some changes in his father's person, but not much in his opinions. The views of life which his son brings forward, he hears with astonishment and not without distrust. They are so much at variance with his own impressions in earlier years, that he cannot but question their correctness. Yet they refer to a state of society so new to him, that he feels he must familiarize his mind with the circumstances before he can be satisfied with the impartiality and the correctness of his judgment. And when, at last, after repeated conversations with his son, after some dispute, and some explanation, his mind settles in certain conclusions, he finds that the current of time has swept away some things that he cannot doubt were good, and some that he must acknowledge were evil; he regrets a few changes which he thinks are for the worse, but he more than suspects that others are for the better; and though he would still warn his son of some dangers he apprehends, and impress on his mind some principles not duly appreciated, he feels that he may improve his own mind, and strengthen his own character, by partially adopting the opinions, and imitating the practice of his younger relative.

And has England nothing to learn from the United States? or has the younger nothing to learn from the 'old country?' How much wiser, how much nobler would it be, if instead of mutual abuse and affected contempt, each profited by the experience of the other, in adopting the good, and shunning the danger, which they may respectively discover in each others' institutions. How much would the national character of the United States be elevated and refined by a respectful bearing towards the land of their fathers, and by the encouraging an intercourse of a higher character than that of mere commercial relations! England too, especially in her present state of transition, when there is an obvious increase of power in the democratical elements of her constitution, and a growing influence exercised by the middle and lower classes of society; England has very much to learn by studying the moral and political condition of the transatlantic states. How much danger may she escape, how much degeneracy may she avoid, if at this critical season, when she is reviewing her institutions, putting them to the test of real utility, and adjusting them to altered circumstances and altered wants, she would consider the debasing evils resulting from a sordid application of the *Cui bono* question, as well as the advantages of basing the national establishments on the affections and approval of a larger portion of the community.

In England, learning and science are cultivated in a higher degree; in the United States the rudiments of knowledge are more generally diffused. If we adopt with them an organized system of national education, let us religiously maintain those institutions in which the higher departments of literature and science are cultivated. For by lowering the standard of intellectual attainment to which the few aspire, we gradually debase the standard of acquirement which the many may reach.

If on the other side the Atlantic there is too little distinction of rank, and too little respect for high station, is there not here too exclusive a spirit, too little sympathy with the poor in those of a higher grade. If we think the working classes in America too much disposed to a rude assertion of equality with their richer neighbours, must we not admit that the wealthy and the high-born of England are too much inclined to regard the lower orders as an inferior race of beings. The general aim of the few is not so much to promote the real welfare of the many, as to keep them in that state of dependence, which will most promote the comfort and ease of their superiors.

It is however beginning to be seen, not only that we ought not, but that we dare not neglect the lower classes of society. Their growing influence we cannot overthrow; it remains for us to turn it into right channels, and confine it by effectual, that is, by moral restraints. If the rich and the noble would not be despoiled and trampled on by a lawless mob, they must do away with the materials of which mobs are formed. They must diffuse the advantages of good education throughout the length and breadth of the land, and train men to submit to the government of others, by teaching them to govern themselves. They must provide suitable instruction, and salutary discipline for the children of mechanics and of shopkeepers, as well as for those of labourers; and thus enlist a large proportion of the most influential classes on the side of order and government, of religion and virtue. It is clear however, that no such fruits can be reasonably expected from an extension of the present National School system. Its utter inadequacy to meet the moral wants of the people, and to train up a decent and a well-informed community, is mournfully evident. The education for which the country calls, is one not only more extensive in its application, but more efficient in its character. To religious instruction must be added religious and moral influence, if we would not mock the supplicant for bread with the offer of a stone. Men have thought that by introducing a religious book, or an orthodox catechism into a school, they based education on religion itself. They are beginning to be disabused. Whether a more extensive system of education in this country shall prove a blessing or a curse, will mainly depend on the treatment of this fundamental point. These are clearly not the times in which a national establishment for education, fettered by the forms of the established church, can be diffused through the mass of the population requiring instruction. This ground then must be at once abandoned. On the other hand, without the characteristic doctrines of the gospel, as held by the Church of England, religious instruction would be devoid of life and power. Happily we can still unite an everwhelming majority of all classes in England, Scotland, and Wales, in the acknowledgment of the leading tenets of Protestant Trinitarianism. And if the Baptist, the Independent, and the Orthodox Presbyterian can unite to form their Mill-hill Academy for the children of the wealthier members of their respective denominations, there need be little difficulty in arranging a course of religious instruction, which shall contain the most essential doctrines, without violating the scruples of one twentieth or of one fiftieth of the population. Some peculiar dogmas, and some particular forms may be safely left to be inculcated in the Sunday School, and yet enough of divine truth, constituting the religious instruction, and animating the moral discipline, may be set forth in the week-day school, to train the children, under the divine blessing, to self-government, and to make them wise unto salvation, through faith which is in Christ Jesus.'

The public mind is now awaking to the truth, that knowledge is not virtue; that it is not enough that a child be made to commit to memory a summary of his duty, he must be trained through the affections of his heart, and the dictates of his conscience to observe it. A stronger moral power than that which the prevailing system of popular education wields, is imperatively called for. Our periodical publications, the great indexes of the current of public opinion and feeling, teem with disquisitions on the subject. It is something gained to know *what* we need; if some assistance in supplying our ascertained want be offered us, by a New England ' Teacher,' let us not refuse to listen to the voice of instruction.

The little volume now presented to the British public, sets forth in a lively and practical manner, the every-day life of a North American school. We are fairly ushered into the class-room, introduced to the pupils, made acquainted with the lights and shades of their characters, and all the physical, moral, and intellectual machinery of the institution, is set in motion before our eyes, and its principles familiarly explained. It is not indeed an elaborate exhibition of abstract truths addressed to a few philosophical minds, but a lively picture of school scenes, a minute detail of lessons, many of which were actually given, and a circumstantial report of cases which have really occurred, and may any day occur again. It is a volume for the practical educator; the teacher in an infant school, the master of a proprietary establishment, the professor in a university, the instructor in a private family, or in a school of any description, may study its lively narratives and judicious remarks with profit to himself and his charge. It exhibits to us how moral discipline and religious influence may be exercised, even in a day-school, and that without violating sectarian prejudices.

I do not contend for the truth of all the opinions expressed, nor the propriety of all the measures described. The author admits in theory that a school should be an absolute monarchy, but in *practice*, his administration is too democratical. His pupils are, in my judgment, too much persuaded or coaxed to adopt the master's views; *he* exercises too little authority, and *they* learn too little submission. The want of discipline at home, and the early indications of the national character may perhaps, render this course, more excusable in New England. Difficulties in moral discipline are sometimes ingeniously evaded, rather than manfully met, and a course sometimes pursued better adapted for the immediate correction of a particular fault, than for the solid improvement of character. Yet with these drawbacks I can conscientiously recommend the perusal of this unpretending work to all who like myself are engaged in tuition, or who as parents or members of society are interested in education. I have derived benefit from its perusal myself, and I must pity or admire very much the instructor who could read it without profit.

Whenever improved principles of popular education are advocated, this difficulty is invariably started, 'where shall we find persons competent to execute these views?' Men must be trained, they must be taught to teach, educated to educate. We have had enough of books adapted to disguise the ignorance of the teacher and perpetuate that of the pupil; we must now form *men*; we must bring the living mind in contact with mind, the living heart in contact with the heart. Whenever the government of the country shall be fully persuaded that an *improved* as well as extended system of education is the greatest boon they can bestow on the people, schools for teachers will doubtless be formed. On the wisdom that presides over their formation, on the moral and religious spirit that pervades their operations, will mainly depend the character of the rising generation. Happy will it be for us, if taught at last by painful experience we seek to diffuse moral discipline and religious influence through all our national institutions for education. A more intelligent population we may expect to find, when the teacher shall feel it a more important work to cultivate reflection and judgment, than to load the memory with ill-digested knowledge. A better and a happier generation we may hope, under the divine blessing, to see, when the educator, whatever rank he may hold, whether instructing our young nobility, training up the children of the middle classes, or labouring in a poor-school, shall feel that he is abandoning the most important post, and compromising his most sacred duty, when he neglects to form the moral character of his pupils on the basis of religious principle. 'L' éducation sans réligion n'est que le vernis.'

C. MAYO.

Cheam,
Feb. 26, 1834.

CHAPTER I.

INTEREST IN TEACHING.

A most singular contrariety of opinion exists in regard to the *pleasantness* of the business of teaching. Some teachers go to their daily task, merely 'on compulsion,' regarding it as intolerable drudgery. Others love the work, lingering in the school-room, and continually talking of their delightful labours. These unfortunately form the less numerous class.

The first object which I propose to myself in this work, is to show my readers, especially those who have been accustomed to look upon the business of teaching as a weary and heartless toil, how it happens, that it is, in any case, so pleasant. The human mind is always, essentially, the same. That which is tedious and joyless to one, will be so to another, if pursued in the same way, and under the same circumstances. And teaching, if it is pleasant, and animating, and exciting to one, may be so to all.

I am met, however, at the outset, in my effort to show why it is that teaching is ever a pleasant work, by the want of a name for a certain faculty or capacity of the human mind through which most of the enjoyment of teaching reaches us. Every mind is so constituted as to take a positive pleasure in the exercise of ingenuity in adapting means to an end, and in watching their operation;—in accomplishing by the intervention of instruments, what we could not accomplish without them;—in devising,—when we see an object to be effected, which is too great for our *direct* and *immediate* power,—and setting at work some *instrumentality*, which may be sufficient to accomplish it.

It is said that when the steam engine was first put into operation, such was the imperfection of the machinery, that a boy was necessarily stationed at it, to open and turn the cock, by which the steam was alternately admitted to the cylinder, and excluded from it. One such boy, after patiently doing his work for many days, contrived to connect this stop-cock with some of the moving parts of the engine, by a wire, in such a manner, that the engine itself did the work, which had been entrusted to him;—and after seeing that the whole business would go regularly forward, he left the wire in charge, and went away to play.

Such is the story; now if it is true, how much pleasure the boy must have experienced in devising this scheme, and witnessing its successful operation. I do not mean the pleasure of relieving himself from a dull and wearisome duty. I do not mean the pleasure of anticipated play. I mean the strong interest he must have taken in the *contriving and executing his plan*. When wearied out with his dull monotonous work, he first noticed those movements of the machinery which he thought adapted to his purpose, and the plan flashed into his mind; how must his eye have brightened, and how soon must the weary listlessness of his employment have vanished. While he was maturing his plan, and carrying it into execution; while adjusting his wires, fitting them to the exact length, and to the exact position, and especially, when at last he was watching the first successful operation of his contrivance, he must have enjoyed a pleasure, which very few, even of the joyous sports of childhood, could have supplied.

It is not, however, exactly the pleasure of exercising *ingenuity in contrivance*, that I refer to here; for the teacher has not, after all, a great deal of absolute *contriving* to do, or rather his *principal business* is not contriving. The greatest and most permanent source of pleasure to the boy, in such a case as I have described, is his feeling that he is accomplishing a great effect by a slight effort of his own; the feeling of *power*; that he is acting through the *intervention of instrumentality*, so as to multiply his power. So great would be this satisfaction, that he would almost wish to have some other similar work assigned him, that he might have another opportunity to contrive some plan for its easy accomplishment.

Looking at an object to be accomplished, or an evil to be remedied, then studying its nature and extent, and devising and executing some means for effecting the purpose desired, is, in all cases, a source of pleasure; especially when, by the process, we bring to view or to operation new powers, or powers heretofore hidden, whether they are our own powers, or those of objects upon which we act. Experimenting has a sort of magical fascination for all. Some do not like the trouble of making preparation, but all are eager to see the results. Contrive a new machine, and everybody will be interested to witness, or to hear of its operation; develope any heretofore unknown properties of matter, or secure some new useful effect, from laws which men have not hitherto employed for their purposes, and the interest of all around you will be excited to observe your results; and especially, you will yourself take a deep and permanent pleasure, in guiding and controlling the power you have thus obtained.

This is peculiarly the case with experiments upon mind, or experiments for producing effects through the medium of voluntary acts of the human mind, so that the contriver must take into consideration the laws of mind in forming his plans. To illustrate this by rather a childish case; I once knew a boy who was employed by his father to remove all the loose small stones, which from the peculiar nature of the ground, had accumulated in the road before the house. He was to take them up and throw them over into the pasture across the way. He soon got tired of picking them up one by one, and sat down upon the bank, to try to devise some better means of accomplishing his work. He at length conceived and adopted the following plan. He set up in the pasture a narrow board for a target, or as boys would call it, a mark, and then collecting all the boys of the neighbourhood, he proposed to them an amusement, which boys are always ready for, firing at a mark. I need not say that the stores of ammunition in the street were soon exhausted; the boys working for their leader, when they supposed they were only finding amusement for themselves.

Here now is experimenting upon the mind; the production of useful effect with rapidity and ease, by the intervention of proper instrumentality; the conversion, by means of a little knowledge of human nature, of that which would have otherwise been dull and fatiguing labour, into a most animating sport, giving pleasure to twenty, instead of tedious labour to one. Now the contrivance and execution of such plans is a source of positive pleasure; it is always pleasant to bring the properties and powers of matter into requisition to promote our designs, but there is a far higher pleasure in controlling, and guiding, and moulding to our purpose the movements of mind.

It is this which gives interest to the plans and operation of human governments. They can do little by actual force. Nearly all the power that is held, even by the most despotic executive, must be based on an adroit management of the principles of human nature, so as to lead men voluntarily to co-operate with the ruler in his plans. Even an army could not be got into battle, in many cases, without a most ingenious arrangement, by means of which half a dozen men can drive, literally drive as many thousands into the very face of danger and death. The difficulty of leading men to battle, must have been for a long time a very perplexing one to generals. It was at last removed by the very simple expedient of creating a greater danger behind, than there is before. Without ingenuity of contrivance like this, turning one principle of human nature against another, and making it for the momentary interest of men to act in a given way, no government could stand a year.

I know of nothing which illustrates more perfectly the way by which a knowledge of human nature is to be turned to account in managing human minds, than a plan which was adopted for clearing the galleries of the British House of Commons. It is well known that a gallery is appropriated to spectators, and that it sometimes becomes necessary to order them to retire, when a vote is to be taken, or private business is to be transacted. When the officer in attendance was ordered to clear the gallery, it was sometimes found to be a very troublesome and slow operation, for those who first went out, remained obstinately as close to the doors as possible, so as to secure the opportunity to come in again first, when the doors should be re-opened. In consequence there was so great an accumulation around the doors outside, that it was almost impossible for the crowd to get out. The whole difficulty arose from the eager desire of every one to remain as near as possible to the door, *through which they were to come back again.* I have been told, that, notwithstanding the utmost efforts of the officers, fifteen minutes were sometimes consumed in effecting the object, when the order was given that the spectators should retire.

The whole difficulty was removed by a very simple plan. One door only was opened when the crowd was to retire, and they were then admitted through the other. The consequence was, that as soon as the order was given to clear the galleries, every one fled as fast as possible through the open door around to the one which was closed, so as to be ready to enter first, when that, in its turn, should be opened; this was usually a few minutes, as the purpose for which the spectators were ordered to retire was usually simply to allow time for taking a vote. Here it will be seen that by the operation of a very simple plan, the very eagerness of the crowd to get back as soon as possible, which had been the *sole cause of the difficulty* was turned to account most effectually to remove it. Before, they were so eager to return, that they crowded around the door so as to prevent others going out. But by this simple plan of ejecting them by one door, and admitting them by another, that very circumstance made them clear the passage at once, and hurried every one away into the lobby, the moment the command was given.

The planner of this scheme must have taken great

pleasure in seeing its successful operation; though the officer who went steadily on, endeavouring to remove the reluctant throng by dint of mere driving, might well have found his task unpleasant. For the exercise of ingenuity in studying the nature of the difficulty with which a man has to contend, and bringing in some antagonist principle of human nature to remove it, or if not an antagonist principle, a similar principle, operating by a peculiar arrangement of circumstances, in an antagonist manner, is always pleasant. From this source a large share of the enjoyment which men find in the active pursuits of life, has its origin.

The teacher has the whole field which this subject opens, fully before him. He has human nature to deal with most directly. His whole work is experimenting upon mind, and the mind which is before him to be the subject of his operation, is exactly in the state to be most easily and pleasantly operated upon. The reason, now, why some teachers find their work delightful, and some find it wearisomeness and tedium itself, is that some do, and some do not take this view of their work. One instructor is like the engine-boy, turning without cessation or change, his everlasting stop-cock in the same ceaseless, mechanical, and monotonous routine. Another is like the little workman in his brighter moments, fixing his invention, and watching with delight its successful and easy accomplishment of his wishes. One is like the officer, driving by vociferation and threats, and demonstrations of violence, the spectators from the galleries. The other, like the shrewd contriver, who converts the very cause which was the whole ground of the difficulty, to a most successful and efficient means of its removal.

These principles show how teaching may in some

cases be a delightful employment, while in others, its tasteless dulness is interrupted by nothing but its perplexities and cares. The school-room is in reality, a little empire of mind. If the one who presides in it, sees it in its true light, studies the nature and tendency of the minds which he has to control, adapts his plans and his measures to the laws of human nature, and endeavours to accomplish his purposes for them, not by mere labour and force, but by ingenuity and enterprise; he will take pleasure in administering his little government. He will watch with care and interest the operation of the moral and intellectual causes which he sets in operation, and find as he accomplishes with increasing facility and power his various objects, that he derives a greater and greater pleasure from his work.

Now when a teacher thus looks upon his school as a field in which he is to exercise skill and ingenuity and enterprise; when he studies the laws of human nature, and the character of those minds upon which he has to act; when he explores deliberately the nature of the field which he has to cultivate, and of the objects which he wishes to accomplish; and applies means, judiciously and skilfully adapted to the object; he must necessarily take a strong interest in his work. But on the other hand, he who goes to his employment, only to perform a certain regular round of daily work, undertaking nothing, and anticipating nothing but this dull and unchangeable routine; and who looks upon his pupils merely as passive objects of his labours, whom he is to treat with simple indifference while they obey his commands, and to whom he is only to apply reproaches and punishment when they disobey; such a teacher never can take pleasure in the school. Weariness and dulness must reign in both master and scholars, when things, as he imagines, are going right, and mutual anger and crimination, when they go wrong.

Scholars never can be instructed by the power of any dull mechanical routine; nor can they be governed by the blind naked strength of the master; such means must fail to accomplish the purposes designed, and consequently the teacher who tries such a course must have constantly upon his mind the discouraging, disheartening burden of unsuccessful and almost useless labour. He is continually uneasy, dissatisfied, and filled with anxious cares; and sources of vexation and perplexity will continually rise. He attempts to remove evils by waging against them a useless and most vexatious warfare of threatening and punishment, and he is trying continually *to drive*, when he might know that neither the intellect nor the heart are capable of being driven.

I will simply state one case, to illustrate what I mean by the difference between blind force, and active ingenuity and enterprise, in the management of a school. I once knew the teacher of a school, who made it his custom to have writing attended to in the afternoon. The boys were accustomed to take their places at the appointed hour, and each one would stick up his pen in the front of his desk for the teacher to pass round and mend it. The teacher would accordingly pass round, mending the pens from desk to desk, and thus enabling the boys, in succession, to begin their task. Of course, each boy before he came to his desk was necessarily idle, and almost necessarily, in mischief. Day after day the teacher went through this regular routine. He sauntered slowly and listlessly through the aisles, and among the benches of the room, wherever he saw the signal of a pen. He paid of course very little attention to the writing, now and then reproving, with an impatient tone, some extraordinary instance of carelessness, or leaving his work to suppress some rising disorder. Ordinarily, however, he seemed to be lost in vacancy of thought—dreaming perhaps of other scenes, or inwardly repining at the eternal monotony and tedium of a teacher's life. His boys took no interest in their work, and of course made no progress. They were sometimes unnecessarily idle, and sometimes mischievous, but never usefully or pleasantly employed; for the whole hour was past before the pens could all be brought down. Wasted time, blotted books, and fretted tempers, were all the results which the system produced.

The same teacher afterwards acted on a very different principle. He looked over the field and said to himself, what are the objects I wish to accomplish in this writing exercise, and how can I best accomplish them? I wish to obtain the greatest possible amount of industrious and careful practice in writing. The first thing evidently is to save the wasted time. He accordingly made preparation for the mending of the pens at a previous hour, so that all should be ready at the appointed time to commence the work together. This could be done quite as conveniently when the boys were engaged in studying, by requesting them to put out their pens at an appointed and *previous* time. He sat at his table, and the pens of a whole bench were brought him, and after being carefully mended, were returned, to be in readiness for the writing hour. Thus the first difficulty, the loss of time, was obviated.

'I must make them *industrious* while they write,' was his next thought. After thinking of a variety of methods he determined to try the following. He required all to begin together at the top of the page, and write the same line, in a hand of the same size. They were all required to begin together, he himself beginning at the same time, and writing about as fast as he thought they ought to write, in order to secure the highest improvement. When he had finished his line, he ascertained how many had preceded him, and how many were behind. He requested the first to write slower, and the others faster, and by this means, after a few trials, he secured uniform, regular, systematic, and industrious employment, throughout the school. Probably there were at first, difficulties in the operation of the plan, which he had to devise ways and means to surmount. But what I mean to present particularly to the reader is, that he was *interested in his experiments*. While sitting in his desk, giving his command to *begin* line after line, and noticing the unbroken silence, and attention, and interest, which prevailed, (for each boy was interested to see how nearly with the master he could finish his work,) while presiding over such a scene, he must have been interested. He must have been pleased with the exercise of his almost military command, and to witness how effectually order and industry, and excited and pleased attention had taken the place of listless idleness, and mutual dissatisfaction.

After a few days he appointed one of the older and more judicious scholars, to give the word for beginning and ending the lines, and he sat surveying the scene, or walking from desk to desk, noticing faults, and considering what plans he could form for securing, more and more fully, the end he had in view. He found that the great object of interest and attention among the boys, was to come out right, and that less pains were taken with the formation of the letters than there ought to be, to secure the most rapid improvement.

But how shall he secure greater pains? By stern

commands and threats, or by going from desk to desk, scolding one, rapping the knuckles of another, and holding up to ridicule a third, making examples of such individuals as may chance to attract his special attention? No; he has learned that he is operating upon a little empire of mind, and he is not to endeavour to drive them as a man drives a herd, by mere peremptory command or half angry blows. He must study the nature of the effect he is to produce, and of the materials upon which he is to work, and adopt, after mature deliberation, a plan to accomplish his purpose, founded upon the principles which ought always to regulate the action of mind upon mind, and adapted to produce the *intellectual effect*, which he wishes to accomplish.

In the case supposed, the teacher concluded to appeal to emulation, and while I describe the measure he adopted, let it be remembered that I am only now approving of the resort to ingenuity, and invention, and the employment of moral and intellectual means for the accomplishment of his purposes, and not of the measures themselves. I do not think the plan I am going to describe a wise one, but I do think that the teacher, while trying it, must *have been interested in his intellectual experiment*. His business, while pursued in such a way, could not have been a mere dull and uninteresting routine.

He purchased, at a small expence, two black lead pencils, an article of great value, in the opinion of the boys of country schools; and he offered them as prizes to the boy who would write most carefully; not to the one who should write *best*, but to the one whose book should exhibit most appearance of *effort* and care for a week. After announcing his plan, he watched with strong interest its operation. He walked round the room while the writing was in progress, to observe the effect of his measure. He did not reprove those who were writing carelessly; he simply noticed who and how many they were. He did not commend those who were evidently making effort; he noticed who and how many they were, that he might understand how far, and upon what sort of minds his experiment was successful, and where it failed. He was taking a lesson in human nature,—human nature as it exhibits itself in boys, and he was preparing to operate more and more powerfully by future plans.

The lesson which he learned by the experiment was this, that one or two prizes will not influence the majority of a large school. A few seemed to think that the pencils were possibly within their reach, and *they* made vigorous efforts to secure them; but the rest wrote on as before. Thinking it certain that they should be surpassed by the others, they gave up the contest at once in despair.

The obvious remedy was to multiply his prizes, so as to bring one within the reach of all. He reflected too that the real prize in such a case, is not the value of the pencil, but the *honour of the victory*; and as the honour of the victory might as well be coupled with an object of less, as well as with one of greater value, the next week he divided his two pencils into quarters, and offered to his pupils eight prizes instead of two. He offered one to every five scholars, as they sat on their benches, and every boy thus saw, now, that a reward would certainly come within five of him. His chance, accordingly, instead of being one in twenty, became one in five.

Now is it possible for a teacher, after having philosophized upon the nature of the minds upon which he is operating, and surveyed the field, and ingeniously formed a plan, which plan he hopes will, through his own intrinsic power, produce certain effects,—is it possible for him when he comes, for the first day, to witness its operations, to come without feeling a strong interest in the result? It is impossible. After having formed such a plan, and made such arrangements, he will look forward almost with impatience, to the next writing hour. He wishes to see whether he has estimated the mental capacities and tendencies of his little community aright; and when the time comes, and he surveys the scene, and observes the operation of his measure, and sees many more are reached by it than were influenced before, he feels a strong gratification, and it is a gratification which is founded upon the noblest principles of our nature. He is tracing on a most interesting field the operation of cause and effect. From being the mere drudge, who drives without intellect or thought, a score or two of boys to their daily tasks, he rises to the rank of an intellectual philosopher, exploring the laws, and successfully controling the tendencies of mind.

It will be observed too, that all the time this teacher was performing these experiments, and watching with intense interest the results, his pupils were going on undisturbed in their pursuits. The exercises in writing were not interrupted or deranged. This is a point of fundamental importance, for, if what I should say on the subject of exercising ingenuity and contrivance in teaching should be the means, in any case, of leading a teacher to break in upon the regular duties of his school, and destroy the steady uniformity with which the great objects of such an institution should be pursued, my remarks had better never have been written. There may be variety in methods and plan, but through all this variety, the school, and every individual pupil of it must go steadily forward in the acquisition of that knowledge which is of the greatest importance in the business of future life. In other words, the variations and changes admitted by the teacher, ought to be mainly confined to the modes of accomplishing those permanent objects at which all the exercises and arrangements of the school ought steadily to aim. More on this subject, however, in another chapter.

I will mention one other circumstance, which will help to explain the difference in interest and pleasure with which they engage in the work. I mean the different views they take *of the offences of their pupils.* One class of teachers, seem never to make it a part of their calculation that their pupils will do wrong; and then, when any misconduct occurs, they are disconcerted and irritated, and look and act as if some unexpected occurrence had broken in upon their plans. Others understand and consider all this beforehand. They seem to think a little before they go into their school, what sort of beings boys and girls are, and any ordinary case of youthful delinquency or dulness does not surprise them. I do not mean that they treat such cases with indifference or neglect, but that they *expect* them, and *are prepared for them.* Such a teacher knows that boys and girls are the *materials* he has to work upon, and he takes care to make himself acquainted with these materials, *just as they are.* The other class however, do not seem to know at all what sort of beings they have to deal with, or if they know, do not *consider.* They expect from them what is not to be obtained, and then are disappointed and vexed at the failure. It is as if a carpenter should attempt to support an entablature by pillars of wood too small and weak for the weight, and then go on, from week to week, suffering anxiety and irritation, as he sees them swelling and splitting under the burden, and finding fault *with the wood*, instead of taking the blame to himself.

It is, of course, one essential part of a man's duty in engaging in any undertaking, whether it will lead him to act upon matter or upon mind, to become first well acquainted with the circumstances of the case,—the materials he is to act upon, and the means which he may reasonably expect to have at his command. If he underrates his difficulties or overrates the power of his means of overcoming them, it is his mistake; a mistake for which *he* is fully responsible. Whatever may be the nature of the effect which he aims at accomplishing, he ought fully to understand it, and to appreciate justly the difficulties which lie in the way.

Teachers however very often overlook this. A man comes home from his school at night, perplexed and irritated by the petty misconduct which he has witnessed, and has been trying to check,—that is, he does not look forward and try to prevent the occasions of it, adapting his measures to the nature of the material upon which he has to operate; but he stands, like the carpenter at his columns, making himself miserable in looking at the mischief after it occurs, and wondering what to do.

'Sir,' we might say to him, 'what is the matter?'

'Why, I have such boys, I can do nothing with them. Were it not for *their misconduct*, I might have a very good school.'

'Were it not for the boys! Why, is there any peculiar depravity in them which you could not have foreseen?'

'No; I suppose they are pretty much like all other

boys,' he replies despairingly; 'they are all hair-brained and unmanageable. The plans I have formed for my school, would be excellent if my boys would only behave properly.'

'Excellent plans,' might we not reply, 'and yet not adapted to the materials upon which they are to operate. No. It is your business to know what sort of beings boys are, and to make your calculations accordingly.'

Two teachers may therefore manage their schools in totally different ways, so that one of them may necessarily find the business a dull, mechanical routine, except as it is occasionally varied by perplexity and irritation, and the other, a successful and happy employment. The one goes on mechanically and monotonously depending for his power on violence, or on threats and demonstrations of violence. The other brings all his ingenuity and enterprise into the field, to accomplish a steady purpose, by means ever varying, and depends for his power, on his knowledge of human nature, and on the adroit adaptation of his plans to her fixed and uniform tendencies.

I am very sorry however to be obliged to say, that probably the latter class of teachers are decidedly in the minority. To practise the art in such a way as to make it an agreeable employment, is difficult, and requires much knowledge of human nature, much attention and skill. And, after all, there are some circumstances necessarily attending the work which constitute a heavy drawback on the pleasures which it might otherwise afford. The almost universal impression that the business of teaching is attended with peculiar trials and difficulties, proves this.

There must be some cause for an impression so

general. It is not right to call it a prejudice, for, although a single individual may conceive a prejudice, whole communities very seldom do, unless in some case, which is presented at once to the whole, so that looking at it, through a common medium, all judge wrong together. But the general opinion in regard to teaching is composed of a vast number of *separate* and *independent* judgments, and there must be some good ground for the universal result.

It is best therefore, if there are any real and peculiar sources of trial and difficulty, in this pursuit, that they should be distinctly known and acknowledged at the outset. Count the cost before going to war. It is even better policy to overrate, than to underrate it. Let us see then what the real difficulties of teaching are.

It is not, however, as is generally supposed, *the confinement.* A teacher is confined, it is true, but not more than men of other professions and employments; not more than a merchant, and probably not as much. A physician is confined in a different way, but more closely than a teacher. He can never leave home : he knows generally no vacation, and nothing but accidental rest.

The lawyer is confined as much. It is true, there are not throughout the year, exact hours which he must keep, but considering the imperious demands of his business, his personal liberty is probably restrained as much by it, as that of the teacher. So with all the other professions. Although the nature of the confinement may vary, it amounts to about the same in all. On the other hand the teacher enjoys, in reference to this subject of confinement, an advantage, which scarcely any other class of men does or can enjoy. I mean vacations. A man in any other business may *force* himself away from it, for a time, but the cares and anxieties of his business will follow him wherever he goes, and it seems to be reserved for the teacher, to enjoy the periodical luxury of a *real and entire release from business and care*. On the whole, as to confinement, it seems to me that the teacher has but little ground of complaint.

There are however some real and serious difficulties which always have, and it is to be feared, always will, cluster round this employment, and which must, for a long time, at least, lead most men to desire some other employment for the business of life. There may perhaps be some, who by their peculiar skill, can overcome, or avoid them, and perhaps the science may, at some future day, be so far improved, that all may avoid them. As I describe them however now, most of the teachers into whose hands this treatise may fall, will probably find that their own experience corresponds in this respect with mine.

1. The first great difficulty which the teacher feels, is a sort of *moral responsibility for the conduct of others*. If his pupils do wrong, he feels almost personal responsibility for it. As he walks out, some afternoon, weary with his labours, and endeavouring to forget for a little time, all his cares, he comes upon a group of boys, in rude and noisy quarrels, or engaged in mischief of some sort, and his heart sinks within him. It is hard enough for any one to witness their bad conduct, with a spirit unruffled and undisturbed, but for their teacher, it is perhaps impossible. He feels *responsible;* in fact he is responsible. If his scholars are disorderly or negligent or idle or quarrelsome, he feels *condemned himself,* almost as if he were, himself, the actual transgressor.

This difficulty is in a great degree, peculiar to a teacher. A physician is called upon to prescribe for a patient; he examines the case, and writes his prescription. When this is done, his duty is ended, and whether the patient obeys the prescription and lives, or neglects it and dies, the physician feels exonerated from all responsibility. He may, and in some cases does feel *anxious concern*, and may regret the infatuation by which in some unhappy case, a valuable life may be hazarded or destroyed. But he feels no *moral responsibility* for another's guilt.

It is so with all the other employments in life. They do indeed often bring men into collision with other men. But though sometimes vexed, and irritated by the conduct of a neighbour, a client, or a patient, they feel not half the bitterness of the solicitude and anxiety which come to the teacher through the criminality of his pupil. In ordinary cases he not only feels responsible for efforts, but for their results; and when, notwithstanding all his efforts, his pupils will do wrong, his spirit sinks, with an intensity of anxious despondency, which none but a teacher can understand.[1]

This feeling of almost *moral accountability for the guilt of other persons*, is a continual burden. The teacher, in the presence of the pupils, never is free from it. It

---

[1] The author does not seem to have clearly defined to his own mind the true character of an instructor's responsibility. He is responsible, in the first place, to Almighty God; and, in the second, to the parents of his pupils, and to society. In the former case he *ought* to feel responsible for endeavours, but he cannot feel so for results; in the latter he may feel himself responsible for both. I know no more effectual relief from the burden of accountability to our fellow-creatures, than the cultivating a strong and continual sense of our accountability to the Creator, so that it be not in a spirit of bondage, but of filial regard to a father's favour and approval. The fear of God is the best remedy against an undue fear of man.

'Lord! may thy fear within me dwell,
Thy love my footsteps guide;
That love shall vainer loves expel,
That fear all fears beside.'   MERRICK.

links him to them by a bond, which, perhaps, he ought not to sunder, and which he cannot sunder if he would do it. And sometimes, when those committed to his charge are idle, or faithless, or unprincipled, it wears away his spirits and his health together. I think there is nothing analogous to this moral connexion between teacher and pupil, unless it be in the case of a parent and child. And here on account of the comparative smallness of the number under the parent's care, the evil is so much diminished that it is easily borne.

2. The second great difficulty of the teacher's employments, is *the immense multiplicity of the objects of his attention and care*, during the time he is employed in his business. His scholars are individuals, and notwithstanding all that the most systematic can do, in the way of classification, they must be attended to in a great measure, as individuals. A merchant keeps his commodities together, and looks upon a cargo composed of ten thousand articles, and worth 100,000 dollars as one: he speaks of it as one, and there is, in many cases, no more perplexity in planning its destination, than if it were a single box of raisins. A lawyer may have a great many important cases, but he has only one at a time; that is, he *attends* to but one at a time. That one may be intricate,—involving many facts and requiring to be examined in many aspects and relations. But he looks at but few of these facts, and regards but few of these relations, at a time. The points which demand his attention come, one after another, in regular succession. His mind may thus be kept calm. He avoids confusion and perplexity. But no skill or classification will turn the poor teacher's hundred scholars into one, or enable him except to a very limited extent, and for a very limited purpose, to regard them as one. He has a distinct, and,

in many respects, a different work to do for every one of the crowd before him. Difficulties must be explained in detail, questions must be answered one by one; and each scholar's own conduct and character must be considered by itself. His work is thus made up of a thousand minute particulars, which are all crowding upon his attention at once, and which he cannot group together, or combine, or simplify. He must by some means or other attend to them in all their distracting individuality. And in a large and complicated school, the endless multiplicity and variety of objects of attention and care, impose a task under which few intellects can long stand.

I have said that this endless multiplicity and variety cannot be reduced and simplified by classification. I mean, of course, that this can be done only to a very limited extent, compared with what may be effected in the other pursuits of mankind. Were it not for the art of classification and system, no school could have more than ten scholars, as I intend hereafter to show. The great reliance of the teacher is upon this art, to reduce to some tolerable order, what would otherwise be the inextricable confusion of his business. He *must be systematic*. He must classify and arrange, but after he has done all that he can, he must still expect that his daily business will continue to consist of a vast multitude of minute particulars, from one to another of which the mind must turn with a rapidity, which, few of the other employments of life ever demand.

These are the essential sources of difficulty with which the teacher has to contend, but, as I shall endeavour to show in succeeding chapters, though they cannot be entirely removed, they can be so far mitigated by the appropriate means, as to render the employment a happy one. I have thought it best however, as this work will doubtless be read by many, who, when they read it, are yet to begin their labours, to describe frankly and fully to them the difficulties which beset the path they are about to enter. "The wisdom of the prudent is to understand his way." It is often wisdom to understand it beforehand.

CHAPTER II.

GENERAL ARRANGEMENTS.

The distraction and perplexity of the teacher's life are, as was explained in the last chapter, almost proverbial. There are other pressing and exhausting pursuits, which wear away the spirit by the ceaseless care which they impose, or perplex and bewilder the intellect by the multiplicity and intricacy of their details. But the business of teaching, by a pre-eminence not very enviable, stands, almost by common consent, at the head of the catalogue.

I have already alluded to this subject in the preceding chapter; and probably the great majority of actual teachers will admit the truth of the view there presented. Some will however doubtless say, that they do not find the business of teaching so perplexing and exhausting an employment. They take things calmly. They do one thing at a time, and that without useless solicitude and anxiety. So that teaching, with them, though it has, indeed, its solicitudes and cares, as every other responsible employment must necessarily have, is, after all, a calm and quiet pursuit, which they follow from month to month, and from year to year, without any extraordinary agitations, or any unusual burdens of anxiety and care.

There are indeed such cases, but they are exceptions; and unquestionably an immense majority, especially of those who are beginners in the work, find it such as I have described. I think it need not be so; or rather, I think the evil may be avoided to *a very great degree.* In this chapter I shall endeavour to show how order may be produced out of that almost inextricable mass of confusion, into which so many teachers, on commencing their labours, find themselves plunged.

The objects then, to be aimed at in the general arrangements of schools are two-fold.

1. That the teacher may be left uninterrupted, to attend to one thing at a time.

2. That the individual scholars may have constant employment, and such an amount and such kinds of study, as shall be suited to the circumstances and capacities of each.

I shall examine each in their order.

1. The following are the principal things which, in a vast number of schools, are all the time pressing upon the teacher: or rather, they are the things which must, every where, press upon the teacher, except so far as, by the skill of his arrangements, he contrives to remove them.

1. Giving leave to whisper or to leave seats.
2. Mending pens.
3. Answering questions in regard to studies.
4. Hearing recitations.
5. Watching the behaviour of the scholars.
6. Administering reproof and punishment for offences as they occur.

A pretty large number of objects of attention and care, one would say, to be pressing upon the mind of the teacher at one and the same time—and *all the time,* too!

There is no doubt that hundreds and hundreds of teachers in every part of our country have all these, crowding upon them from morning to night, without cessation, except perhaps some accidental and momentary respite. During the winter months, while the principal common schools in our country are in operation, it is sad to reflect how many teachers come home, every evening, with bewildered and aching heads, having been vainly trying all the day, to do six things at a time, while He, who made the human mind, has determined that it shall do but one. How many become discouraged and disheartened by what they consider the unavoidable trials of a teacher's life, and give up in despair, just because their faculties will not sustain a six-fold task. There are multitudes who, in early life, attempted teaching, and, after having been worried, almost to distraction, by the simultaneous pressure of these multifarious cares, gave up the employment in disgust, and forever after wonder how any body can like teaching. I know multitudes of persons to whom the above description will exactly apply.

I once heard a teacher who had been very successful, even in large schools, say that he could hear two classes recite, mend pens, and watch his school, all at the same time; and that, without any distraction of mind, or any unusual fatigue. Of course the recitations in such a case must be memoriter. There are very few minds however, which can thus perform triple or quadruple work, and probably none which can safely be tasked so severely. For my part, I can do but one thing at a time; and I have no doubt that the true policy for all, is, to learn, not *to do every thing at once,* but so to classify and arrange their work, that *they shall have but one thing to do.* Instead of vainly attempting to attend simultaneously to a dozen things, they should so plan their work, that only *one* will demand attention.

Let us then examine the various particulars above mentioned in succession, and see how each can be disposed of, so as not to be a constant source of interruption and derangement.

1. *Whispering* and *leaving seats*. In regard to this subject, there are very different methods now in practice in different schools. In some, especially in very small schools, the teacher allows the pupils to act according to their own discretion. They whisper and leave their seats whenever they think it necessary. This plan may possibly be admissible in a very small school; that is, one of ten or twelve pupils. I am convinced, however, that it is very bad even here. No vigilant watch, which, it is possible for any teacher to exert, will prevent a vast amount of mere talk, entirely foreign to the business of the school. I tried this plan very thoroughly, with high ideas of the dependence which might be placed upon conscience and a sense of duty, if these principles are properly brought out to action in an effort to sustain the system. I was told by distinguished teachers, that it would not be found to answer. But predictions of failure in such cases only prompt to greater exertions, and I persevered. But I was forced at last to give up the point, and adopt another plan. My pupils would make resolutions enough; they understood their duty well enough. They were allowed to leave their seats and whisper to their companions, whenever, *in their honest judgment, it was necessary for the prosecution of their studies*. I knew that it sometimes would be necessary, and I was desirous to adopt this plan to save myself the constant interruption of hearing and replying to requests. But it would not

do. Whenever, from time to time, I called them to account, I found that a large majority, according to their own confession, were in the habit of holding daily and deliberate communication with each other, on subjects entirely foreign to the business of the school. A more experienced teacher would have predicted this result, but I had very high ideas of the power of cultivated conscience, and in fact, still have. But then, like almost all other persons who become possessed of a good idea, I could not be satisfied without carrying it to an extreme.

Still it is necessary to give pupils, sometimes, the opportunity to whisper and leave seats. Cases occur where this is unavoidable. It cannot therefore be forbidden altogether. How then, you will ask, can the teacher regulate this practice, so as to prevent the evils which will otherwise flow from it, without being continually interrupted by the request for permission?

By a very simple method. *Appropriate particular times at which all this business is to be done*, and *forbid it altogether* at every other time. It is well on other accounts to give the pupils of a school a little respite, at least every hour:—and if this is done, an intermission of study for two minutes each time, will be sufficient. During this time, *general* permission should be given to speak or to leave seats provided they do nothing at such a time to disturb the studies of others. This has been my plan for two or three years, and has operated more entirely to my satisfaction than any other arrangement which I ever pursued so uninterruptedly, and for so long a time. It of course will require some little time, and no little firmness, to establish the new order of things, where a school has been accustomed to another course; but where this is once done, I know no one plan so simple and so easily put into execution, which will do so much towards relieving the teacher of the distraction and perplexity of his pursuits.

In making the change however, it is of fundamental importance that the pupils should themselves be interested in it. Their co-operation, or rather the co-operation of the majority, which it is very easy to obtain, is absolutely essential to success. I say, this is very easily obtained. Let us suppose that some teacher, who has been accustomed to require his pupils to ask and obtain permission, every time they wish to speak to a companion, is induced by these remarks to introduce this plan. He says accordingly to his school:

'You know that you are now accustomed to ask me whenever you wish to obtain permission to whisper to a companion, or to leave your seats. Now I have been thinking of a plan which will be better for both you and me. By our present plan, you are sometimes obliged to wait before I can attend to your request. Sometimes I think it is unnecessary, and deny you, when perhaps I was mistaken, and it was really necessary. At other times, I think it very probable, that when it is quite desirable for you to leave your seat, you do not ask, because you think you may not obtain permission, and you do not wish to ask and be refused. Do you, or not, experience these inconveniences from our present plans?'

The boys would undoubtedly answer in the affirmative.

'I experience great inconvenience, too. I am very frequently interrupted when busily engaged, and it also occupies a great portion of my time and attention. It requires as much mental effort to consider and decide sometimes whether I ought to allow a pupil to leave his seat, as it would to decide a much more important question. Therefore I do not like our plan, and I have another to propose.'

The boys are all attention to know what the new plan is. It will always be of great advantage to the school, for the teacher to propose his new plans from time to time to his pupils in such a way as this. It interests them in the improvement of the school, exercises their judgment, establishes a common feeling between teacher and pupil, and in many other ways will assist very much in promoting the welfare of the school.

'My plan,' continues the teacher, 'is this: to allow you all, besides the recess, a short time, two or three minutes perhaps every hour;' (or every half hour, according to the character of the school, the age of the pupils, or other circumstances to be judged of by the teacher,) 'during which you may all whisper or leave your seats, without asking permission.'

Instead of deciding the question of the *frequency* of this general permission, the teacher may, if he pleases, leave it to the pupils to decide. It is often useful to leave the decision of such a question to them. On this subject, however, I shall speak in another place. It is only necessary here, to say that this point may be safely left to them, since the time is so small which is to be thus appropriated. Even if they vote to have the general permission to whisper every half hour, it will make but eight minutes in the forenoon. There being six half hours in the forenoon, and one of them ending at the close of school, and another at the recess, only *four* of these *halts*, as a military man would call them, would be necessary; and four, of two minutes each, would make eight minutes. If the teacher thinks that evil would result from the interruption of the studies so often, he may offer the pupils *three* minutes rest every *hour*, instead of *two* minutes every *half hour*, and let them take their choice, or he may decide the case altogether himself.

Such a change from *particular permission on individual requests* to *general permission* at *stated times*, would unquestionably be popular in every school, if the teacher managed the business properly. And by presenting it as an object of common interest, an arrangement proposed for the common convenience of teacher and pupils, the latter may be much interested in carrying the plan into effect. We must not rely, however, entirely upon their *interest in it*. All that we can expect from such an effort to interest them, as I have described and recommended, is to get a *majority* on our side, so that we may have only a small minority to deal with by other measures. Still *we must calculate on having this minority, and form our plans accordingly*, or we shall be sadly disappointed. I shall, however, in another place, speak of this principle of interesting the pupils in our plans, for the purpose of securing a majority in our favour, and explain the methods by which the minority is then to be governed. I only mean here to say, that by such means the teacher may easily interest a large proportion of the scholars, in carrying his plans into effect, and that he must expect to be prepared with other measures for those who will not be governed by these.

You cannot reasonably expect, however, that immediately after having explained your plan, it will at once go into full and complete operation. Even those who are firmly determined to keep the rule, will, from inadvertence, for a day or two, make communication with each other. They must be *trained*, not by threatening and punishment, but by your good-humoured assistance, to their new duties. When I first adopted this plan in my school, something like the following proceedings took place.

'Do you suppose that you will perfectly keep this rule from this time?'

'No, sir,' was the answer.

'I suppose you will not. Some, I am afraid, may not really be determined to keep it, and others will forget. Now I wish every one would keep an exact account to-day, of all the instances of speaking and leaving seats out of the regular times, and be prepared to report them at the close of the school. Of course, I shall have no punishment for it, but it will very much assist you to watch yourselves, if you expect to make a report at the end of the forenoon. Do you like this plan?'

'Yes, sir,' was the answer, and all seemed to enter into it with spirit.

In order to mark more definitely the times for communication, I wrote in large letters, on a piece of pasteboard, 'STUDY HOURS,' and making a hole over the centre of it, I hung it upon a nail over my desk. At the close of each half hour, a little bell was to be struck, and this card was to be taken down. When it was up, they were, on no occasion whatever, (except some such extraordinary occurrence, as sickness, or my sending one of them on a message to another, or something clearly out of the common course,) to speak to each other, but were to wait, whatever they wanted, until the *study card*, as they called it, was taken down.

'Suppose now,' said I, ' that a young lady has come into school, and has accidentally left her book in the entry, the book from which she is to study during the first half hour of the school. She sits near the door, and she might, in a moment, slip out and obtain it: if she does not, she must spend the half hour in idleness, and be unprepared in her lesson. What would it be her duty to do?'

'To go;' 'not to go;' answered the scholars simultaneously.

'It would be her duty *not* to go; but I suppose it will be very difficult for me to convince you of it. The reason is this,' I continued. 'If the one case I have supposed, were the *only* one which would be likely to occur, it would undoubtedly be better for her to go; but if it is understood, that in such cases, the rule may be dispensed with, there will be many others where it will be equally necessary to lay it aside. Scholars will differ in regard to the degree of inconvenience which they must submit to rather than break the rule. They will gradually do it on slighter and slighter occasions, until at last the rule will be disregarded entirely. We must, therefore, draw a *precise line*, and individuals must submit to a little inconvenience sometimes, to promote the general good.'

At the close of the day, I desired all in the school to rise. While they were standing, I called them to account in the following manner.

'Now it is very probable that some have, from inadvertence, or from design, omitted to keep an account of the number of transgressions of the rule which they have committed during the day; others, perhaps, do not wish to make a report of themselves. Now as this is a common and voluntary effort, I wish none to render assistance, who do not, of their own accord, desire to do so. All those, therefore, who are not able to make a report, from not having been correct in keeping it, and all those who are unwilling to report themselves, may sit.'

A very small number hesitatingly took their seats.

'I am afraid that all do not sit, who really wish not to report themselves. Now I am honest in saying I wish you to do just as you please. If a great majority of the school really wish to assist me in accomplishing the object, why, of course, I am glad; still, I shall not call upon any for such assistance, unless it is freely and voluntarily rendered.'

One or two more took their seats while these things were saying. Among such, there would generally be some who would refuse to have any thing to do with the measure, just from a desire to thwart and impede the plans of the teacher. If so, it is best to take no notice of them. If the teacher can contrive to obtain a great majority upon his side, so as to let them see that any opposition which they can raise, is of no consequence, and is not even noticed, they will soon be ashamed of it.

The reports then of those who remained standing, were called for. First, those who had whispered only once were requested to sit; then those who had whispered more than once, and less than five times, &c. &c. until at last all were down. In such a case, the pupils might, if thought expedient, again be desired to rise, for the purpose of asking some other questions, with reference to ascertaining whether they had spoken most in the former or latter part of the forenoon. The number who had spoken inadvertently, and the number who had done it by design, might be ascertained. These inquiries accustom the pupils to render honest and faithful accounts of themselves. They become, by such means, familiarized to the practice, and by means of it, the teacher can, many times, receive most important assistance.

All however, should be done in a pleasant tone, and

with a pleasant and cheerful air. It should be considered by the pupils, not a reluctant confession of guilt, for which they are to be rebuked or punished, but the voluntary and free report of the result of *an experiment*, in which all are interested.

Some will have been dishonest in their reports. To diminish the number of these, the teacher may say, after the report is concluded:

'We will drop the subject here to-day. To-morrow we will make another effort, when we shall be more successful. I have taken your reports as you have offered them, without any inquiry, because I had no doubt, that a great majority of this school would be honest at all hazards. They would not, I am confident, make a false report, even if, by a true one, they were to bring upon themselves punishment; so that I think I may have confidence that nearly all these reports have been faithful. Still, it is very probable, that, among so large a number, some may have made a report, which, they are now aware, was not perfectly fair and honest. I do not wish to know who they are; if there are any such cases, I only wish to say to the rest, how much pleasanter it is for you, that you have been honest and open. The business is now all ended; you have done your duty; and though you reported a little larger number than you would, if you had been disposed to conceal, yet you go away from school with a quiet conscience. On the other hand, how miserable must any boy feel, if he has any nobleness of mind whatever, to go away from school, to-day, thinking that he has not been honest; that he has been trying to conceal his faults, and thus to obtain a credit which he did not justly deserve. Always be honest, let the consequence be what it may.'

The reader will understand that the object of such measures is, simply *to secure as large a majority as possible*, to make *voluntary* efforts to observe the rule. I do not expect that by such measures, *universal* obedience can be exacted. The teacher must follow up the plan, after a few days, by other measures, for those who will not yield to such inducements as these. On this subject, however, I shall speak more particularly at a future time.

In my own school, it required two or three weeks to exclude whispering and communication by signs. The period necessary to effect the revolution will be longer or shorter, according to the circumstances of the school and the dexterity of the teacher. And, after all, the teacher must not hope *entirely* to exclude it. Approximation to excellence is all that we can expect; for unprincipled and deceiving characters will perhaps always be found, and no system whatever can prevent their existence. Proper treatment may indeed be the means of their reformation, and before this process has arrived at a successful result, others similar in character will have entered, so that the teacher can never expect perfection in the operation of any of his plans.

I found so much relief from the change which this plan introduced, that I soon took measures for rendering it permanent; and though I am not much in favour of efforts to bring all teachers and all schools to the same plans, this principle of *whispering at limited and prescribed times alone*, seems to me well suited to universal adoption.

The following simple apparatus has been used in several schools where this principle has been adopted. A drawing and description of it is inserted here, as by this means, some teachers, who may like to try the course

GENERAL ARRANGEMENTS.

here recommended, may be saved the time and trouble of contriving something of the kind themselves.

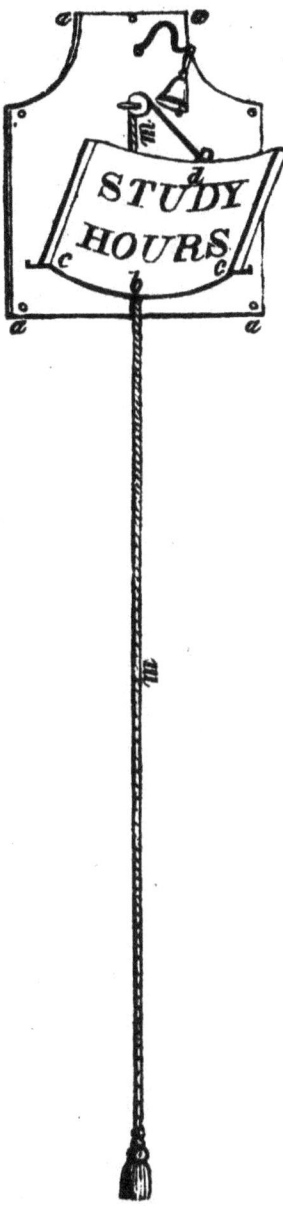

The figure *a a a a* is a board, about 18 inches by 12, to which the parts are to be attached, and which is to be nailed against the wall, at the height of about 8 feet; *b c d c* is a plate of tin or brass, 8 inches by 12, of the form represented in the drawing. At *c c* the lower extremities of the parts at the sides, the metal is bent round, so as to clasp a wire which runs from *c* to *c*, the ends of which wire are bent at right angles and run into the board. The plate will consequently turn on this axis, as on a hinge. At the top of the plate *d*, a small projection of the tin turns inwards, and to this, one end of the cord *m m* is attached. This cord passes back from *d* to a small pulley at the upper part of the board, and at the lower end of it a tassel, loaded so as to be an exact counterpoise to the card, is attached. By raising the tassel, the plate will of course fall over forward, till it is stopped by the part *b* striking the board, when it will remain in a horizontal position. On the other hand, by pulling down the tassel, the plate will be raised and drawn upwards against the board, so as to present its convex surface, with the words STUDY HOURS upon it, distinctly to the school. In the drawing it is represented in an inclined position, being not quite drawn up, that the parts might be more easily seen. At *d* there is a small projection of the tin, upwards, which touches the clapper of the bell suspended above, every time the plate passes up or down, and thus gives notice of its motions.

Of course the construction might be varied very much, and it may be more or less expensive, according to the wishes of the teacher. In the first apparatus of this kind which I used, the plate was simply a card of pasteboard, from which the machine took its name. This was cut out with a pen-knife, and after being covered with marble paper, a strip of white paper was pasted along the middle, with the inscription upon it. The wire *c e* and a similar one at the top of the plate, were passed through a perforation in the pasteboard and thence into the board. Instead of a pulley, the cord, which was a piece of twine, was passed through a little staple made of wire and driven into the board. The whole was made in one or two recesses in school, with such tools and materials as I could then command. The bell was a common table bell, with a wire passing through the handle. The whole was attached to such a piece of pine board as I could get on the occasion. This coarse contrivance was, for more than a year, the grand regulator of all the movements of the school.

I afterwards had one made in a better manner. The plate is of tin, gilded; the border and the letters of the inscription being black. A parlour bell rope passes over a brass pulley, and then runs downward in a groove made in the mahogany board to which the card is attached.

A little reflection will, however, show the teacher that the form and construction of the apparatus for marking the times of study and of rest, may be greatly varied. The chief point is simply to secure the *principle*, of whispering at definite and limited times, and at those alone. If such an arrangement is adopted, and carried faithfully into effect, it will be found to relieve the teacher of more than half of the confusion and perplexity which would otherwise be his hourly lot. I have detailed so particularly the method to be pursued in carrying this principle into effect, because I am so convinced of its importance, and of the incalculable assistance which such an arrangement will afford to the teacher in all his plans. Of course, I would not be understood to recommend its adoption in those cases, where teachers from their own experience, have devised and adopted *other* plans, which accomplish as effectually the same purpose. All that I mean, is to insist upon the absolute necessity of *some* plan, to remove this very common source of interruption and confusion, and I recommend this mode where a better is not known.

2. The second of the sources of interruption, as I have enumerated them, is mending pens. This business ought, if possible, to have a specific time assigned to it. Scholars are in general far too particular in regard to their pens. The teacher ought to explain to them that, in the transaction of the ordinary business of life, they cannot always have exactly such a pen as they would like. They must learn to write with various kinds of pens, and when furnished with one such as the teacher himself would consider suitable to write a letter to a friend with, they must be content. They should under-

stand that the *form* of the letters is more important, in learning to write, than the smoothness and clearness of the hair lines, and that though writing looks better, when executed with a perfect pen, a person may *learn* to write, nearly as well with one which is not absolutely perfect. So certain is this, though often overlooked, that a person would perhaps learn faster with chalk upon a black board, than with the best goose-quill that ever was mended.

I do not make these remarks to shew that it is of no consequence, whether scholars have good or bad pens, but only that this subject deserves very much less of the time and attention of the teacher, than it usually receives. When the scholars are allowed, as they very generally are, to come when they please, to present their pens, some four, five, or six times in a day—breaking in upon any business—interrupting any classes —perplexing and embarrassing the teacher, however he may be employed—there is a very serious obstruction to the progress of the scholars, which is by no means repaid by the improvement in this branch.

There are several ways by which this evil may be remedied, or at least be very effectually curtailed. Some teachers take their pens with them, and mend them in the evening at home. For various reasons, this cannot always be practised. There may, however, be a time set apart in the school specially for this purpose. But the best plan is, for the teacher not to mend the pens himself.

Let him choose from among the older and more intelligent of his scholars, four or five, whom he will teach. They will be very glad to learn, and to mend every day twenty-five or fifty pens each. Very little ingenuity will be necessary to devise some plan, by which the scholars may be apportioned among these, so that each shall supply a given number, and the teacher be relieved entirely.

3. *Answering questions about studies.* A teacher who does not adopt some system in regard to this subject, will be always at the mercy of his scholars. One boy will want to know how to parse a word, another where the lesson is, another to have a sum explained, and a fourth will wish to show his work, to see if it is right. The teacher does not like to discourage such inquiries. Each one, as it comes up, seems necessary; each one too is answered in a moment; but the endless number, and the continual repetition of them consume his time and exhaust his patience.

There is another view of the subject, which ought to be taken. Perhaps it would not be far from the truth, to estimate the average number of scholars in the schools in our country, at fifty. At any rate, this will be near enough for our present purpose. There are three hours in each session, making one hundred and eighty minutes, which divided among fifty, give about three minutes and a half to each individual. If the reader has in his own school, a greater or a less number, he can easily correct the above, so as to adapt it to his own case, and ascertain the portion, which may justly be appropriated to each pupil. It will probably vary from two to four minutes. Now a period of four minutes slips away very fast while a man is looking over perplexing problems, and if he exceeds that time at all, he is doing injustice to his other pupils. I do not mean that a man is to confine himself, rigidly, to the principle suggested by this calculation, of cautiously appropriating no more time to any one of his pupils, than such a calculation would assign to each; but simply that this is a point which should be kept in view, and have a very strong influence in deciding how far it is right to devote attention, exclusively, to individuals. It seems to me that it shows very clearly, that one ought to teach his pupils, as much as possible, *in masses*, and as little as possible, by private attention to individual cases.

The following directions will help the teacher to carry these principles into effect. When you assign a lesson, glance over it yourself, and consider what difficulties are likely to arise. You know the progress which your pupils have made, and can easily anticipate their difficulties. Tell them all together, in the class, what their difficulties will be, and how they may surmount them. Give them directions how they are to act in the emergencies, which will be likely to occur. This simple step will remove a vast number of the questions, which would otherwise become occasions for interrupting you. With regard to other difficulties, which cannot be foreseen and guarded against, tell them to bring them to the class the next recitation. Half a dozen might, and very probably would meet with the same difficulty. If they bring it to you one by one, you have to answer it over and over again, whereas, when it is brought to the class, one explanation answers for all.

As to all questions about the lesson,—where it is, and what it is, and how long it is,—never answer them. Require each pupil to remember for himself, and if he was absent when the lesson was assigned, let him ask his classmate in a recess.

You may refuse to give particular individuals the private assistance they ask for, in such a way as to discourage and irritate them, but it is not necessary. It can be done in such a manner, that the pupil will see the propriety of it, and acquiesce pleasantly in it.

A child comes to you, for example, and says,

'Will you tell me, sir, where the next lesson is?'

'Were you not in the class at the time?'

'Yes, sir, but I have forgotten.'

'Well, I have forgotten too. I have a great many classes to hear, and of course a great many lessons to assign, and I never remember them; it is not necessary for me to remember.'

'May I speak to one of the class, to ask about it?'

'You cannot speak, you know, till the Study Card is down; you may, then.'

'But I want to get my lesson now.'

'I don't know what you will do, then: I am sorry you don't remember.'

'Besides,' continues the teacher, looking pleasantly, however, while he says it, 'if I knew, I should think I ought not to tell you.'

'Why, sir?'

'Because, you know, I have said I wish the scholars to remember where the lessons are, and not come to me. You know it would be very unwise for me, after assigning a lesson in the class, to spend my time in telling the individuals over again here. Now if I should tell *you*, I should have to tell others, and thus adopt a practice, which I have condemned.'

Take another case. You assign to a class of little girls a subject of composition, requesting them to copy their writing upon a sheet of paper, leaving a margin an inch wide at the top, and one of half an inch at the sides and bottom. The class take their seats, and, after a short time, one of them comes to you, saying she does not know how long an inch is.

'Don't you know any thing about it?'

'No sir, not much.'

'Should you think *that* is more or less than an inch?' (pointing to a space on a piece of paper much too large.)

'More.'

'Then you know something about it. Now I did not tell you to make the margins *exactly* an inch, and half an inch, but only as near as you could tell.'

'Would that be about right?' asks the girl, showing a distance.

'I must not tell you, because you know I never in such cases help individuals; if that is as near as you can get it, you may make it so.'

It may be well, after assigning a lesson to a class, to say that all those who do not distinctly understand what they have to do, may remain after the class have taken their seats, and ask. The task may then be distinctly assigned again, and the difficulties so far as they can be foreseen, explained.

By such means, these sources of interruption and difficulty may, like the others, be almost entirely removed. Perhaps not altogether, for many cases may occur where the teacher may choose to give a particular class permission to come to him for help. Such permission, however, ought never to be given, unless it is absolutely necessary, and should never be allowed to be taken, unless it is distinctly given.

4. Hearing recitations. I am aware that many attempt to do something else at the same time that they are hearing a recitation, and there may perhaps be some individuals who can succeed in this. If the exercise to which the teacher is attending consists merely in listening to the reciting, from memory, some passage committed, it

can perhaps be done. I hope, however, to show in a future chapter, that there are other and far higher objects which every teacher ought to have in view, and he who understands these objects, and aims at accomplishing them,—who endeavours to *instruct* his class, to enlarge and elevate their ideas, to awaken a deep and paramount interest in the subject which they are examining, will find that his time must be his own, and his attention uninterrupted, while he is presiding at a class. All the other exercises and arrangements of the school are, in fact, preparatory and subsidiary to this. Here, that is, in the classes, the real business of teaching is to be done. Here the teacher comes in contact with his scholars, mind with mind; and here consequently, he must be uninterrupted and undisturbed. I shall speak more particularly on this subject hereafter, under the head of instruction; all I wish to secure in this place is, that the teacher should make such arrangements, that he can devote his exclusive attention to his classes, while he is actually engaged with them.

Each recitation, too, should have its specified time, which should be adhered to with rigid accuracy. If anything like the plan I have suggested for allowing rests of a minute or two every half hour should be adopted, it will mark off the forenoon into parts, which ought to be precisely and carefully observed. I was formerly accustomed to think, that I could not limit the time for my recitations without great inconvenience, and occasionally allowed one exercise to encroach upon the succeeding, and this upon the next, and thus sometimes the last was excluded altogether. But such a lax and irregular method of procedure is ruinous to the discipline of a school. On perceiving it, at last I put the bell into the hands of a pupil, commissioning her to ring regularly, having myself fixed the times, saying that I would show my pupils that I could myself be confined to system, as well as they. At first I experienced a little inconvenience, but this soon disappeared, and at last the hours and half hours of our artificial division, entirely superseded in the school-room, the divisions of the clock face.

But in order that I may be specific and definite, I will draw up a plan for the regular division of time, for a common school, not to be *adopted*, but to be *imitated*; i. e. I do not recommend exactly this plan, but that some plan, precise and specific, should be determined upon, and exhibited to the school by a diagram like the following.

FORENOON.

IX	X	XI	XII
Reading.	Writing. R. G.	Arithmetic.

AFTERNOON.

II	III	IV	V
Grammar.	Writing. R. G.	Geography.

A drawing on a large sheet, made by some of the older scholars, (for a teacher should never do any thing of this kind which his scholars can do for him,) should be made and pasted up to view, the names of the classes being inserted in the columns, under their respective heads. At the double lines at ten and three, there might be a rest of two minutes. An officer appointed for the purpose, ringing a bell at each of the parts marked on the plan, and making the signal for the *rest*, whatever signal might be determined upon. It is a good plan to have a bell rung five minutes before each half hour expires, and then exactly at its close. The first one would be to notify the teacher, or teachers, if there are more than one in the school, that the time for their respective recitations is drawing to a close. At the second bell the new classes should take their places without waiting to be called for. The scholars will thus see that the arrangements of the school are based upon system, to which the teacher himself conforms, and not subjected to his own varying will. They will thus not only go on more regularly, but they will yield more easily and pleasantly to the necessary arrangements.

The fact is, children love system and regularity. Each one is sometimes a little uneasy under the restraint which it imposes upon him, individually, but they all love to see its operation upon others, and they are generally very willing to submit to its laws, if the rest of the community are required to submit too. They show this in their love of military parade; what allures them is chiefly the *order* of it: and even a little child creeping upon the floor will be pleased when he gets his playthings in a row. A teacher may turn this principle to most useful account, in forming his plans for his school.

It will be seen by reference to the foregoing plan, that I have marked the time for the recesses, by the letter R. at the top. Immediately after them, both in the forenoon and in the afternoon, twenty minutes are left, marked G., the initial standing for General Exercise. They are intended to denote periods during which all the scholars are in their seats, with their work laid aside, ready to attend to what the teacher has to bring before the whole. There are so many occasions, on which it is necessary to address the whole school, that it is very desirable to appropriate a particular time for it. In most of the best schools, I believe this plan is adopted. I will mention some of the subjects which would come up at such a time.

1. There are some studies which can be advantageously attended to by the whole school together; such as Punctuation, and to some extent, Spelling.

2. Cases of discipline which it is necessary to bring before the whole school, ought to come up at a regularly appointed time. By attending to them here, there will be a greater importance attached to them. Whatever the teacher does, will seem to be more deliberate, and in fact *will be* more deliberate.

3. General remarks, bringing up classes of faults which prevail, also any general directions which may at any time be needed: and in fact any business relating to the general arrangements of the school.

4. Familiar lectures from the teacher on various subjects,—very familiar in their form, and perhaps accompanied by questions addressed to the whole. The design of such lectures should be to extend the *general knowledge* of the pupils in regard to those subjects on which they will need information in their progress through life. In regard to each of these particulars, I shall speak more particularly hereafter in the chapters to which they respectively belong. My only object here is to show in the general arrangements of the school,

how a place is to be found for them. My practice has been to have two periods of short duration each day appropriated to these objects: the first to the *business of the school*, and the second to such studies or lectures as could be most profitably attended to at such a time.

We come now to one of the most important subjects which present themselves to the teacher's attention, in settling the principles upon which he shall govern his school. I mean the degree of influence which the boys themselves shall have in the management of its affairs. Shall the government of a school be a *monarchy* or a *republic?* To this question, after much inquiry and many experiments, I answer, a monarchy; an absolute, unlimited monarchy; the teacher possessing exclusive power, as far as the pupils are concerned, though strictly responsible to the committee, or the trustees, under whom he holds his office.

While, however, it is thus distinctly understood that the power of the teacher is supreme, that all the power rests in him, and that he alone is responsible for its exercise, there ought to be a very free and continual *delegation* of power to the pupils. As much business as is possible, should be committed to them. They should be interested as much as possible in the affairs of the school, and led to take an active part in carrying them forward; though they should, all the time, distinctly understand that it is only *delegated* power which they exercise, and that the teacher can, at any time revoke what he has granted, and alter or annul at pleasure, any of their decisions. By this plan, we have the responsibility resting where it ought to rest, and yet the boys are trained to business, and led to take an active interest in the welfare of the school. Trust is reposed in them, which may be greater or less as they are able to bear. All the good effects of reposing trust and confidence, and committing the management of important business to the pupils will be secured, without the dangers which would result from the entire surrender of the management of the institution into their hands.

There have been, in several cases, experiments made with reference to ascertaining how far a government, strictly republican, would be admissible in a school. A very fair experiment of this kind was made at the Gardiner Lyceum, in Maine. At the time of its establishment, nothing was said of the mode of government which it was intended to adopt. For some time the attention of the instructors was occupied in arranging the course of study, and attending to the other concerns of the institution, and in the infant state of the Lyceum, few cases of discipline occurred, and no regular system of government was necessary.

Before long, however, complaints were made that the students at the Lyceum were guilty of breaking windows in an old building used as a town-house. The Principal called the students together, mentioned the reports, and said that he did not know, and did not wish to know who were the guilty individuals. It was necessary, however, that the thing should be examined, and that restitution should be made; and relying on their faithfulness and ability, he should leave them to manage the business alone. For this purpose, he nominated one of the students as judge, some others as jury-men, and appointed the other officers necessary, in the same manner. He told them, that in order to give them time to make a thorough investigation, they were excused from farther exercises during the day.

The principal then left them, and they entered on the

trial. The result was, that they discovered the guilty individuals, ascertained the amount of mischief done by each, and sent to the *select men* a message, by which they agreed to pay a sum equal to three times the value of the injury sustained.

The students were soon after informed that this mode of bringing offenders to justice, would hereafter be always pursued, and arrangements were made for organizing a *regular republican government* among the young men. By this government, all laws which related to the internal police of the institution, were to be made, all officers were appointed, and all criminal cases were to be tried. The students finding the part of a judge too difficult for them to sustain, one of the Professors was appointed to hold that office, and for similar reasons, another of the Professors was made President of the Legislative assembly. The Principal was the executive, with power to *pardon*, but not to *sentence*, or even *accuse*.

Some time after this, a student was indicted for profane swearing; he was tried, convicted and punished. After this he evinced a strong hostility to the government. He made great exertions to bring it into contempt, and when the next trial came on, he endeavoured to persuade the witnesses that giving evidence was dishonourable, and he so far succeeded, that the defendant was acquitted for want of evidence, when it was generally understood that there was proof of his guilt, which would have been satisfactory, if it could have been brought forward. For some time after this, the prospect was rather unfavourable, though many of the students themselves opposed with great earnestness these efforts, and were much alarmed lest they should lose their free government, through the perverseness of one of their number. The attorney general, at this juncture, conceived the idea of indicting the individual alluded to, for an attempt to overturn the government. He obtained the approbation of the principal, and the Grand Jury found a bill. The court, as the case was so important, invited some of the trustees of the Lyceum who were in town, to attend the trial. The parent of the defendant was also informed of the circumstances and requested to be present, and he accordingly attended. The prisoner was tried, found guilty, and sentenced, if I mistake not, to an expulsion. At his earnest request however, to be permitted to remain in the Lyceum and redeem his character, he was pardoned and restored, and became perfectly exemplary in his conduct and character. After this occurrence, the system went on in successful operation, for some time.

The legislative power was vested in the hands of a general committee, consisting of eight or ten, chosen by the students from their own number. They met about once a week to transact such business as appointing officers, making and repealing regulations, and inquiring into the state of the Lyceum. The Instructors had a negative upon all their proceedings, but no direct and positive power. They could pardon, but they could assign no punishments, nor make laws inflicting any.

Now such a plan as this may succeed for a short time, and under very favourable circumstances; and the circumstance, which it is chiefly important should be favourable, is, that the man who is called to preside over such an association, should possess such a share of *generalship*, that he can really manage the institution *himself*, while the power is *nominally* and *apparently* in the hands of the boys. Should this not be the case, or should the teacher, from any cause, lose his personal influence in the school, so that the institution should really be surrendered into the hands of the pupils, things must be on a very unstable footing. And accordingly where such a plan has been adopted, it has I believe, in every instance, been ultimately abandoned.

Real self-government is an experiment sufficiently hazardous among men; though Providence, in making a daily supply of food necessary for every human being, has imposed a most powerful check upon the tendency to anarchy and confusion. Let the populace of London materially interrupt the order, and break in upon the arrangements of the community, and in eight and forty hours, nearly the whole of the mighty mass will be in the hands of the devourer, hunger; and they will be soon brought to submission. On the other hand, a month's anarchy and confusion in a college or an academy, would be delight to half the students, or else times have greatly changed, since I was within college walls.

Although it is thus evident that the important concerns of a literary institution cannot be safely committed into the hands of the students, very great benefits will result from calling upon them to act upon, and to decide questions relative to the school, within such limits, and under such restrictions, as may appear best. Such a practice will assist the teacher very much, if he manages it with any degree of dexterity: for it will interest his pupils in the success of the school, and secure, to a very considerable extent, their co-operation. It will teach them self-control and self-government, and will accustom them to submit to the majority,—that lesson, which, of all others, it is important for a republican to learn.

In endeavouring to interest the pupils of a school in

the work of co-operating with the teacher in its administration, no little dexterity will be necessary, at the outset. In all probability, the formal announcement of this principle, and the endeavour to introduce it, by a sudden revolution, would totally fail. Boys, like men, must be gradually prepared for power, and they must exercise it only so far as they are prepared. This however, can very easily be done. The teacher should say nothing of his general design, but when some suitable opportunity presents, he should endeavour to lead his pupils to co-operate with him, in some particular instance.

For example, let us suppose that he has been accustomed to distribute the writing-books with his own hand, when the writing hour arrives, and that he concludes to delegate this simple business first to his scholars. He accordingly states to them, just before the writing exercise of the day on which he proposes the experiment, as follows:

'I have thought that time will be saved, if you will help me to distribute the books; and I will accordingly appoint four distributors, one for each division of the seats, who may come to me, and receive the books and distribute them, each to his own division. Are you willing to adopt this plan?'

The boys answer, 'Yes sir,' and the teacher then looks carefully around the room, and selects four pleasant and popular boys, boys who, he knows, would gladly assist him, and who would, at the same time, be agreeable to their school-mates. This latter point is necessary, in order to secure the popularity and success of the plan.

Unless the boys are very different from any I have ever met with, they will be pleased with the duty thus assigned them. They will learn system and regularity by being taught to perform this simple duty in a proper manner. After a week, the teacher may consider their term of service as having expired, and thanking them in public for the assistance they have rendered him, he may ask the scholars if they are willing to continue the plan, and if the vote is in favour of it, as it unquestionably would be, each boy probably hoping that he should be appointed to the office, the teacher may nominate four others, including perhaps upon the list, some boy popular among his companions, but whom he has suspected to be not very friendly to himself or the school. I think the most scrupulous politician would not object to securing influence, by conferring office in such a case. If any difficulties arise from the operation of such a measure, it can easily be dropped or modified. If it is successful, it may be continued, and the principle extended, till it very considerably modifies all the arrangements, and the whole management of the school.

Or let us imagine the following scene to have been the commencement of the introduction of the principle of limited self-government into a school.

The preceptor of an academy was sitting at his desk, at the close of school, while the pupils were putting up their books and leaving the room, when a boy came in with angry looks, and with his hat in his hands, bruised and dusty, advanced to the master's desk, and complained that one of his companions had thrown down his hat upon the floor, and had almost spoiled it.

The teacher looked calmly at the mischief, and then asked how it happened.

'I don't know sir; I hung it up on my nail, and he pulled it down.'

'I wish you would ask him to come here,' said the teacher. 'Ask him pleasantly.'

The accused soon came in, and the two boys stood together before the master.

'There seems to be some difficulty between you boys, about a nail to hang your hats upon. I suppose each of you think it is your own nail.'

'Yes sir,' said both the boys.

'It will be more convenient for me to talk with you about this to-morrow, than to night, if you are willing to wait. Besides, we can examine it more calmly then. But if we put it off till then, you must not talk about it in the mean time, blaming one another, and keeping up the irritation that you feel. Are you both willing to leave it just where it is till to-morrow, and try to forget all about it till then? I expect I shall find you both a little to blame.'

The boys rather reluctantly consented. The next day the master heard the case and settled it, so far as it related to the two boys. It was easily settled in the morning, for they had had time to get calm, and were, after sleeping away their anger, rather ashamed of the whole affair, and very desirous to have it forgotten.

That day, when the hour for the transaction of business came, the teacher stated to the school that it was necessary to take some measures to provide each boy with a nail for his hat. In order to show that it was necessary, he related the circumstances of the quarrel which had occurred the day before. He did this, not with such an air and manner as to convey the impression that his object was to find fault with the boys, or to expose their misconduct, but to show the necessity of doing something to remedy the evil, which had been the cause of so unpleasant an occurrence. Still, though he said nothing in the way of reproach or reprehension, and did not name the boys, but merely gave a cool and impartial narrative of the facts, the effect, very evidently, was to bring such quarrels into discredit. A calm review of misconduct, after the excitement has gone by, will do more to bring it into disgrace, than the most violent invectives and reproaches, directed against the individuals guilty of it.

'Now boys,' continued the master, ' will you assist me in making arrangements to prevent the recurrence of all temptations of this kind hereafter. It is plain that every boy ought to have a nail appropriated expressly to his use. The first thing to be done, is to ascertain whether there are enough for all. I should like, therefore, to have two committees appointed; one to count and report the number of nails in the entry, and also how much room there is for more; the other, is to ascertain the number of scholars in school. They can count all who are here, and by observing the vacant desks, they can ascertain the number absent. When this investigation is made, I will tell you what to do next.'

The boys seemed pleased with the plan, and the committees were appointed, two members on each. The master took care to give the quarrellers some share in the work, apparently forgetting, from this time, the unpleasant occurrence which had brought up the subject.

When the boys came to tell him their results, he desired them to make a little memorandum, in writing, as he might forget, before the time came for reading them. They brought him presently a rough scrap of paper, with the figures marked upon it. He told them he should forget which was the number of nails, and which the number of scholars, unless they wrote it down.

'It is the custom among men,' said he, ' to make out their report, in such a case, fully, so that it would explain itself; and I should like to have you, if you are willing, make out yours a little more distinctly.'

Accordingly, after a little additional explanation, the boys made another attempt, and presently returned, with something like the following:

>The Committee for counting the nails report as follows :
>Number of nails - 35
>Room for - - - 15

The other report was very similar, though somewhat rudely written and expressed, and both were perfectly satisfactory to the preceptor, as he plainly showed by the manner in which he received them.

I need not finish the description of this case, by narrating particularly, the reading of the reports, the appointment of a committee to assign the nails, and to paste up the names of the scholars, one to each. The work, in such a case, might be done in recesses, and out of school hours; and though, at first, the teacher will find that it is as much trouble to accomplish business in this way, as it would be to attend to it directly himself; yet after a little experience, he will find that his pupils will acquire dexterity and readiness, and will be able to render him very material assistance in the accomplishment of his plans.

The *assistance rendered to the teacher*, is however not the object. The main design is to *interest the pupils* in the management and welfare of the school, and to identify them, as it were, with it. It will accomplish this object: and every teacher who will try the experiment, and carry it into effect, with any tolerable degree of skill, will find that it will in a short time, change the whole aspect of the school, in regard to the feelings subsisting between himself and his pupils.

Each teacher who tries such an experiment, will find himself insensibly repeating it, and after a time he may have a large number of officers and committees, who are entrusted with various departments of business. He will have a secretary, chosen by ballot by the scholars, to keep a record of all the important transactions in the school for each day. At first he will dictate to the secretary, telling him precisely what to say, or even writing it for him, and merely requiring him to copy it into the book provided for the purpose. Afterwards he will give him less and less assistance, till he can keep the record properly himself. The record of each day will be read on that succeeding, at the hour for business. He will have a committee of one or two to take care of the fire, and another to see that the room is constantly in good order. He will have distributors for each division of seats, to distribute books, and compositions, and pens, and to collect votes. And thus, in a short time, his school will become *regularly organized as a society*, or *legislative assembly*. The boys will learn submission to the majority, in such *unimportant* things as may be committed to them, they will learn system and regularity, and every thing else that belongs to the science of political self-government.[1]

There are dangers, however:—what useful practice has not its dangers? One of these is, that the teacher may allow these arrangements to take up too much time. He must guard against this. I have found from experience, that fifteen minutes each day, with a school

---

[1] It must be remembered that these expressions are from the pen of a citizen of the United States.

of 135, is time enough. This ought never to be exceeded.

Another danger is, that the boys will be so engaged in the duties of their *offices*, as to neglect their *studies*. This would be, and ought to be, fatal to the whole plan. Avoid it in this manner; state publicly that you will not appoint any to office who are not good scholars, always punctual, and always prepared; and when any boy who holds any office is going behindhand in his studies, say to him kindly, 'You have not time to get your lessons, and I am afraid it is owing to the time you spend in helping me. Now if you wish to resign your office, so as to have a little more time for your lessons, you can: in fact, I think you ought to do it. You may try it for a day or two, and I will notice how you recite, and then we can decide.'

Such a communication will generally be found to have a powerful effect. If it does not remedy the evil, the resignation must be insisted on. A few decided cases of this kind, will effectually remove the evil I am considering.

Another difficulty which is likely to attend the plan of allowing the pupils of the school to decide some of the cases which occur, is, that it may tend to make them insubordinate; so that they will, in many instances, submit with less good humour, to such decisions as you may consider necessary. I do not mean that this will be the case with all, but that there will be a few who will be ungenerous enough, if you allow them to decide, sometimes, to endeavour to make trouble, or at least to show symptoms of impatience and vexation, because you do not allow them to decide always.

Sometimes this feeling may show itself by the discontented looks, or gestures, or even words, with which some unwelcome decision is received. Such a spirit should be checked with promptitude and decision. It will not be difficult to check, or even entirely to remove it. On one occasion, when, after learning the wishes of the scholars on some subject which had been brought before them, I decided otherwise than they wished, there arose a murmur of discontent from all parts of the room. This was the more distinct, because I have always accustomed my pupils to answer questions asked, and to express their wishes and feelings on any subject I may present to them, with great freedom.

I desired all those who had expressed their dissatisfaction, to rise.

About one third of the scholars arose.

'Perhaps you understood, that when I put the question to vote, I meant to abide by your decision, and that, consequently, I ought not to have reversed it, as I did, afterwards.'

'Yes, sir;' 'Yes, sir;' they replied.

'Do you suppose it would be safe to leave the decision of important questions to the scholars in this school?'

'Yes, sir;' 'No, sir.' The majority were, however, in the affirmative.

Thus far, only those who were standing, had answered. I told them, that as they were divided in opinion, they might sit, and I would put the question to the whole school.

'You know,' I continued, addressing the whole, 'what sort of persons the girls, who compose this school are. You know about how many are governed, habitually, by steady principle, and how many by impulse and feeling. You know, too, what proportion have judgment and foresight necessary to consider and decide independently, such questions as continually arise in the management of a school. Now suppose I should resign the school into your own hands, as to its management, and only come in to give instruction to the classes, leaving all general control of its arrangements with you; would it go on safely, or not?'

As might have been foreseen, there was, when the question was fairly proposed, scarcely a solitary vote in favour of government by scholars. They seemed to see clearly the absurdity of such a scheme.

'Besides,' I continued, ' the Trustees of this school have committed it to my charge; they hold me responsible; the public hold *me* responsible, not you. Now if I should surrender it into your hands, and you, from any cause, should manage the trust unfaithfully, or unskilfully, I should still be held accountable. I could never shift the responsibility upon you. Now it plainly is not just nor right, that one party should hold the power, and another be held accountable for its exercise. It is clear, therefore, in every view of the subject, that I should retain the management of this school in my own hands. Are you not satisfied that it is?'

The scholars universally answered, 'Yes, sir.' They seemed satisfied; and doubtless were.

It was then stated to them, that the object in asking them to vote, was, in some cases, to obtain an expression of their opinion or their wishes, in order to help *me* to decide; and only in those cases where it was expressly stated, did I mean to give the final decision to them.

Still, however, if cases are often referred to them, the feeling will gradually creep in among them, that the school is managed on republican principles, as they call it, and they will, unless this point is specially guarded, gradually lose that spirit of entire and cordial subordination, so necessary for the success of any school. It should often be distinctly explained to them, that a republican government is one, where the power essentially resides in the community, and is exercised by a ruler, only so far as the community delegates it to him; whereas in a school, the government is based on the principle, that the power, primarily and essentially, resides in the teacher, the scholars exercising only such as he may delegate to them.

With these limitations and restrictions, and with this express understanding, in regard to what is, in all cases, the ultimate authority, I think there will be no danger in throwing a very large share of the business which will, from time to time, arise in the school, upon the scholars for decision. In my own experience, this plan has been adopted with the happiest results. A small red morocco wrapper lies constantly on a little shelf, accessible to all. By its side is a little pile of papers, about one inch by six, on which any one may write her motion, or her *proposition*, as they call it, whatever it may be, and when written, it is enclosed in the wrapper, to be brought to me at the appointed time for attending to the general business of the school. Through this wrapper, all questions are asked, all complaints entered, all proposals made. Is there discontent in the school? It shows itself by '*propositions*' in the wrapper. Is any body aggrieved or injured? I learn it through the wrapper. In fact it is a little safety valve, which lets off, what, if confined, might threaten explosion,—an index,—a thermometer, which reveals to me, from day to day, more of the state of public opinion in the little community, than any thing beside.

These propositions are generally read aloud; some cases are referred to the scholars for decision; some I decide myself; others are laid aside without notice of any kind; others still, merely suggest remarks on the subjects to which they allude.

The principles, then, which this chapter has been intended to establish, are simply these. In making your general arrangements, look carefully over your ground, consider all the objects which you have to accomplish, and the proper degree of time and attention, which each deserves. Then act upon system. Let the mass of particulars which would otherwise crowd upon you in promiscuous confusion, be arranged and classified. Let each be assigned to its proper time and place; that your time may be your own—under your own command—and not, as is too often the case, at the mercy of the thousand accidental circumstances, which may occur.

In government, be yourself supreme, and let your supremacy be that of *authority*. But delegate power, as freely as possible, to those under your care. Show them that you are desirous of reposing trust in them, just so far as they show themselves capable of exercising it. Thus interest them in your plans, and make them feel that they participate in the honour of success or the disgrace of failure.

I have gone much into detail in this chapter, proposing definite measures by which the principles I have recommended may be carried into effect. I wish, however, that it may be distinctly understood, that all I contend for, is the *principles* themselves; no matter what the particular measures are, by which they are secured. Every good school must be systematic; but they need not all be on precisely the same system. As this work is intended almost exclusively for beginners, much detail has been admitted: and many of the specific measures here proposed, may perhaps be safely adopted, where no others are established. There may also perhaps be cases, where teachers, whose schools are already in successful operation, may engraft, upon their own plans, some things which are here proposed. If they should attempt it, it must be done cautiously and gradually. There is no other way by which they can be safely introduced, or even introduced, at all. This is a point of so much importance, that I must devote a paragraph to it, before closing the chapter.

Let a teacher propose to his pupils, formally, from his desk, the plan of writing *propositions*, for example, and procure his wrapper, and put it in its place;—and what would be the result? Why, not a single paper, probably, could he get, from one end of the week to the other. But let him, on the other hand, when a boy comes to him to ask some question, the answer to which, many in the school would equally wish to hear, say to the inquirer—

'Will you be so good as to write that question, and put it on my desk, and then, at the regular time, I will answer it to all the school.'

When he reads it, let him state, that it was written at his request, and give the other boys permission to leave their proposals or questions on his desk, in the same way. In a few days, he will have another, and thus the plan may be gently and gradually introduced.

So with officers. They should be appointed among the scholars, only *as fast as they are actually needed*, and the plan should thus be cautiously carried into execution, only so far as it proves good on trial. Be always cautious about innovations and changes. Make no rash experiments, on a large scale, but always test your principle, in a small way, and then, if it proves good, gradually extend its operation, as circumstances seem to require.

By thus cautiously and slowly introducing plans, founded on the systematic principles here brought to view, a very considerable degree of quiet and order and regularity may be introduced into the largest and most miscellaneous schools. And this order and quiet are absolutely necessary, to enable the teacher to find that interest and enjoyment in his work which were exhibited in the last chapter; the pleasure of *directing and controlling mind*, and doing it, not by useless and anxious complaints, or stern threats and painful punishments; but by regarding the scene of labour in its true light, as a community of intellectual and moral beings, and governing it by moral and intellectual power. It is, in fact, the pleasure of exercising *power*. I do not mean arbitrary, personal authority, but the power to produce, by successful but quiet contrivance, extensive and happy results; the pleasure of calmly considering every difficulty, and without irritation or anger, devising the moral means to remedy the moral evil: and then the interest and pleasure of witnessing its effects.

CHAPTER III.

INSTRUCTION.

There are three kinds of human knowledge which stand strikingly distinct from all the rest. They lie at the foundation. They constitute the roots of the tree. In other words they are the *means*, by which all other knowledge is acquired. I need not say, that I mean Reading, Writing, and Calculation.[1]

---

[1] There is much incorrectness and want of precision in these remarks. Reading, writing, and calculation, do not lie at the foundation of human knowledge. An hour's conversation with a North American Indian might have convinced the writer, that without any knowledge of these three arts, which he calls fundamental, and indispensible for the attainment of knowledge, much valuable knowledge may be acquired and communicated. Again, were he to endeavour to teach a child of two or three years old these arts, he would find that certain attainments must be mastered, and a certain developement of the faculties made, before any successful prosecution of these branches can be reasonably expected. But let us suppose that by the term *knowledge*, the writer means *learning*; still, those other studies which are grouped together, as necessarily coexisting, and of equal importance for the attainment of knowledge, are in fact of very different value in themselves, and tending in very different degrees to the attainment of knowledge. Hence, if it be admitted that Reading should be regarded as a matter of primary importance, and that a greater facility in this branch is more valuable, than a proportionate increase of Geographical or Historical knowledge; the conclusion is not necessarily to be made as respects Arithmetic, and still less as respects Writing. Had I the same conduct of a school in which a very limited time were to be appropriated to instruction, I should certainly, on the Author's principles, be most anxious that a mechanical facility in the art of reading should be secured to all the pupils. But this point attained, or fairly in prospect, the next

Teachers do not perhaps always consider how entirely and essentially distinct these three are from all the rest. They are arts—the acquisition of them is not to be considered as Knowledge, so much as the means by which knowledge may be obtained. A child who is studying geography, or history, or natural science, is learning *facts*—gaining information; on the other hand, the one who is learning to write, or to read, or to calculate, may be adding little or nothing to his stock of knowledge. He is acquiring *skill*, which, at some future time, he may make the means of increasing his knowledge, to any extent.

This distinction ought to be kept constantly in view, and the teacher should feel that these three fundamental branches stand by themselves, and they stand first in importance. I do not mean to undervalue the others, but only to insist upon the superior value and importance of these. Teaching a pupil to read, before he enters upon the active business of life, is like giving a new settler an axe, as he goes to seek his new home in the forest. Teaching him a lesson in history, is, on the other hand, only cutting down a tree or two for him. A knowledge of natural history is like a few bushels of grain, gratuitously placed in his barn; but the art of ready reckoning, is the plough, which will remain by

---

consideration should be, such a measure of intellectual developement as would render the mechanical act of reading more available to its true end. Some practice in calculation would form a very important branch, on account of its application to the business of life, and still more on account of its peculiar efficacy when properly conducted, in imparting quickness and clearness to the mind. Writing I should regard as of far less moment than such studies as tend more directly to the improvement of the mind. I am convinced that many of our peasantry lose altogether the capacity of reading, in consequence of their understandings having been too much neglected to allow of their taking pleasure in the perusal of a book; and further, that the preaching of our clergy is often unprofitable to them because for the same reason, little understood.

him for years, and help him to draw out from the soil an annual treasure.

The great object then, of the common schools in our country, is to teach the whole population to read, to write, and to calculate. In fact, so essential is it, that the accomplishment of these objects should be secured, that it is even a question whether common schools should not be confined to them. I say it is a *question*, for it is sometimes made so, though public opinion has decided, that some portion of attention, at least, should be paid to the acquisition of additional knowledge. But after all, the amount of *knowledge*, which is actually acquired at schools, is very small. It must be very small. The true policy is, to aim at making all good readers, writers, and calculators, and to consider the other studies of the school important, chiefly as practice, in turning these arts to useful account. In other words, the scholars should be taught these arts thoroughly, first of all, and in the other studies, the main design should be to show them how to use, and interest them in using, the arts they have thus acquired.

A great many teachers feel a much stronger interest in the one or two scholars they may have, in Surveying, or in Latin, than they do in the large classes in the elementary branches, which fill the school. But a moment's reflection will show, that such a preference is founded on a very mistaken view. Leading forward one or two minds, from step to step, in an advanced study, is certainly far inferior, in real dignity and importance, to opening all the stores of written knowledge, to fifty or a hundred. The man who neglects the interests of his school, in these great branches, to devote his time to two or three, or half a dozen older scholars, is unjust both to his employers and to himself.

It is the duty, therefore, of every teacher, who commences a common district school, even for a single season, to make, when he commences, an estimate of the state of his pupils, in reference to these three branches. How do they all write? How do they all read? How do they calculate? It would be well if he would make a careful examination of the school, in this respect. Let them all write a specimen, Let all read, and let him make a memorandum of the manner, noticing how many read fluently, how many with difficulty, how many know only their letters, and how many are to be taught these. Let him ascertain also, what progress they have made in arithmetic—how many can readily perform the elementary processes, and what number need instruction in these. After thus surveying the ground, let him form his plan, and lay out his whole strength in carrying forward, as rapidly as possible, the *whole school*, in these studies. In this manner he is acting, most directly and powerfully, on the intelligence of the whole future community in that place. He is opening to fifty or a hundred minds, stores of knowledge, which they will go on exploring, for years to come. What a descent now from such a work as this, to the mere hearing of the recitation of half a dozen boys in Surveying!

I repeat it, that a thorough and enlightened survey of the whole school should be taken, and plans formed for elevating the whole mass in those great branches of knowledge which are to be of immediate practical use to them in future life.

If the school is of a higher order, the teacher should, in the same manner, before he forms his plans, consider well what are the great objects which he has to accomplish. He should ascertain what is the existing state of his school, both as to knowledge and character;—how long, generally, his pupils are to remain under his care—what are to be their future stations and conditions in life, and what objects he can reasonably hope to effect for them, while they remain under his influence. By means of this forethought and consideration, he will be enabled to work judiciously.

It is desirable, also, that what I have recommended, in reference to the whole school, should be done with each individual. Ascertain, (by other means however than formal examination,) to what stage his education has advanced, and deliberately consider what objects you can reasonably expect to effect for him, while he remains under your care. You cannot indeed always form your plans so as to promote to the fullest extent the general advancement of the school, and yet to consult the interests of particular individuals;—but these general views will, in a thousand cases, modify your plans, or affect in a greater or less degree, all your arrangements. They will keep you to a steady purpose, and your work will go on far more systematically and regularly, than it would, if, following a too common practice, you were to come headlong into your school, take things just as you find them, and carry them forward at random, without end or aim.

This survey of your field being made, you are prepared to commence definite operations, and the great difficulty in carrying your plans into effect, is, to act more efficiently on *the greatest number at a time*. The whole business of public instruction, if it goes on at all, must go on by the teacher's skill in multiplying his power, by acting on *numbers at once*. In most books on education, we are taught almost exclusively, how to operate on the *individual*. It is the error into which theoretic writers almost always fall. We meet in every periodical, and in every treatise, and in fact in almost every conversation on the subject, with remarks which sound very well by the fire-side, but they are totally inefficient and useless in school, from their being apparently based upon the supposition, that the teacher has but *one* pupil to attend to at a time. The great question in the management of schools, is not, how you can take *one* scholar, and lead him forward most rapidly in a prescribed course, but how you can classify and arrange *numbers*, comprising every possible variety, both as to knowledge and capacity, so as to carry them all forward effectually together.

The extent to which a teacher may multiply his power, by acting on numbers at a time, is very great. In order to estimate it, we must consider carefully what it is, when carried to the greatest extent to which it is capable of being carried, under the most favourable circumstances. Now it is possible for a teacher to speak so as to be easily heard by three hundred persons, and three hundred pupils can be easily so seated as to see his illustrations or diagrams. Now suppose that three hundred pupils, all ignorant of the method of reducing fractions to a common denominator, and yet all old enough to learn, are collected in one room. Suppose they are all attentive and desirous of learning, it is very plain that the process may be explained to the whole at once, so that half an hour spent in that exercise would enable a very large proportion of them to understand the subject. So, if a teacher is explaining to a class in grammar, the difference between a noun and verb, the explanation would do as well for several hundred as for the dozen who constitute the class, if arrangements could only be made to have the hundreds hear it. But there are, perhaps, only a hundred in the school, and of these a large part understand already the point to be explained, and another large part are too young to attend to it. I wish the object of these remarks not to be misunderstood. I do not recommend the attempt to teach on so extensive a scale; I admit that it is impracticable; I only mean to show in what the impracticability consists, namely, in the difficulty of making such arrangements as to derive the full benefit from the instructions rendered. They are, in the nature of things, available to the extent I have represented, but in actual practice, the full benefit cannot be derived. Now so far as we thus fall short of this full benefit, so far there is, of course, waste; and it is difficult or impossible to make such arrangements as will prevent the waste, in this manner, of a large portion of every effort, which the teacher makes.

A very small class instructed by an able teacher, is like a factory of a hundred spindles, with a water-wheel of power sufficient for a thousand. In such a case, even if the owner from want of capital or any other cause, cannot add the other nine hundred, he ought to know how much of his power is in fact unemployed, and make arrangements to bring it into useful exercise, as soon as he can. The teacher in the same manner, should understand what is the full beneficial effect, which it is possible *in theory*, to derive from his instructions. He should understand too, that just so far as he falls short of this full effect, there is waste. It may be unavoidable; part of it unquestionably is, like the friction of machinery, unavoidable. Still, it is waste; and it ought to be so understood, that by the gradual perfection of the machinery, it may be more and more fully prevented.

Always bear in mind then, when you are devoting your time to two or three individuals in a class, that you are losing a very large part of your labour. Your instructions are conducive to good effect, only to the one tenth or one twentieth of the extent, to which, under more favourable circumstances, they might be made available. And though you cannot always avoid this loss, you ought always to be aware of it, and so to shape your measures, as to diminish it as much as possible.

We come now to consider the particular measures to be adopted, in giving instruction.

The objects which are to be secured, in the management of classes, are twofold,

1. Recitation.
2. Instruction.

These two objects are, it is plain, entirely distinct. Under the latter, is included all the explanation and assistance and additional information, which the teacher may give his pupils, and under the former, such an *examination* of individuals, as is necessary to secure their careful attention to their lessons. It is unsafe to neglect either of these points. If the class meetings are mere *recitations*, they soon become dull and mechanical: the pupils generally take little interest in their studies, and imbibe no literary spirit. Their intellectual progress will, accordingly suddenly cease, the moment they leave school, and cease to be called upon to recite lessons. On the other hand, if *instruction* is all that is aimed at, and *recitation*, (by which I mean, as above explained, such an examination of individuals as is necessary to ascertain that they have faithfully performed the tasks assigned,) is neglected, the exercise soon becomes not much more than a lecture, to which those, and those only, will attend, who please.

The business therefore of a thorough examination of the class must not be omitted. I do not mean that each individual scholar must every day be examined; but simply that the teacher must in some way or other satisfy himself by reasonable evidence, that the whole class are really prepared. A great deal of ingenuity may be exercised in contriving means for effecting this object, in the shortest possible time. I know of no part of the field of a teacher's labours, which may be more facilitated by a little ingenuity than this.

One teacher, for instance, has a spelling lesson to hear, he begins at the head of the line, and putting one word to each boy, he goes regularly down, each successive pupil calculating the chances whether a word, which he can accidentally spell, will or will not come to him. If he spells it, the teacher cannot tell whether he is prepared or not. That word is only one among fifty, constituting the lesson. If he misses it, the teacher cannot decide that he was unprepared. It might have been a single accidental error.

Another teacher, hearing the same lesson, requests the boys to bring their slates, and as he dictates the words, one after another, requires all to write them. After they are all written, he calls upon them to spell aloud as they have written them, simultaneously; pausing a moment after each, to give those who are wrong, an opportunity to indicate it, by some mark opposite the word misspelt. They all count the number of errors and report them. He passes down the class, glancing his eye at the work of each one, to see that all is right, noticing particularly those slates, which from the character of the boys, need a more careful inspection. A teacher who had never tried this experiment, would be surprised at the rapidity with which such work will be done by a class, after a little practice.

Now how different are these two methods, in their actual results! In the latter case the whole class are thoroughly examined. In the former, not a single member of it is. Let me not be understood to recommend exactly this method of teaching spelling, as the best one to be adopted in all cases. I only bring it forward as an illustration of the idea, that a little machinery, a little ingenuity, in contriving ways of acting on the *whole*, rather than on individuals, will very much promote the teacher's designs.

In order to facilitate such plans, it is highly desirable that the classes should be trained to military precision and exactness in these manipulations. What I mean by this, may perhaps be best illustrated by describing a case. It will show, in another branch, how much will be gained by acting upon numbers at once, instead of upon each individual in succession.

Imagine, then, that a teacher requested all the pupils of his school, who could write, to take out their slates, at the hour for a general exercise. As soon as the first bustle of opening and shutting the desks was over, he looked around the room, and saw some ruling lines across their slates, others wiping them all over on both sides with sponges, others scribbling, or writing, or making figures.

'All those,' says he, with a pleasant tone and look, ' who have taken out any thing besides slates, may rise.'

Several, in various parts of the room, stood up.

'All those who have written any thing since they took out their slates, may rise too, and those who have wiped their slates.'

When all were up, he said to them, though not with a frown or a scowl, as if they had committed some very great offence:

'Suppose a company of soldiers should be ordered to *form a line*, and instead of simply obeying that order, they should all set at work, each in his own way, doing something else. One man, at one end of the line, begins to load and fire his gun, another takes out his knapsack, and begins to eat his luncheon; a third amuses himself by going as fast as possible through the exercise; and another still, begins to march about, hither and thither, facing to the right and left, and performing all the evolutions he can think of. What should you say to such a company as that?'

The boys laughed.

'It is better,' said the teacher, 'when numbers are acting under the direction of one, that they should all act *exactly together*. In this way we advance much faster than we otherwise should. Be careful therefore to do exactly what I command, and nothing more.'

'*Provide a place on your slates, large enough to write a single line*,' added the teacher, in a distinct voice. [I print his orders in Italics, and his remarks and explanations in Roman letter.]

'*Prepare to write.*'

'I mean by this,' he continued, 'that you place your slates before you, with your pencils at the place where you are to begin, so that all may commence precisely at the same instant.

The teacher who tries such an experiment as this, will find at such a juncture, an expression of fixed and pleased attention upon every countenance in school. All will be intent; all will be interested. Boys love order and system, and acting in concert, and they will obey, with great alacrity, such commands as these, if they are good-humouredly, though decidedly expressed.

The teacher observed in one part of the room, a hand raised, indicating that the boy wished to speak to him. He gave him liberty by pronouncing his name.

'I have no pencil,' said the boy.

A dozen hands all around him were immediately seen fumbling in pockets and desks, and in a few minutes several pencils were reached out for his acceptance.

The boy looked at the pencils, and then at the teacher; he did not exactly know whether he was to take one or not.

'All those boys,' said the teacher, pleasantly, 'who have taken out pencils, may rise.'

'Have these boys done right or wrong?'

'Right,' 'wrong,' 'right,' answered their companions, variously.

'Their motive was to help their classmate out of his difficulties; that is a good feeling, certainly.'

'Yes sir, right,' 'right.'

'But I thought you promised me a moment ago,' replied the teacher, 'not to do any thing unless I commanded it. Did I ask for pencils?'

A pause.

'I do not blame these boys at all in this case, still it is better to adhere rigidly to the principle of *exact obedience*, when numbers are acting together. I thank them, therefore, for being so ready to assist a companion, but they must put their pencils away, as they were taken out without orders.'

Now such a dialogue as this, if the teacher speaks in a good-humoured, though decided manner, would be universally well received in any school. Whenever strictness of discipline is unpopular, it is rendered so simply by the ill-humoured and ill-judged means by which it is attempted to be introduced. But all children will love strict discipline, if it is pleasantly, though firmly maintained. It is a great, though very prevalent mistake, to imagine that boys and girls like a lax and inefficient government, and dislike the pressure of steady control. What they dislike, is sour looks and irritating language, and they therefore very naturally dislike every thing introduced or sustained by their means. If, however, exactness and precision in all the operations of a class, and of the school, are introduced and enforced in the proper manner, i. e. by a firm, but mild and good-humoured authority, scholars will universally be pleased with them. They like to see the uniform appearance, the straight line, the simultaneous movement. They like to feel the operation of system, and to realize, while they are in the school room, that they form a community, governed by fixed and steady laws, firmly but pleasantly administered. On the other hand, laxity of discipline, and the disorder which will result from it, will only lead the pupils to despise their teacher, and to hate their school.

By introducing and maintaining such a discipline as I have described, great facilities will be secured for examining the classes. For example, to take a case different from the one before described; let us suppose that a class have been performing a number of examples in Addition: they come together to the recitation, and under *one* mode of managing classes, the teacher is immediately beset by a number of the pupils, with excuses. One had no slate, another was absent when the lesson was assigned; a third performed the work, but it got rubbed out; and a fourth did not know what was to be done. The teacher stops to hear all these, and to talk about them, fretted himself, and fretting the delinquents by his impatient remarks. The rest of the class are waiting, and having nothing good to do, the temptation is almost irresistible to do something bad. One boy is drawing pictures on his slate, to make his neighbours laugh, another is whispering, and two more are at play. The disorder continues, while the teacher goes round examining slate after slate, his whole attention being engrossed by each individual as the pupils come to him successively, while the rest are left to themselves, interrupted only by an occasional harsh, or even angry, but utterly useless rebuke from him.

But under *another* mode of managing classes and schools, a very different result would be produced.

A boy approaches the teacher to render an excuse; the teacher replies, addressing himself, however, to the whole class, 'I shall give all an opportunity to offer their excuses presently. No one must come till he is called.'

The class then regularly take their places in the recitation seats; the prepared and unprepared together. The following commands are given and obeyed promptly. They are spoken pleasantly, but still in the tone of command.

'The class may rise.'

'All those that are not fully prepared with this lesson, may sit.'

A number sit, and others, doubtful whether they are prepared or not, or thinking that there is something peculiar in their cases, which they wish to state, raise their hands, or make any other signal which is customary to indicate a wish to speak. Such a signal ought always to be agreed upon, and understood in school.

The teacher shakes his head; saying, 'I will hear you presently. If there is on any account whatever, any doubt whether you are prepared, you must sit.'

'Those that are standing may read their answers to No. 1. Unit figure?'

Boys. 'Five.'

Teacher. 'Tens?'

B. 'Six.'

T. 'Hundreds?'

B. 'Seven.'

While these numbers are thus reading, the teacher looks at the boys, and can easily see whether any are not reading their own answers, but only following the rest. If they have been trained to speak exactly together, his ear will also at once detect any erroneous answer which any one may give. He takes down the figures given by the majority on his own slate, and reads them aloud.

'This is the answer obtained by the majority. It is undoubtedly right. Those who have different answers may sit.'

These directions if understood and obeyed, would divide the class evidently into two portions. Those standing have their work done, and done correctly; and those sitting, have some excuse or error to be examined. A new lesson may now be assigned, and the first portion may be dismissed; which, in a well-regulated school, will be two-thirds of the class. Their slates may be slightly examined as they pass by the teacher on their way to their seats, to see that all is fair; but it will be safe to take it for granted, that a result in which a majority agree, will be right. Truth is consistent with itself, but error, in such a case, never is. This the teacher can at any time shew, by comparing the answers that are wrong, they will always be found, not only to differ from the correct result, but to contradict each other.

The teacher may now if he pleases, after the majority of the class have gone, hear the reasons of those who were unprepared, and look for the errors of those whose work was incorrect; but it is better to spend as little time as possible in such a way. If a scholar is not prepared, it is not of much consequence, whether it is because he forgot his book, or mistook the lesson; or if it is ascertained that his answer is incorrect, it is ordinarily, a mere waste of time, to search for the particular error.

'I have looked over my work, Sir,' says the boy, perhaps, 'and I cannot find where it is wrong.' He means by it, that he does not believe that it is wrong.

'It is no matter if you cannot,' would be the proper reply, 'since it certainly is wrong; you have made a mistake in adding somewhere, but it is not worth while for me to spend two or three minutes apiece with all of you to ascertain where. Try to be careful next time.'

The cases of those who are unprepared at a recitation ought, by no means, to be passed by unnoticed, although it would be unwise to spend much time in examining each in detail.

'It is not of much consequence,' the teacher might say, 'whether you have good excuses or bad, so long as you are not prepared. In future life you will certainly be unsuccessful, if you fail, no matter for what reason, to discharge the duties which devolve upon you. A carpenter, for instance, would certainly lose his work, if he should not perform it faithfully, and in season. Excuses, no matter how reasonable, will do him little good. So in this school. I want good recitations, not good excuses. I hope every one will be prepared to-morrow.'

It is not probable, however, that every one would be prepared the next day, in such a case,—but, by acting steadily on these principles, the number of delinquencies would be so much diminished, that the very few which should be left, could easily be examined in detail, and the remedies applied.

Simultaneous recitation, by which I mean the practice of addressing a question to all the class, to be answered by all together, is a practice which has been for some years rapidly extending in our schools, and if adopted with proper limits and restrictions, is attended with great advantage. The teacher must guard against some dangers, however, which will be likely to attend it.

1. Some will answer very eagerly,—instantly after the question is completed. They wish to show their superior readiness. Let the teacher mention this,—expose kindly the motive which leads to it, and tell them it is as irregular to answer before the rest, as after them.

2. Some will defer their answers until they can catch those of their comrades for a guide. Let the teacher mention this fault,—expose the motive which leads to it, and tell them that if they do not answer independently, and at once, they had better not answer at all.

3. Some will not answer at all. The teacher can tell by looking round the class who do not, for they cannot counterfeit the proper motion of the lips with promptness and decision, unless they know what the answer is to be. He ought occasionally to say to such a one, ' I perceive you do not answer; ' and ask him questions individually.

4. In some cases there is danger of confusion in the answers, from the fact that the question may be of such

a nature, that the answer is long, and may, by different individuals, be differently expressed. This evil must be guarded against, by so shaping the question as to admit of a reply in a single word. In reading large numbers, for example, each figure may be called for by itself, or they may be given one after another, the pupils keeping exact time. When it is desirable to ask a question to which the answer is necessarily long, it may be addressed to an individual, or the whole class may write their replies, which may then be read in succession.

In a great many cases where simultaneous answering is practised, after a short time the evils above specified are allowed to grow, until at last some half dozen bright members of a class answer for all, the rest dragging after them echoing their replies, or ceasing to take any interest in an exercise, which brings no personal and individual responsibility upon them. To prevent this, the teacher should exercise double vigilance at such a time. He should often address questions to individuals alone, especially to those most likely to be inattentive and careless, and guard against the ingress of every abuse, which might without close vigilance appear.

With these cautions the method here alluded to, will be found to be of very great advantage in many studies; for example, all the arithmetical tables may be recited in this way; words may be spelt, answers to sums given; columns of figures added, or numbers multiplied; and many questions in History, Geography, and other miscellaneous studies, answered, especially the general questions asked for the purpose of a review.

But besides being useful as a mode of examination, this plan of answering questions simultaneously, is a very important means of fixing in the mind any facts which the teacher may communicate to his pupils. If for instance, he says, some day to a class, that Vasco de Gama, was the discoverer of the passage round the Cape of Good Hope, and leaves it here, in a few days not one in twenty will recollect the name. But let him call upon them all to spell it simultaneously, and then to pronounce it distinctly three or four times in concert, and the word will be very strongly impressed upon the mind. The reflecting teacher will find a thousand cases in the instruction of his classes, and in his general exercises in the school, in which this principle will be of great utility. It is universal in its application. What we *say*, we fix by the very act of saying it in the mind. Hence reading aloud, though a slower, is a far more thorough method than reading silently; and it is better in almost all cases, whether in the family, or in sabbath, or common schools, when general instructions are given, to have the leading points fixed in the mind by questions answered simultaneously.

But we are wandering a little from our subject; which is, in this part of our chapter, the methods of *examining* a class, not of giving or fixing instructions.

Another mode of examining classes, which it is important to describe, consists in requiring *written answers* to the questions asked. The form and manner in which this plan may be adopted, is various. The class may bring their slates to the recitation, and the teacher may propose questions successively, the answers to which all the class may write, numbering them carefully. After a dozen answers are written, the teacher may call for them at random, or he may repeat a question, and ask each pupil to read the answer he had written, or he may examine the slates. Perhaps this method may be very successfully employed in reviews, by dictating to the class a list of questions relating to the ground they have gone over for a week, and to which they are to prepare answers, written out at length, and to be brought in at the next exercise. This method may be made more formal still, by requiring a class to write a full and regular abstract of all they have learned during a specified time. The practice of thus reducing to writing what has been learned, will be attended with many advantages, so obvious that they need not be described.

It will be perceived that three methods of examining classes have now been named, and these will afford the teacher the means of introducing a very great variety in his mode of conducting his recitations, while he still carries his class forward steadily in their prescribed course. Each is attended with its peculiar advantages. The *single replies*, coming from individuals specially addressed, are more rigid, and more to be relied upon; but they consume a great deal of time, and while one is questioned, it requires much skill to keep up interest in the rest. The *simultaneous answers* of a class, awaken more general interest, but it is difficult, without special care, to secure by this means a thorough examination of all. The *written replies*, are more thorough, but they require more time and attention; and while they habituate the pupil to express his thoughts in writing, they would, if exclusively adopted, fail to accustom him to an equally important practice, that of the oral communication of his thoughts. A constant variety, of which these three methods should be the elements, is unquestionably the best mode. We not only, by this means, secure in a great degree the advantages which each is fitted to produce, but we gain also the additional advantage and interest of variety.

By these, and perhaps by other means, it is the duty of the teacher to satisfy himself that his pupils are really attentive to their duties. It is not perhaps necessary, that every individual should be every day minutely examined. This is in many cases impossible, but the system of examination should be so framed, and so administered, as to be daily felt by all, and to bring upon every one a daily responsibility.

We come now to consider the second general head, which was to be discussed in this chapter.

The study of books alone, is insufficient to give knowledge to the young. In the first stage, learning to read a book is of no use whatever, without the voice of the living teacher. The child cannot take a step alone. But as the pupil advances in his course, his dependence upon his teacher for guidance and help continually diminishes, until, at last, the scholar sits in his solitary study, with no companion but his books, and desiring, for a solution of every difficulty, nothing but a larger library. In schools, however, the pupils have made so little progress in this course, that they all need more or less of this oral assistance. Difficulties must be explained, questions must be answered, the path must be smoothed, and the way pointed out by a guide who has travelled it before, or it will be impossible for the pupil to go on. This is the part of our subject which we now approach.

The great principle which is to guide the teacher in this part of his duty, is this; *assist your pupils in such a way as to lead them, as soon as possible, to do without assistance.* This is fundamental; in a short time they will be away from your reach; they will have no teacher to consult; and unless you teach them how to understand books themselves, they must necessarily stop suddenly in their course the moment you cease to help them forward. I shall proceed, therefore, to consider the subject in the following plan :—

1. Means of exciting interest in study.
2. The kind and degree of assistance to be rendered.
3. Miscellaneous suggestions.

1. Interesting the pupils in their studies. There are various principles of human nature, which may be of great avail in accomplishing this object. Making intellectual effort, and acquiring knowledge, are always pleasant to the human mind, unless some peculiar circumstances render them otherwise. The teacher has, therefore, only to remove obstructions, and sources of pain, and the employment of his pupils will be, of itself, a pleasure.

'I am going to give you a new exercise to day,' said a teacher to a class of boys, in Latin. 'I am going to have you parse your whole lesson, in writing. It will be difficult, but I think you may be able to accomplish it.'

The class looked surprised; they did not know what *parsing in writing* could be.

'You may first, when you take your seats, and are ready to prepare the lesson, write upon your slates a list of the first ten nouns, arranging them in a column. Do you understand so far?'

'Yes, sir.'

'Then rule lines for another column just beyond this. In parsing nouns, what is the first particular to be named?'

'What the noun is from.'

'Yes, that is its nominative. Now you may write at the head of the first column, the word *Nouns,* and at the head of the second, *Nom.* for nominative. Then rule a line for the third column. What shall this contain?' 'The declension.' 'Yes, and the fourth?' 'Gender.' 'The fifth?' 'Number.'

In the same manner, the other columns were designated; the sixth was to contain case; the seventh, the word with which the noun was connected in construction; and the eighth, a reference to the rule.

'Now I wish you,' continued the teacher, 'to fill up such a table as this, with *ten* nouns. Do you understand how I mean?'

'Yes, sir,' 'no, sir,' they answered, variously.

'All who do understand may take their seats, as I wish to give as little explanation as possible. The more you can depend upon yourselves the better.'

Those who saw clearly what was to be done, left the class, and the teacher continued his explanation to those who were left behind. He made the plan perfectly clear to them, by taking a particular noun, and running it through the table, showing what should be written opposite to the word, in all the columns, and then dismissed them.

The class separated, as every class would, in such a case, with strong interest in the work before them. It was not so difficult as to perplex them, and yet it required attention and care. They were interested and pleased; pleased with the effort which it required them to make, and they anticipated, with interest and pleasure, the time of coming again to the class to report and compare their work.

When the time for the class came, the teacher addressed them somewhat as follows:

'Before looking at your slates, I am going to predict what the faults are. I have not seen any of your work, but shall judge altogether from my general knowledge of school-boys, and the difficulties I know they meet with. Do you think I shall succeed?'

The scholars made no reply, and an unskilful teacher would imagine, that time spent in such remarks would be wholly wasted. By no means; the influence of it was to awaken universal interest in the approaching examination of the slates. Every scholar would be intent, watching with eager interest to see whether the imagined faults would be found upon his work. The class was, by that single pleasant remark, put into the best possible state for receiving the criticisms of the teacher.

'The first fault, which I suppose will be found, is, that some are unfinished.'

The scholars looked surprized. They did not expect to have that called a fault.

'How many plead guilty to it?'

A few raised their hands, and the teacher continued.

'I suppose that some will be found partly effaced. The slates were not laid away carefully, or they were not clean, so that the writing is not distinct. How many find this the case with their work?'

'I suppose that, in some cases, the lines will not be perpendicular, but will slant, probably towards the left, like writing.'

'I suppose also, that in some cases, the writing will be careless, so that I cannot easily read it. How many plead guilty to this?'

After mentioning such other faults as occurred to him, relating chiefly to the form of the table, and the mere mechanical execution of the work, he said—

'I think I shall not look at your slates to-day. You can all see, I have no doubt, how you can considerably improve them, in mechanical execution, in your next lesson; and I suppose you would a little prefer that I should not see your first imperfect efforts. In fact, I should rather not see them. At the next recitation, they probably will be much better.'

One important means by which the teacher may make his scholars careful of their reputation, is to show them thus, that he is careful of it himself.

Now, in such a case as this, for it is, except in the principles which it is intended to illustrate, imaginary, a very strong interest would be awakened in the class, in the work assigned them. Intellectual effort, in new and constantly varied modes, is in itself a pleasure, and this pleasure the teacher may deepen and increase very easily, by a little dexterous management, designed to awaken curiosity, and concentrate attention. It ought, however, to be constantly borne in mind, that this variety should be confined to the modes of pursuing an object, which is permanent, and constant, and steadily pursued. For instance, if a little class are to be taught simple Addition, after the process is once explained, which may be done, perhaps, in two or three lessons, they will need many days of patient practice, to render it familiar, to impress it firmly in their recollection, and to enable them to work with rapidity. Now this object must be steadily pursued. It would be very unwise for the teacher to say to himself; my class are tired of Addition, I must carry them on to Subtraction, or give them some other study. It would be equally unwise, to keep them many days performing example after example, in monotonous succession, each lesson a mere repetition of the last. He must steadily pursue his object, of familiarizing them fully with this elementary process, but he may give variety and spirit to the work, by changing occasionally the modes. One week he may dictate examples to them, and let them come together to compare their results; one of the class being appointed to keep a list of all who are correct, each day. At another time, each one may write an example, which he may read aloud to all the others, to be performed and brought in at the next time. Again, he may let them work on paper, with pen and ink, that he may see how few mistakes they make, as mistakes in ink cannot be easily removed. He may excite interest by devising ingenious examples, such as finding out how much all the numbers from one to fifty will make when added together, or the amount of the ages of the whole class; or any such example, the result of which they might feel a little interest in learning. Thus the object is steadily pursued, though the means of pursuing it, are constantly changing. We have the advantage of regular progress in the acquisition of knowledge truly valuable, while this progress is made, with all the spirit and interest which variety can give.

The necessity of making such efforts as this, however, to keep up the interest of the class in their work, and to make it pleasant to them, will depend altogether upon circumstances; or rather, it will vary much with circumstances. A class of pupils somewhat advanced in their studies, and understanding and feeling the value of knowledge, will need very little of such effort as this; while young and giddy children, who have been accustomed to dislike books and school, and every thing connected with them, will need more. It ought, however, in all cases, to be made a means, not an end;— the means to lead on a pupil to an *interest in progress in knowledge itself*, which is, after all, the great motive which ought to be brought to operate in the school-room as soon and as extensively as possible.

Another way to awaken interest in the studies of the school, is to bring out, as frequently and as distinctly as possible, the connexion between these studies and the practical business of life. The events which are occurring around you, and which interest the community in which you are placed, may, by a little ingenuity, be connected, in a thousand ways, with the studies of the school. If the practice, which has been already repeatedly recommended, of appropriating a quarter of an hour, each day, to a general exercise, should be adopted, it will afford great facilities for doing this.

Suppose, for example, while the question between the General Government and the State of South Carolina, was pending, and agitating the whole country, almost every one looking, with anxious interest, every day, for intelligence from the scene of the conflict, that the teacher of a school had brought up the subject, at such a general exercise as has been mentioned. He describes in a few words, the nature of the question, and in such a manner, as to awaken throughout the school, a strong interest in the result of the contest. He then says,

'I wish now to make you all more fully acquainted with this case, and the best way of doing it, which occurs to me, is as follows—

'There are several studies in school, which throw light upon this controversy; especially History, Geography, and Political Economy. Now, I shall take the classes in these studies, for a day or two, out of their regular course, and assign them lessons which relate to this subject, and then hear them recite in the General Exercise, that you may all hear. The first class in Geography may take therefore for their next lesson, the State of South Carolina; to-morrow they will recite in the hearing of the whole school, when I shall make such additional explanations as will occur to me. The next day, I shall assign to the class in History, a passage giving an account of the formation of this government; and afterwards lessons will be recited from the Political Class Book, explaining the mode of collecting money for the use of our government, by duties, and the relative powers of the General and State Governments. After hearing all these lessons recited, with my remarks in addition, you will be the better able to understand the subject, and then I shall bring in a newspaper now and then, and keep you acquainted with the progress of the affair.'

Now the propriety of taking up the particular subject, which I have here introduced, by way of illustration, in such a way, would depend altogether upon the character and standing of the school, the age and mental maturity of the scholars, and their capacity to understand the circumstances of such a case, and to appreciate those considerations which give interest to it. The principle however, is applicable to all; and one such experiment, dexterously carried through, will do more towards giving boys and girls, clear and practical ideas of the reason why they go to school, and of the importance of acquiring knowledge, than the best lecture on such a subject, which ever was delivered.

There is no branch of study attended to in school, which may, by judicious efforts, be made more effectual in accomplishing this object,—leading the pupils to see the practical utility, and the value of knowledge, than composition. If such subjects as are suitable themes for *moral essays*, are assigned, the scholars will indeed dislike the work of writing, and derive little benefit from it. The mass of pupils in our schools, are not to be writers of moral essays or orations, and they do not need to form that style of empty, florid, verbose declamation, which the practice of writing composition in our schools, as it is too frequently managed, tends to form. Assign practical subjects—subjects relating to the business of the school—or the events taking place around you. Is there a question before the community on the subject of the location of a new school house? Assign it to your pupils, as a question for discussion, and direct them not to write empty declamation, but to obtain, from their parents, the real arguments in the case, and to present them, distinctly and clearly, and in simple language, to their companions. Was a building burnt by lightning in the neighbourhood? Let those who saw the scene, describe it; their productions to be read by the teacher aloud; and let them see that clear descriptions please, and that good legible writing can be read fluently, and that correct spelling and punctuation and grammar, make the article go smoothly and pleasantly, and enable it to produce its full effect. Is a public building going forward in the neighbourhood of your school? You can make it a very fruitful source of subjects and questions, to give interest and impulse to the studies of the school-room. Your classes in geometry may measure—your arithmeticians may calculate, and make estimates—your writers may describe its progress, from week to week, and anticipate the scenes, which it will in future years exhibit.

By such means, the practical bearings and relations of the studies of the school-room may be constantly kept in view; but I ought to guard the teacher, while on this subject, most distinctly against the danger of making the school-room a scene of literary amusement, instead of study. These means of awakening interest, and relieving the tedium of the uninterrupted and monotonous study of text books, must not encroach on the regular duties of the school. They must be brought forward with judgment and moderation, and made subordinate and subservient to these regular duties. Their design is, to give spirit and interest, and a feeling of practical utility, to what the pupils are doing, and if resorted to, with these restrictions, and within these limits, they will produce powerful, but safe results.

Another way to excite interest, and that of the right kind in school, is not to *remove* difficulties, but to teach the pupils how to *surmount* them. A text book so contrived as to make study mere play, and to dispense with thought and effort, is the worst text book that can be made, and the surest to be in the end a dull one. The great source of literary enjoyment, which is the successful exercise of intellectual power, is, by such a mode of presenting a subject, cut off. Secure therefore severe study. Let the pupils see that you are aiming to secure it, and that the pleasure which you expect that they will receive, is that of firmly and patiently encountering and overcoming difficulty; of penetrating, by steady and persevering effort, into regions from which the idle and the inefficient are debarred; and that it is your province to lead them forward, not to carry them. They will soon understand this, and like it.

Never underrate the difficulties which your pupils will have to encounter, or try to persuade them that what you assign is *easy*. Doing easy things is generally dull work, and it is especially discouraging and disheartening for a pupil to spend his strength in doing what is really difficult for him, when his instructor, by calling his work easy, gives him no credit for what may have been severe and protracted labour. If a thing is really hard for the pupil, his teacher ought to know it, and admit it. The child then feels that he has some sympathy.

It is astonishing how great an influence may be exerted over a child, by his simply knowing that his efforts are observed and appreciated. You pass a boy in the street, wheeling a heavy load in a barrow; now simply stop to look at him, with a countenance which says, 'that is a heavy load; I should not think that boy could wheel it;' and how instantaneously will your look give fresh strength and vigour to his efforts. On the other hand, when in such a case, the boy is faltering under his load, try the effect of telling him, 'Why, that is not heavy; you can wheel it easily enough; trundle it along.' The poor boy will drop his load, disheartened and discouraged, and sit down upon it in despair. No, even if the work you are assigning to a class is easy, do not tell them so, unless you wish to destroy all their spirit and interest in doing it; and if you wish to excite their spirit and interest, make your work difficult, and let them see that you know it is so. Not so difficult as to tax their powers too heavily, but enough so, to require a vigorous and persevering effort. Let them distinctly understand too, that you know it is difficult,—that you mean to make it so,—but that they have your sympathy and encouragement, in the efforts which it calls them to make.

You may satisfy yourself that human nature is in this respect what I have described, by some such experiment as the following :—Select two classes, not very familiar with elementary arithmetic, and offer to each of them the following example in Addition :—

$$1\ 2\ 3\ 4\ 5\ 6\ 7\ 8\ 9$$
$$2\ 3\ 4\ 5\ 6\ 7\ 8\ 9\ 1$$
$$3\ 4\ 5\ 6\ 7\ 8\ 9\ 1\ 2$$

The numbers may be continued, according to the obvious law regulating the above, until each one of the nine digits has commenced the line. Or, if you choose Multiplication let the example be this:—

  Multiply 123456789
  by   123456789

Now, when you bring the example to one of the classes, address the pupils as follows:—

'I have contrived for you a very difficult sum. It is the most difficult one that can be made, with the number of figures contained in it, and I do not think that any of you can do it, but you may try. I shall not be surprised, if every answer should contain mistakes.'

To the other class, say as follows:—

'I have prepared an example for you, which I wish you to be very careful to perform correctly. It is a little longer than those you have had heretofore, but it is to be performed upon the same principles, and you can all do it correctly, if you really try.'

Now under such circumstances the first class will go to their seats with ardour and alacrity; determined to shew you that they can do work, even if it is difficult work. And if they succeed, they come to the class, the next day, with pride and pleasure. They have accomplished something which you admit it was not easy to accomplish. On the other hand, the second class will go to their seats with murmuring looks and words; and with a hearty dislike of the task you have assigned them. They know that they have something to do, which, however easy it may be to the teacher, is really difficult for them, and they have to be perplexed and wearied with the work, without having at last, even the little satisfaction of knowing that the teacher appreciates the difficulties with which they had to contend.

2. We now come to consider the subject of rendering assistance to the pupil, which is one of the most important and delicate parts of a teacher's work. The great difference which exists among teachers in regard to the skill they possess in this part of their duty, is so striking that it is very often noticed by others; and perhaps skill is here of more avail in deciding the question of success or failure, than any thing besides. The first great principle is however, simple and effectual.

(1.) *Divide and subdivide a difficult process, until your steps are so short, that the pupil can easily take them.*

Most teachers forget the difference between the pupil's capacity and their own, and they pass rapidly forward, through a difficult train of thought, in their own ordinary gait, their unfortunate followers vainly trying to keep up with them. The case is precisely analagous to that of the father, who walks with the step of a man, while his little son is by his side, wearying and exhausting himself with fruitless efforts to stretch his feet as far, and to move them as rapidly as a full-grown man.

But to show what I mean by subdividing a difficult process, so as to make each step simple, I will take a case which may serve as an example. I will suppose that the teacher of a common school, undertakes to show to his boys, who we will suppose are acquainted with nothing but elementary arithmetic, how longitude is ascertained, by means of the eclipses of Jupiter's satellites; not a *very* simple question,—as it would, at first view, strike one, but still one which like all others, may be easily explained merely by the power of the subdivision alluded to. I will suppose that the subject has come up at a general exercise,—perhaps the question was asked in writing by one of the older boys. I will present the explanation, chiefly in the form of question and answer, that it may be seen that the steps are so short, that the boys may take them themselves.

'Which way,' asked the teacher, 'are the Rocky Mountains from us?'

'West,' answer two or three of the boys.

In such cases as this, it is very desirable that the answers should be general, so that throughout the school there should be a spirited interest in the questions and replies. This will never be the case, if a small number of the boys only take part in the answers, and many teachers complain, that when they try this experiment, they can seldom induce many of the pupils to take a part.

The reason ordinarily is, that they say that *any* of the boys may answer, instead of that *all* of them may. The boys do not get the idea that it is wished that an universal reply should come from all parts of the room in which every one's voice should be heard. If the answer were feeble in the instance we are supposing, the teacher would perhaps say;

'I only heard one or two answers: do not more of you know where the Rocky Mountains are? Will you all think, and answer together? Which way are they from us?'

'West,' answer a large number of boys.

'You do not answer fully enough yet; I do not think more than forty answered, and there are about sixty here. I should like to have *every one in the room* answer, and all precisely together.'

He then repeats the question, and obtains a full response. A similar effort will always succeed.

'Now, does the sun in going round the earth, pass over the Rocky Mountains or over us first?'

To this question the teacher hears a confused answer.

Some do not reply; some say, 'Over the Rocky Mountains,' others, 'Over us,' and others still, 'The sun does not move at all.'

'It is true that the sun, strictly speaking, does not move; the earth turns round, presenting the various countries in succession to the sun, but the effect is precisely the same as it would be, if the sun moved, and accordingly I use that language. Now, how long does it take the sun to pass round the earth?'

'Twenty-four hours.'

'Does he go towards the west, or towards the east from us?'

'Towards the west.'

But it is not necessary to give the replies. The questions alone will be sufficient. The reader will observe that they inevitably lead the pupil by short and simple steps, to a clear understanding of the point to be explained.

'Will the sun go towards, or from, the Rocky Mountains, after leaving us?'

'How long did you say it takes the sun to go round the globe, and come to us again?'

'How long to go half round?' 'Quarter round?'

'How long will it take him to go to the Rocky Mountains?'

No answer.

'You cannot tell. It would depend upon the distance. Suppose then the Rocky Mountains were half round the globe, how long would it take the sun to go to them?'

'Suppose they were quarter round?'

'The whole distance is divided into portions called degrees, 360 in all. How many will the sun pass in going half round? In going quarter round? In going one-eighth round?'

'Forty-five degrees then, make one-eighth of the circumference of the globe. This you have already said will take three hours. In one hour then, how many degrees will the sun pass over?'

Perhaps no answer. If so, the teacher will subdivide the question on the principle we are explaining, so as to make the steps such that the pupils *can* take them.

'How many degrees will the sun pass over in three hours?'

'Forty-five.'

'How large a part of that then will he pass in one hour?'

'One third of it.'

'And what is one third of forty-five?'

The boys would readily answer fifteen, and the teacher would then dwell for a moment on the general truth thus deduced, that the sun, in passing round the earth, passes over fifteen degrees every hour.

'Suppose then it takes the sun one hour to go from us to the river Mississippi, how many degrees west of us would the river be?'

Having thus familiarized the pupils to the fact, that the motion of the sun is a proper measure of the difference of longtitude between two places, the teacher must dismiss the subject for a day, and when the next opportunity of bringing it forward occurs, he would perhaps take up the subject of the sun's motion as a measure of *time*.

'Is the sun ever exactly over our heads?'

'Is he ever exactly south of us?'

'When he is exactly south of us, or in other words, exactly opposite to us in his course round the earth, he is said to be in our meridian. For the word meridian means a line drawn exactly north or south from any place.'

There is no limit to the simplicity which may be imparted, even to the most difficult subjects, by subdividing the steps. This point for instance, the meaning of meridian, may be the subject if it were necessary of many questions, which would render it simple to the youngest child. The teacher may point to the various articles in the room or buildings, or other objects without, and ask if they are or are not in his meridian. But to proceed:

'When the sun is exactly opposite to us in the south, at the highest point to which he rises, what o'clock is it?'

'When the sun is exactly opposite to us, can he be opposite to the Rocky Mountains?'

'Does he get opposite to the Rocky Mountains before or after he is opposite to us?'

'When he is opposite to the Rocky Mountains, what o'clock is it there?'

'Is it twelve o'clock here, then, before or after it is twelve o'clock there?'

'Suppose the river Mississippi is fifteen degrees from us, how long is it twelve o'clock here before it is twelve o'clock there?'

'When it is twelve o'clock here then, what time will it be there?'

Some will probably answer 'one,' and some 'eleven.' If so, the step is too long, and may be subdivided thus:

'When it is noon here, is the sun going towards the Mississippi, or has he passed it?'

'Then has noon gone by at that river, or has it not yet come?'

'Then will it be one hour before, or one hour after noon?'

'Then will it be eleven or one?'

Such minuteness and simplicity would not in ordinary cases be necessary. I go into it here, merely to show how a subject ordinarily perplexing, may, by simply subdividing the steps, be made plain. The reader will observe, that in the above there are no explanations by the teacher, there are not even leading questions; that is, there are no questions whose form suggests the answers desired. The pupil goes on from step to step, simply because he has but one short step to take at a time.

'Can it be noon, then,' continues the teacher, 'here and at a place fifteen degrees west of us at the same time?'

'Can it be noon here, and at a place ten miles west of us at the same time?'

It is unnecessary to continue the illustration, for it will be very evident to every reader, that by going forward in this way, the whole subject may be laid out before the pupils, so that they shall perfectly understand it. They can, by a series of questions like the above, be led to see by their own reasoning, that time, as denoted by the clock, must differ in every two places, not upon the same meridian, and that the difference must be exactly proportional to the difference of longitude. So that a watch which is right in one place, cannot, strictly speaking, be right in any other place, east or west of the first: and that, if the time of day at two places can be compared, either by taking a chronometer from one to another, or by observing some celestial phenomenon, like the eclipses of Jupiter's satellites, and ascertaining precisely the time of their occurrence, according to the reckoning at both; the distances east or west by degrees may be determined. The reader will observe too, that the method by which this explanation is made, is strictly in accordance with the principle I am illustrating,—which is by simply *dividing the process into short steps*. There is no ingenious reasoning on the part of the teacher, no happy illustrations; no apparatus, no diagrams. It is a pure process of mathematical reasoning, made clear and easy by *simple analysis*.

In applying this method however, the teacher should be careful not to subdivide too much. It is best that the pupils should walk as fast as they can. The object of the teacher should be to smooth the path, not much more than barely enough to enable the pupil to go on. He should not endeavour to make it very easy.

(2.) Truths must not only be taught to the pupils, but they must be *fixed* and *made familiar*. This a point which seems to be very generally overlooked.[1]

'Can you say the Multiplication Table?' said a teacher to a boy, who was standing before him in his class.

'Yes, sir.'

'Well, I should like to hear you say the line beginning nine times one.'

The boy repeated it slowly, but correctly.

'Now I should like to hear you try again; and I will at the same time, say another line, to see if I can put you out.'

The boy looked surprised. The idea of his teacher's trying to perplex and embarrass him, was entirely new.

'You must not be afraid,' said the teacher; 'you will

---

[1] Where? In the United States? In *England* the importance of *grounding* pupils, i. e. of rendering first principles *fixed and familiar*, is generally recognized. The best mode of acquiring fresh knowledge seems to have been well considered and judiciously practised in the schools of the United States; here the principal attention has been paid to the *retaining and applying* the knowledge acquired. Is it not desirable to unite the characteristic features of each system?

undoubtedly not succeed in getting through, but you will not be to blame for the failure. I only try it, as a sort of intellectual experiment.'

The boy accordingly began again, but was soon completely confused by the teacher's accompaniment; he stopped in the middle of his line saying,

'I could say it, only you put me out.'

'Well, now try to say the Alphabet, and let me see if I can put you out there.'

As might have been expected the teacher failed. The boy went regularly onward to the end.

'You see now,' said the teacher, to the class, which had witnessed the experiment, 'that this boy knows his Alphabet, in a different sense, from that in which he knows his Multiplication Table. In the latter, his knowledge is only imperfectly his own; he can make use of it only under favourable circumstances. In the former it is entirely his own; circumstances have no control over him.'

A child has a lesson in Latin grammar to recite. She hesitates and stammers, miscalls the cases, and then corrects herself, and if she gets through at last, she considers herself as having recited well; and very many teachers would consider it well too. If she hesitates a little longer than usual in trying to summon to her recollection a particular word, she says perhaps, 'Don't tell me,' and if she happens at last to guess right, she takes her book with a countenance beaming with satisfaction.

'Suppose you had the care of an infant school,' might the instructor say to such a scholar, 'and were endeavouring to teach a little child to count, and she should recite her lesson to you in this way: 'One, two, four, no, three;—one, two, three,'—— stop, don't tell me,—

five—no, four—four—, five, — — — I shall think in a minute,—six—is that right? five, six, &c.' Should you call that reciting well?'

Nothing is more common than for pupils to say when they fail of reciting their lesson, that they could say it at their seats, but that they cannot now say it before the class. When such a thing is said for the first time, it should not be severely reproved, because nine children in ten honestly think, that if the lesson was learned so that it could be recited any where, their duty is discharged. But it should be kindly, though distinctly explained to them, that in the business of life, they must have their knowledge so much at command, that they can use it at all times, and in all circumstances, or it will do them little good.

One of the most common causes of difficulty in pursuing mathematical studies, or studies of any kind, where the succeeding lessons depend upon those which precede, is the fact that the pupil, though he may understand what precedes, is not *familiar* with it. This is very strikingly the case with Geometry. The class study the definitions, and the teacher supposes they fully understand them; in fact, they do *understand* them, but the name and the thing are so feebly connected in their minds, that a direct effort and a short pause, are necessary to recall the idea, when they hear or see the word. When they come on therefore to the demonstrations, which, in themselves, would be difficult enough, they have double duty to perform. The words used do not readily suggest the idea, and the connexion of the ideas requires careful study. Under this double burden, many a young geometrician sinks discouraged.

A class should go on slowly, and dwell on details, so long as to fix firmly, and make perfectly familiar, whatever they undertake to learn. In this manner, the knowledge they acquire will become their own. It will be incorporated, as it were, into their very minds, and they cannot afterwards be deprived of it.

The exercises which have for their object the rendering familiar that which has been learned, may be so varied as to interest the pupil very much, instead of being tiresome, as it might at first be supposed.

Suppose, for instance, a teacher has explained to a large class in grammar, the difference between an adjective and an adverb. If he leave it here, in a fortnight one half would have forgotten the distinction, but by dwelling upon it a few lessons, he may fix it for ever. The first lesson might be to write twenty short sentences containing only adjectives. The second to write twenty, containing only adverbs. The third, to write sentences in two forms, one containing the adjective, and the other expressing the same idea, by means of the adverb, arranging them in two columns, thus,

He writes well. | His writing is good.

Again, they may make out a list of adjectives, with the adverbs derived from each, in another column. Then they may classify adverbs on the principle of their meaning, or according to their termination. The exercise may be infinitely varied, and yet the object of the whole may be, to make *perfectly familiar*, and to fix for ever in the mind, the distinction explained.

These two points seem to me to be fundamental, so far as assisting pupils through the difficulties which lie in their way, is concerned. Diminish the difficulties as far as is necessary, by merely shortening and simplifying the steps, and make thorough work as you go on. These principles carried steadily into practice, will be effectual, in leading any mind through any difficulties which may occur. And though they cannot, perhaps be fully applied to every mind in a large school, yet they can be so far acted upon, in reference to the whole mass, as to accomplish the object for a very large majority.

3. *General cautions.* A few miscellaneous suggestions, which we shall include under this head, will conclude this chapter.

(1.) Never do any thing *for* a scholar, but teach him to do it for himself. How many cases occur, in the schools of our country, where the boy brings his slate to the teacher, saying he cannot do a certain sum. The teacher takes the slate and pencil, performs the work in silence,—brings the result,—returns the slate to the hands of his pupil,—who walks off to his seat, and goes to work on the next example; perfectly satisfied with the manner in which he is passing on. A man who has not done this a hundred times himself, will hardly believe it possible that such a practice can prevail. It is so evidently a waste of time, both for master and scholar.

(2.) Never get out of patience with dulness. Perhaps I ought to say, never get out of patience with any thing, that would perhaps be the wisest rule; but above all things, remember that dulness and stupidity, (and you will certainly find them in every school,) are the very last things to get out of patience with. If the Creator has so formed the mind of a boy, that he must go through life slowly and with difficulty, impeded by obstructions, which others do not feel, and depressed by discouragements which others never know, his lot is surely hard enough, without having you to add to it the trials and suffering, which sarcasm and reproach from you can heap upon him. Look over your school-room, therefore, and wherever you find one whom you perceive the Creator to have endued with less intellectual power than others, fix your eye upon him with an expression of kindness and sympathy. Such a boy will have suffering enough from the selfish tyranny of his companions; he ought to find in you a protector and friend. One of the greatest pleasures which a teacher's life affords, is the interest of seeking out such an one, bowed down with burdens of depression and discouragement, unaccustomed to sympathy and kindness, and expecting nothing for the future but a weary continuation of the cheerless toils, which have embittered the past; and the pleasure of taking off the burden, of surprising the timid disheartened sufferer by kind words and cheering looks, and of seeing, in his countenance, the expression of ease and even of happiness, gradually returning.

(3.) The teacher should be interested in *all* his scholars, and aim equally to secure the progress of all. Let there be no neglected ones in the school room. We should always remember, that however unpleasant in countenance and manners that bashful boy in the corner may be, or however repulsive in appearance, or unhappy in disposition, that girl, seeming to be interested in nobody, and nobody appearing interested in her, they still have each of them a mother who loves her own child, and takes a deep and constant interest in its history. Those mothers have a right too, that their children should receive their full share of attention in a school which has been established for the common and equal benefit of all.[1]

(4.) Do not hope or attempt to make all your pupils alike. Providence has determined that human minds

[1] Yes; but anterior to the consideration of the parent, is the consideration of the child itself. It is at least as important for the pupil of little abilities to have them cultivated, and advanced, if possible, to respectable mediocrity, as for one more highly gifted to have his talents cherished and pushed on to superior brilliancy.

should differ from each other, for the very purpose of giving variety and interest to this busy scene of life. Now if it were possible for a teacher so to plan his operations, as to send his pupils forth upon the community, formed on the same model, as if they were made by machinery, he would do so much towards spoiling one of the wisest of the plans which the Almighty has formed for making this world a happy scene. Let it be the teacher's aim to co-operate with, not vainly to attempt to thwart the designs of providence. We should bring out those powers with which the Creator has endued the minds placed under our control. We must open our garden to such influences as shall bring forward all the plants, each in a way corresponding to its own nature. It is impossible, if it were wise, and it would be foolish if it were possible, to stimulate by artificial means, the rose, in hope of its reaching the size and magnitude of the apple-tree, or to try to cultivate the fig and the orange, where wheat only will grow. No, it should be the teacher's main design to shelter his pupils from every deleterious influence, and to bring every thing to bear upon the community of minds before him, which will encourage in each one the developement of its own native powers. For the rest, he must remember that his province is to cultivate, not to create.

Error on this point is very common. Many teachers, even among those who have taken high rank, through the success with which they have laboured in this field, have wasted much time in attempting to do what can never be done; to form the character of those brought under their influence, after a certain uniform model, which they have conceived as the standard of excellence. Their pupils must write just such a hand, they must compose in just such a style; they must be similar in sentiment and feeling, and their manners must be formed according to a fixed and uniform model; and when, in such a case, a pupil comes under their charge whom providence has designed to be entirely different from the beau ideal adopted as the standard, more time and pains, and anxious solicitude are wasted in vain attempts to produce the desired conformity, than half the school require beside.

(5.) Do not allow the faults or obliquities of character, or the intellectual or moral wants of any individual of your pupils, to engross a disproportionate share of your time. I have already said, that those who are peculiarly in need of sympathy or help, should receive the special attention they seem to require; what I mean to say now, is, do not carry this to an extreme. When a parent sends you a pupil, who, in consequence of neglect or mismanagement at home, has become wild and ungovernable, and full of all sorts of wickedness, he has no right to expect, that you shall turn your attention away from the wide field, which in your whole school-room lies before you, to spend your time, and exhaust your spirits and strength, in endeavouring to repair the injuries which his own neglect has occasioned. When you open a school, you do not engage, either openly or tacitly, to make every pupil who may be sent to you, a learned or a virtuous man. You do engage to give them all faithful instruction, and to bestow upon each such a degree of attention, as is consistent with the claims of the rest: but it is both unwise and unjust to neglect the many trees in your nursery, which by ordinary attention may be made to grow straight and tall, and to bear good fruit, that you may waste your labour upon a crooked stick, from which all your toil can secure very little beauty or fruitfulness.[1]

Let no one now understand me to say, that such cases are to be neglected. I admit the propriety, and in fact, have urged the duty, of paying to them a little more than their due share of attention. What I now condemn is the practice, of which all teachers are in danger, of devoting such a disproportionate and unreasonable degree of attention to them, as to encroach upon their duties to others. The school, the whole school is your field, the elevation *of the mass*, in knowledge and virtue, and no individual instance, either of dulness or precosity, should draw you away from its steady pursuit.

(6.) The teacher should guard against unnecessarily imbibing those faulty mental habits to which his station and employment expose him. Accustomed to command, and to hold intercourse with minds which are immature and feeble, compared with our own, we gradually acquire habits, that the rough collisions and the friction of active life, prevent from gathering around other men. Narrow-minded prejudices and prepossessions are imbibed, through the facility with which, in our own little community, we adopt and maintain opinions. A too strong confidence in our own views on every subject, almost inevitably comes, from never hearing our opinions contradicted or called in question; and we express those opinions in a tone of authority, and even sometimes of arrogance, which we acquire in the school-room: for there, when we speak, nobody can reply.

These peculiarities show themselves first, and in fact,

---

[1] True; but if an educator has no reasonable prospect of correcting the vicious propensities of a pupil, he is bound in conscience to inform the parent, and offer to resign his charge.

most commonly in the school-room; and the opinions thus formed, very often relate to the studies and management of the school. One has a peculiar mode of teaching spelling, which is successful almost entirely through the magic influence of his interest in it, and he thinks no other mode of teaching this branch, is even tolerable. Another must have all his pupils write on the angular system, or the anti-angular system, and he enters with all the zeal into a controversy on the subject, as if the destiny of the whole rising generation depended upon its decision. Tell him that all that is of any consequence in any hand-writing, is that it should be legible, rapid, and uniform, and that for the rest, it would be better that every human being should write a different hand—and he looks upon you with astonishment, wondering that you cannot see the vital importance of the question, whether the vertex of an *o* should be pointed or round. So in every thing; he has *his way* in every minute particular, a way from which he cannot deviate, and to which he wishes every one else to conform.

This set, formal mannerism is entirely inconsistent with that commanding intellectual influence which the teacher should exert in the administration of his school. He should work, with what an artist calls boldness and freedom of touch. Activity and enterprise of mind should characterize all his measures, if he wishes to make bold, original and efficient men.

(7.) Assume no false appearances in your school, either as to knowledge or character. Perhaps it may justly be said to be the common practice of teachers in this country, to affect dignity of deportment in the presence of their pupils, which in other cases is laid aside; and to pretend to superiority in knowledge, and an infallibility of judgment, which no sensible man would claim before other sensible men, but which an absurd fashion seems to require of the teacher. It can however scarcely be said to be a fashion, for the temptation is almost exclusively confined to the young and the ignorant, who think they must take up by appearance, what they want in reality. Very few of the older and more experienced and successful instructers in our country, fall into it at all. But some young beginner, whose knowledge is very limited, and who, in manner and habits, has only just ceased to be a boy, walks into his school-room with a countenance of forced gravity, and with a dignified and solemn step, which is ludicrous even to himself. I describe accurately, for I describe from recollection. This unnatural, and forced, and ludicrous dignity, cleaves to him like disease, through the whole period of his duty. In the presence of his scholars, he is always under restraint—assuming a stiff, and formal dignity, which is as ridiculous as it is unnatural. He is also obliged to resort the arts, which are certainly not very honourable, to conceal his ignorance.

A scholar, for example, brings him a sum in arithmetic, which he does not know how to perform. This may be the case with a most excellent teacher,—and one well qualified for his business. In order to be successful as a teacher, it is not necessary to understand every thing. Instead however, of saying frankly, 'I do not understand that example, I will look at it and examine it,' he looks at it embarrassed and perplexed, not knowing how he shall escape the exposure of his ignorance. His first thought will be, to give some general directions to the pupil, and send him to his seat to make a new experiment, hoping that in some way or other, he scarcely knows how, he will get through; and at any rate, if he does not, the teacher at least gains time by manœuvre, and is glad to postpone his trouble, though he knows it must soon return.

All efforts to conceal ignorance, and all affectation of knowledge not possessed, are as unwise as they are dishonest. If a scholar asks a question which you cannot answer, or brings you a difficulty which you cannot solve, say frankly, 'I do not know.' It is the only way to save continual anxiety and irritation, and the surest means of securing real respect. Let the scholars understand that the superiority of the teacher does not consist in his infallibility, or in his universal acquisitions, but in a well-balanced mind, where the boundary between knowledge and ignorance is distinctly marked; in a strong desire to go forward in mental improvement; and in fixed principles of action, and systematic habits. You may even take up in school, a study entirely new to you, and have it understood at the outset, that you know no more of it than the class commencing, but that you can be their guide, on account of the superior maturity and discipline of your powers, and the comparative ease with which you can meet and overcome difficulties. This is the understanding which ought always to exist, between master and scholars. The fact that the teacher does not know every thing, cannot long be concealed, if he tries to conceal it; and in this, as in every other case, HONESTY IS THE BEST POLICY.

Some years ago, while I was passing a few days at Wiesbaden, in Germany, with a disciple of Pestalozzi, who had founded there a large institution, I learned from him some interesting particulars of his early career. As a boy, he had been much struck with Pestalozzi's work, entitled, 'Leonard and Gertrude,' and the accounts which reached him of the author and of his establishment, excited the most ardent desire to study his method of education, and put in practice his views. But his parents were poor, they had no means of defraying the expences of a journey of a hundred leagues, or of supporting him when arrived at his destination. He had recourse to a plan very commonly pursued in Germany, where the advantages of education are far more highly appreciated by the working classes than they are in England. A subscription was set on foot in his native village, and a sum was soon raised which he thought sufficient for his purpose. Staff in hand, he set out on his long journey; but scarcely had he traversed a third part of his way, when he was robbed of his whole treasure. What was now to be done? to go forward was to measure twice the distance; to brave hunger, exhaustion, perhaps sickness, without pecuniary resources, and far from every friend; and then to arrive without the means of support, and to cast himself on the compassion of a stranger? but that stranger was Pestalozzi; and to return, was to abandon his favourite day-dreams, and settle down to some humble occupation of village life. He resolved to proceed; and at last almost famished, having eaten nothing for many hours, he arrived at Yverdon, told his story to the benevolent Pestalozzi, was admitted to teach the little he knew, and to learn the much he desired. After a residence of two or three years in Switzerland, he returned to his native country and formed his school. There was in him a remarkable union of energy of character, and sweetness of disposition; he was respected as a master, and beloved as a father; his pupils made rapid progress, and after a time his Geometry class reached the utmost bound of their teacher's attainments. He frankly told them so; 'Now, my children,' said he, 'we will all learn together; I will read the questions, and we will see whether I or the class can solve them first.' Never had the pupils displayed so much energy; never had the lessons been followed with so much interest. There was indeed an emulation on both sides, but the proper dignity was never violated on the one, nor the due respect forgotten on the other. It was an experiment eminently successful in that instance, but it is an experiment rather to be admired than repeated. Indeed, nothing requires a more mature and comprehensive knowledge of a subject, than the giving instruction in it. To set children to teach children, may be an economical system of education; but its economy is, in my judgment, its solitary recommendation.

CHAPTER IV.

MORAL DISCIPLINE.

Under the title which I have placed at the head of this chapter, I intend to discuss the Methods by which the teacher is to secure a moral ascendency over his pupils, so that he may lead them to do what is right, and bring them back to duty, when they do what is wrong. I shall use, in what I have to say, a very plain and familiar style; and as very much depends, not only on the general principles, by which the teacher is actuated, but also on the tone and manner, in which, in cases of discipline, he addresses his pupils, I shall describe particular cases, real and imaginary, because by this method, I can better illustrate the course to be pursued. I shall also present and illustrate the various principles which I consider important, and in the order in which they occur to my mind.

1. The first duty then, of the teacher, when he enters his school, is, to beware of the danger of making an unfavourable impression, at first, upon his pupils. Many years ago, when I was a child, the teacher of the school where my early studies were carried on, closed his connexion with the establishment, and, after a short vacation, another master was expected. On the appointed day, the boys began to collect, some from

curiosity, at an early hour, and many speculations were started, as to the character of the new instructer. We were standing near a table with our hats on, and our position, and the exact appearance of the group, is indelibly fixed on my memory, when a small and youthful-looking man, entered the room, and walked up towards us. Supposing him to be some stranger, or rather, not making any supposition at all, we stood looking at him as he approached, and were thunderstruck at hearing him accost us with a stern voice and sterner brow, 'Take off your hats. Take off your hats, and go to your seats.' The conviction immediately rushed upon our minds, that this must be our new teacher. The first emotion was that of surprise, and the second was that of the ludicrous; though I believe we contrived to smother the laugh, until we got out into the open air.

So long since was this little occurrence, that I have entirely forgotten the name of the teacher, and have not the slightest recollection of any other act in his administration of the school. But this recollection of his first greeting of his pupils, and the expression of his countenance at the moment, will go with me to the end of life. So strong are first impressions.

Be careful then, when you first see your pupils, that you meet them with a smile, and that not of pretended, but of real cordiality. Think of the relation which you are to sustain to them, and think of the very interesting circumstances, under which, for some months at least, your destinies are to be united to theirs, until you cannot help feeling a strong interest in them. Shut your eyes, for a day or two, to their faults, if possible, and take an interest in all their pleasures and pursuits, that the first attitude, in which you exhibit yourself before them, may be one, which shall allure, and not repel.

2. In endeavouring to correct the faults of your pupils, do not, like many teachers, seize only upon *those particular cases* of transgression, which may happen to come under your notice. These individual instances are very few, probably, compared with the whole number of faults, against which you ought to exert an influence. And though you perhaps ought not to neglect those, which may accidentally come under your notice, yet the observing and punishing such cases, is a very small part of your duty.

You accidentally hear, I will suppose, as you are walking home from school, two of your boys in earnest conversation, one of whom uses profane language. Now, the course to be pursued in such a case is most evidently, not to call the boy to you the next day and punish him, and there let the matter rest. This would perhaps be better than nothing. But the chief impression which it would make upon the individual, and upon the other scholars would be, ' I must take care how I *let the master hear me* use such language again.' A wise teacher, who takes enlarged and extended views of his duty in regard to the moral progress of his pupils, would act very differently. He would look at the whole subject. ' Does this fault,' he would say to himself, ' prevail among my pupils? If so, how extensively? It is comparatively of little consequence to punish the particular transgression. The great point is, to devise some plan to reach the whole evil, and to correct it if possible.'

In one case where such a circumstance occurred, the teacher managed it most successfully in the following way :—

He said nothing to the boy, and in fact the boy did not know that he was overheard. He allowed a day or two to elapse, so that the conversation might be forgotten; and then took an opportunity one day after school, when all things had gone on pleasantly, and the school was about to be closed, to bring forward the whole subject. He told the boys that he had something to say to them after they had laid by their books, and were ready to go. The desks were soon closed, and every face in the room was turned towards the master with a look of fixed attention. It was almost evening. The sun had gone down. The boys' labours were over. The day was done, and their minds were at rest, and every thing was favourable for making a deep and permanent impression.

'A few days ago,' says the teacher, when all was still, 'I accidentally overheard some conversation between two of the boys of this school, and one of them swore.'

There was a pause.

'Perhaps you expect that I am now going to call the boy out, and punish him. Is that what I ought to do?'

There was no answer.

'I think a boy who uses bad language of any kind, does what he knows is wrong. He disobeys God. He does what he knows would be displeasing to his parents, and he sets a bad example. He does wrong, therefore, and justly deserves punishment.'

There were of course, many boys who felt that they were in danger. Every one who had used profane language, was aware that he might be the one who had been overheard, and of course, all were deeply interested in what the teacher was saying.

'He might, I say,' continued the teacher, 'justly be punished, but I am not going to punish him; for if I should, I am afraid that it would only make him a little more careful hereafter, not to commit this sin when I could possibly be within hearing, instead of persuading him, as I wish to do, to avoid such a sin in future altogether.[1] I am satisfied that that boy would be far happier, even in this world, if he would make it a principle always to do his duty, and never in any case, to do wrong. And then when I think how soon he, and all of us will be in another world, where we shall all be judged for what we do here, I feel strongly desirous of persuading him to abandon entirely this practice. I am afraid that punishing him now would not do that.

'Besides,' continues the teacher, 'I think it very probable that there are many other boys in this school who are sometimes guilty of this fault, and I have thought that it would be a great deal better and happier for us all, if, instead of punishing this particular boy whom I have accidentally overheard, and who probably is not more to blame than many other boys in the school, I should bring up the whole subject, and endeavour to persuade all to reform.'

I am aware that there are unfortunately in our country, a great many teachers, from whose lips such an appeal as this would be wholly in vain. The man who is accustomed to scold, and storm, and punish, with unsparing severity every transgression, under the influence of irritation and anger, must not expect that he can win over his pupils to confidence in him, and to the principles of duty by a word. But such an appeal will not be lost, when it comes from a man whose daily and habitual management corresponds with it. But to return to the story.

---

[1] It cannot, however, be very judicious to suggest such a train of thought.

The teacher made some farther remarks, explaining the nature of the sin, not in the language of execration, and affected abhorrence, but calmly, temperately, and without any disposition to make the worst of the occurrence which had taken place. In concluding what he said, he addressed the boys as follows:

'Now boys, the question is, do you wish to abandon this habit or not; if you do, all is well.[1] I shall immediately forget all the past, and will do all I can to help you to resist and overcome temptation in future. But all I can do is, only to help you; and the first thing to be done, if you wish to engage in this work of reform is, to acknowledge your fault; and I should like to know how many are willing to do this.'

'I wish all those who are willing to tell me whether they use profane language would rise.'

Every individual but one rose.

'I am very glad to see so large a number,' said the teacher; 'and I hope you will find that the work of confessing and forsaking your faults is, on the whole, pleasant, not painful business. Now those who can truly and honestly say, that they never do use profane language of any kind may take their seats.'

Three only of the whole number, which consisted of not far from twenty, sat down. It was in a sea-port town, where the temptation to yield to this vice is even greater than in the interior of our country, would be supposed possible.

[1] '*All is well.*' Indeed! Has there then been no guilt contracted? must there not be pardon obtained for the past, as well as amendment purposed for the future? Oh, let us take heed, lest in such unhallowed attempts to bring about an external propriety of conduct, we weaken in the minds of the young the fundamental truths of revelation. That caution which the author subsequently recommends will, if it be a holy caution, lead us to a very different mode altogether of treating the subject.

'Those who are now standing,' pursued the teacher, 'admit that they do sometimes at least, commit this sin. I suppose all, however, are determined to reform; for I do not know what else should induce you to rise and acknowledge it here, unless it is a desire, hereafter to break yourselves of the habit. But do you suppose that it will be enough for you merely to resolve here, that you will reform?'

'No, sir,' said the boys.

'Why? If you now sincerely determine never more to use a profane word, will you not easily avoid it?'

The boys were silent. Some said faintly, 'No, sir.'

'It will not be easy for you to avoid the sin hereafter,' continued the teacher, 'even if you do now sincerely and resolutely determine to do so. You have formed the habit of sin, and the habit will not be easily overcome. But I have detained you long enough now. I will try to devise some method by which you may carry your plan into effect, and to-morrow I will tell you what it is.'

So they were dismissed for the day. The pleasant countenance, and cheerful tone of the teacher conveying to them the impression, that they were engaging in the common effort to accomplish a most desirable purpose, in which they were to receive the teacher's help; not that he was pursuing them with threatening and punishment for the forbidden practice into which they had wickedly strayed. Great caution is, however, in such a case necessary to guard against the danger, that the teacher in attempting to avoid the tones of irritation and anger, should so speak of the sin, as to blunt their sense of its guilt, and lull their consciences into slumber.

At the appointed time on the following day, the subject was again brought before the school, and some plans proposed, by which the resolutions now formed, might be more certainly kept. These plans were readily and cheerfully adopted by the boys, and in a short time the vice of profaneness was in a great degree banished from the school. This whole account is substantially fact.

I hope the reader will keep in mind the object of the above illustration, which is to show, that it is the true policy of the teacher not to waste his time and strength in contending against *such accidental instances* of transgression as may chance to fall under his notice, but to take an enlarged and extended view of the whole ground, endeavouring to remove *whole classes of faults,*—to elevate and improve *multitudes together*.

By these means, his labours will not only be more effectual, but far more pleasant. You cannot come into collision with an individual scholar, to punish him for a mischievous spirit, or even to rebuke him for some single act, by which he has given you trouble, without an uncomfortable and uneasy feeling, which makes, in ordinary cases, the discipline of a school, the most unpleasant part of a teacher's duty. But you can plan a campaign against a whole class of faults, and put into operation a system of measures to correct them, and watch from day to day the operation of that system, with all the spirit and interest of a game.[1] It is in fact a game, where your ingenuity and moral power are brought into the field, in opposition to the evil tendencies of the hearts which are under your influence. You will notice the success or the failure of the means you may put into operation, with all the interest with which the

---

[1] But surely the state of feeling implied here is incompatible with that abhorrence of sin, without which no man can exercise a sound moral influence.

experimental philosopher observes the curious processes he guides; though your interest may be much purer and higher; for he works upon matter, but you are experimenting upon mind.

Remember then, as for the first time, you take your new station, that it is not your duty, simply to watch with an eagle eye for those accidental instances of transgression, which may chance to fall under your notice. You are to look over the whole ground. You are to make yourself acquainted, as soon as possible, with the classes of character, and classes of faults, which may prevail in your dominions, and to form deliberate and well digested plans, for improving the one and correcting the other.

And this is to be the course pursued, not only with great delinquencies, such as those to which I have already alluded, but to every little transgression against the rules of order and propriety. You can correct them far more easily and pleasantly in the mass, than in detail.

To illustrate this principle by another case. A teacher who takes the course I am condemning, approaches the seat of one of his pupils, and asks to see one of his books. As the boy opens his desk, the teacher observes that it is in complete disorder. Books, maps, papers, playthings, are there in promiscuous confusion; and from the impulse of the moment, the displeased teacher pours out upon the poor boy a torrent of reproach.

'What a sloven's desk! Why, John! I am really ashamed of you. Look,' continues he, holding up the lid, so that the boys in the neighbourhood can look in; 'see what a mass of disorder and confusion! If ever I see your desk in such a state again, I shall most certainly punish you.'

The boys around laugh; very equivocally, however, for with the feeling of amusement, there is mingled the fear that the angry master may take it into his head to inspect their dominions. The boy accidentally exposed, looks sullen, and begins to throw his books into some sort of arrangement, just enough to shield himself from the charge of absolutely disobeying, and there the matter ends.

Another teacher takes no apparent notice of the confusion he thus accidentally witnesses. 'I must take up,' thinks he to himself, 'the subject of order, before the whole school. I have not yet spoken of it.' He thanks the boy for the book he borrowed, and goes away. He makes a memorandum of the subject, and the boy does not know that the condition of his desk was noticed; perhaps he does not even know that there was any thing amiss.

A day or two after, at a time regularly appropriated to such subjects, he addresses the boy as follows.

'In our efforts to improve the school as much as possible, there is one subject which we must not forget. I mean the order of the desks.'

The boys all begin to open their desk-lids.

'You may stop a moment,' says the teacher. 'I shall give you all an opportunity to examine your desks presently.'

'I do not know what the condition of your desks are. I have not examined them, and have not in fact, seen the inside of more than one or two. As I have not brought up this subject before, I presume that there are a great many which can be arranged better than they are. Will you all now look into your desks, and see whether you consider them in good order. Stop a moment however. Let me tell you what good order is.

All those things which are alike, should be arranged together. Books should be in one place, papers in another, and thus every thing should be classified. Again, every thing should be so placed, that it can be taken out without disturbing other things. There is another principle also, which I will mention. The various articles should have *constant* places,—that is, they should not be changed from day to day. By this means, you soon remember where every thing belongs, and you can put away your things much more easily every night, than if you had every night to arrange them, in a new way. Now will you look into your desks, and tell me whether they are, on these three principles, well arranged.'

The boys of most schools, where this subject had not been regularly attended to, would nearly all answer in the negative.

'I will allow you then, some time to-day, fifteen minutes, to arrange them, and I hope you will try to keep them in good order hereafter. A few days hence, I shall examine them. If any of you wish for assistance or advice from me, in putting them in order, I shall be happy to render it.'

By such a plan, which will occupy but little more time than the irritating and useless scolding, which I supposed in the other case, how much more will be accomplished. Such an address would of itself, probably be the means of putting in order, and keeping in order, at least one half; and following up the plan in the same manner, and in the same spirit, with which it was begun, would secure the rest.

I repeat it, therefore, make it a principle, in all cases, to aim as much as possible, at the correction of those faults, which are likely to be general, by *general measures*. You avoid by this means, a vast amount of irritation and impatience, both on your own part, and on the part of your scholars, and you produce at least twenty times the useful effect.

3. The next principle which occurs to me, as deserving the teacher's attention in the outset of his course, is this:

Interest your scholars in doing something themselves to elevate the moral character of the school: so as to secure *a decided majority, who will of their own accord, co-operate with you.*

Let your pupils understand, not by any formal speech you make to that effect, but by the manner in which, from time to time, you incidentally allude to the subject, that you consider the school, when you commence it, as *at par,* so to speak—that is, on a level with other schools, and that your various plans for improving and amending it, are not to be considered in the light of finding fault, and punishing transgressions, and controling evil propensities, so as just to keep things in a tolerable state; but as efforts to improve and carry forward to a state of excellence, not yet attained, all the affairs of the institution. Such is the tone and manner of some teachers, that they never appear to be more than merely satisfied. When the scholars do right, nothing is said about it. The teacher seems to consider that a matter of course. It does not appear to interest or please him at all. Nothing rouses him, but their misconduct and that only excites him to anger and frowns. Now, in such a case, there can of course be no stimulus to effort on the part of the pupils, but the cold and heartless stimulus of fear.

Now, it is wrong for the teacher to expect that things will go right in his school, as a matter of course. All that he can expect, as a matter of course is, that things should go on as well as they do ordinarily in schools,—the ordinary amount of idleness,—the ordinary amount of misconduct. This is what he should expect, and let his pupils know that he expects it; and then, all he can gain which will be better than this, should be a source of positive pleasure; a pleasure which his pupils have procured for him, and which consequently they should share. They should understand that the teacher is engaged in various plans for improving the school, in which he invites them to engage, not from the selfish desire of thereby saving himself trouble, but because it will really be happy employment for them to engage in such an enterprise, and because by such efforts, their own moral powers will be exercised and strengthened, in the best possible way.

In another chapter, I have explained to what extent, and in what manner, the assistance of the pupils may be usefully and successfully employed, in carrying forward the general arrangements of the school. The same *principles* will apply here, though perhaps a little more careful and delicate management is necessary, in interesting them in subjects which relate to moral discipline.

One important method of doing this, is to present these plans before the minds of the scholars, as experiments,—moral experiments, whose commencement, progress, and results, they may take a great interest in witnessing. Let us take, for example, the case alluded to under the last head,—the plan of effecting a reform in regard to keeping desks in order. Suppose the teacher were to say, when the time had arrived, at which he had promised to give them an opportunity to put them in order,—

' I think it would be a good plan to keep some account of our efforts for improving the school in this respect.

We might make a record of what we do to-day, noting the day of the month, and the number of desks which may be found to be disorderly. Then at the end of any time you may propose, we will have the desks examined again, and see how many are disorderly. We can then see how much improvement has been made, in that time. Should you like to adopt the plan?'

If the boys should appear not much interested in the proposal, the teacher might, at his own discretion, waive it. In all probability, however, they would like it, and would indicate their interest by their countenances, or perhaps by a response. If so, the teacher might proceed.

'You may all examine your desks then, and decide whether they are in order or not. I do not know, however, but that we ought to appoint a committee to examine them; for perhaps all the boys would not be honest, and report their desks as they really are.'

'Yes, sir;' 'Yes, sir;' say the boys.

'Do you mean that you will be honest, or that you would like to have a committee appointed?'

There was a confused murmur. Some answer one, and some the other.

'I think,' proceeds the teacher, 'the boys will be honest, and report their desks just as they are. At any rate, the number of dishonest boys in this school, cannot be so large as materially to affect the result. I think we had better take your own statements. As soon as the desks are all examined, those who have found theirs in a condition which does not satisfy them, are requested to rise and be counted.'

The teacher then looks round the room, and selecting some intelligent boy, who has influence among his companions, and whose influence he is particularly desirous of enlisting on the side of good order, says,

'Shall I nominate some one to keep an account of this plan?'

'Yes, sir,' say the boys.

'Well, I nominate William Jones. How many are in favour of requesting William Jones to perform this duty?'

'It is a vote. William, I will thank you to write upon a piece of paper, that on the 8th of December, the subject of order in the desks was brought up, and that the boys resolved on making an effort to improve the school in this respect. Then say, that the boys reported all their desks, which they thought were disorderly, and that the number was 35; and that after a week or two, the desks are to be examined again, and the disorderly ones counted, that we may see how much we have improved. After you have written it, you may bring it to me, and I will tell you whether it is right.'

'How many desks do you think will be found to be disorderly, when we come to make the examination?'

The boys hesitate.

The teacher names successively several numbers, and asks, whether they think the real number will be greater or less. He notices their votes upon them, and at last fixes upon one, which seems to be about the general sense of the school. Then the teacher himself mentions the number, which he supposes will be found to be disorderly. His estimate will ordinarily be larger than that of the scholars; because he knows better how easily resolutions are broken. This number too, is recorded, and then the whole subject is dismissed.

Now, of course, no reader of these remarks will understand me to be recommending, by this imaginary dialogue, (for the whole of it is imaginary,) a particular course to be taken in regard to this subject, far less the particular language to be used. All I mean is, to show, by a familiar illustration, how the teacher is to endeavour to enlist the interest, and to excite the curiosity of his pupils, in his plans for the improvement of his school, by presenting them as moral experiments, which they are to assist him in trying,—experiments, whose progress they are to watch, and whose results they are to predict. If the precise steps which I have described, should actually be taken, although it would occupy but a few minutes, and would cause no thought, and no perplexing care, yet it would undoubtedly be the means of awakening a very general interest in the subject of order, throughout the school. All would be interested in the work of arrangement.

All would watch, too, with interest, the progress and the result of the experiment; and if, a few days after, the teacher should accidentally, in recess, see a disorderly desk, a pleasant remark, made with a smile to the bystanders, 'I suspect my prediction will turn out the correct one,' would have far more effect, than the most severe reproaches, or the tingling of a rap over the knuckles with a rattan.

I know, from experience, that scholars of every kind, can be led by such measures as these, or rather by such a spirit as this, to take an active interest, and to exert a most powerful influence, in regard to the whole condition of the institution. I have seen the experiment successful in boy's schools, and in girl's schools; among very little children, and among the seniors and juniors at college.

In one of the colleges of New England, a new and beautiful edifice was erected. The lecture rooms were fitted up in handsome style, and the officers when the time for the occupation of the building approached, were anticipating with regret, what seemed to be the unavoidable defacing, and cutting, and marking of the seats and walls. It was however thought, that if the subject was properly presented to the students, they would take an interest in preserving the property from injury. They were accordingly addressed somewhat as follows:

'It seems, young gentlemen, to be generally the custom in colleges, for the students to ornament the walls and benches of their recitation rooms, with various inscriptions and carricatures, so that after the premises have been for a short time in the possession of a class, every thing within reach, which will take an impression from a penknife, or a trace from a pencil, is covered with names, and dates, and heads, and inscriptions of every kind. The faculty do not know what you wish in this respect, in regard to the new accommodations, which the trustees have now provided for you, and which you are soon to enter. They have had them fitted up for you handsomely, and if you wish to have them kept in good order, we will assist you. If the students think proper to express by a vote, or in any other way, their wish to keep them in good order, we will engage to have such incidental injuries, as may from time to time occur, immediately repaired. Such injuries will of course be done; for whatever may be the wish and general opinion of the whole, it is not to be expected that every individual, in so large a community, will be careful. If, however, as a body, you wish to have the building preserved in its present state, and will, as a body, take the necessary precautions, we will do our part.'

The students responded to this appeal most heartily. They passed a vote, expressing a desire to preserve the premises in order, and for many years, and for aught I know, to the present hour, the whole is kept as a room occupied by gentlemen should be kept. At some other colleges, and those, too, sustaining the very highest rank among the institutions of the country, the doors of the public buildings are sometimes *studded with nails, as thick as they can possibly be driven, and then covered with a thick coat of sand, dried into the paint, as a protection from the knives of the students!!*

The particular methods by which the teacher is to interest his pupils in his various plans, for their improvement, cannot be very fully described here. In fact, it does not depend so much on the methods he adopts, as upon the view which he himself takes of these plans, and the *tone and manner in which he speaks of them to his pupils.*

A teacher, for example, perhaps on the first day of his labours in a new school, calls a class to read. They pretend to form a line, but it crooks in every direction. One boy is leaning back against a desk, another comes forward as far as possible, to get near the fire, the rest lounging in every position, and in every attitude. John is holding up his book high before his face, to conceal an apple, from which he is endeavouring to secure an enormous bite. James is by the same sagacious device, concealing a whisper, which he is addressing to his next neighbour, and Moses is seeking amusement by crowding and elbowing the little boy who is unluckily standing next him.

'What a spectacle!' says the master to himself, as he looks at this sad display. 'What shall I do?' The first impulse is to break forth upon them at once, with all the artillery of reproof, and threatening, and punishment. I have seen in such a case, a scolding and frowning master walk up and down before such a class, with a stern and angry air, commanding this one to stand back, and that to come forward, ordering one boy to put down his book, and scolding at a second for having lost his place, and knocking the knees of another with his rule, because he was out of the line. The boys scowl at their teacher, and with ill-natured reluctance, they obey just enough to escape punishment.

Another teacher looks calmly at the scene, and says to himself, ' What shall I do to remove effectually these evils? If I can but interest the boys in reform, it will be far more easy to effect it, than if I attempt to accomplish it, by the mere exercise of my authority.'

In the mean time things go on during the reading, in their own way. The teacher simply *observes*. He is in no haste to commence his operations. He looks for the faults; watches, without seeming to watch, the movements which he is attempting to control. He studies the materials with which he is to work, and lets their true character develope itself. He tries to find something to approve in the exercise, as it proceeds, and endeavours to interest the class, by narrating some fact connected with the reading, or making some explanation which interests the boys. At the end of the exercise, he addresses them perhaps as follows.

' I have observed, boys, in some military companies, that the officers are very strict, requiring implicit and precise obedience. The men are required to form a precise line.' (Here there is a sort of involuntary movement all along the line by which it is very sensibly straightened.) ' They make all the men stand erect' (At this word heads go up, and straggling feet draw in all along the class,) ' in the true military posture. They allow nothing to be done in the ranks, but to attend to the exercise,' (John hastily crams his apple into his pocket,) ' and thus they regulate every thing in exact and steady discipline, so that all things go on in a most systematic and scientific manner. This discipline is so admirable in some countries, especially in Europe, where much greater attention is paid to military tactics, than in our country, that I have heard it said by travellers, that some of the soldiers who mount guard at public places, look as much like statues as they do like living men.

'Other commanders act differently, they let the men do pretty much as they please. So you will see such a company lounging into a line when the drum beats, as if they took little interest in what was going on. While the captain is giving his commands, one is eating his luncheon, another is talking with his next neighbour. Part are out of the line, part lounge on one foot; they hold their guns in every position, and on the whole, present a very disorderly and unsoldier-like appearance.

'I have observed too, that boys very generally prefer to *see* the strict companies, but perhaps they would prefer to *belong* to the lax ones.'

'No, sir;' 'no, sir;' say the boys.

'Suppose you all had your choice, either to belong to a company like the first one I described, where the captain was strict in all his requirements, or to one like the latter, where you could do pretty much as you pleased, which should you prefer?'

Unless I am entirely mistaken in my idea of the inclinations of boys, it would be very difficult to get a single honest expression of preference for the latter. They would say with one voice,

'The first.'

'I suppose it would be so. You would be put to some inconvenience, by the strict commands of the captain, but then you would be more than paid by the beauty of regularity and order, which you would all witness. There is nothing so pleasant as regularity, and nobody likes regularity more than boys do. To show this, I should like to have you now form a line as exact as you can.'

After some unnecessary shoving and pushing, increased by the disorderly conduct of a few bad boys, a line is formed. Most of the class are pleased with the experiment, and the teacher takes no notice of the few exceptions. The time to attend to *them* will come by and by.

'Hands down.' The boys obey.

'Shoulders back.'

'There; there is a very perfect line.'

'Do you stand easily in that position?'

'Yes, sir.'

'I believe your position is a military one now, pretty nearly; and military men study the postures of the human body, for the sake of finding the one most easy; for they wish to preserve as much as possible of the soldiers' strength for the time of battle. I should like to try the experiment of your standing thus at the next lesson. It is a very great improvement upon your common mode. Are you willing to do it?'

'Yes, sir;' say the boys.

'You will get tired, I have no doubt. In fact, I do not expect you will succeed the first day very well. You will probably become restless and uneasy before the end of the lesson, especially the smaller boys. I must excuse it I suppose, if you do, as it will be the first time.'

By such methods as these, the teacher will certainly secure a majority in favour of all his plans. But perhaps some experienced teacher, who knows from his own repeated difficulties with bad boys, what sort of spirits the teacher of district schools has sometimes to deal with, may ask as he reads this:

'Do you expect that such a method as this, will succeed in keeping your school in order? Why, there are boys in almost every school, whom you would no more coax into obedience and order in this way, than you would persuade the north-west wind to change its course by reasoning.'

I know there are. And my readers are requested to bear in mind, that my object is not now to show how the whole government of the school may be secured, but how one important advantage may be gained, which will assist in accomplishing the object. All I should expect or hope for, by such measures as these, is *to interest and gain over to our side the majority*. What is to be done with those who cannot be reached by such kinds of influence, I shall endeavour presently to show. The object now is simply to gain the *majority*—to awaken a general interest, which you can make effectual in promoting your plans, and thus to narrow the field of discipline by getting those right, who can be got right by such measures.

The securing a majority to be on your side in the general administration of the school, is absolutely indispensable to success. A teacher may by the force of mere authority so control his pupils, as to preserve order in the school-room, and secure a tolerable progress in study, but the heart will not be in it. The progress in knowledge must accordingly be in ordinary cases slow, and the cultivation of moral principle must be in such a case entirely neglected. The principles of duty cannot be inculcated by fear; and though pain and terror must, in many instances be called in to coerce an individual offender, whom milder measures will not reach, yet these agents, and others like them, can never be successfully employed as the ordinary motives to action. They cannot produce any thing but mere external and heartless obedience in the presence of the teacher, with an inclination to throw off all restraint when the pressure of stern authority is removed.

We should all remember that our pupils are but for a very short time under our direct control. Even when they are in school, the most unceasing vigilance will not enable us to watch, except for a very small portion of the time, any individual. Many hours of the day too, they are entirely removed from our inspection, and a few months will take them away from us altogether: so that subjecting them to mere external restraint, is a very inadequate remedy for the moral evil to which they are exposed. What we aim at, is to bring forward and strengthen an internal principle, which will act when both parent and teacher are away, and control where external circumstances are all unfavourable.

I have thus far under this head been endeavouring to show the importance of securing, by gentle measures, a majority of the scholars, to co-operate with the teacher in his plans. The methods of doing this demand a little attention.

1. The teacher should study human nature as it exhibits itself in the school-room, by taking an interest in the sports and enjoyments of the pupils, and connecting as much as possible what is interesting and agreeable with the pursuits of the school, so as to lead the scholars to like the place. An attachment to the institution and to the duties of it, will give the teacher a very strong hold upon the community of mind which exists there.

2. Every thing which is unpleasant in the discipline of the school should be attended to as far as possible, privately. Sometimes it is necessary to bring a case forward in public for reproof or punishment, but this is seldom. In some schools it is the custom to postpone cases of discipline till the close of the day, and then just before the boys are dismissed at night, all the difficulties are settled. Thus, day after day, the impression which is last made upon their minds, is received from a season of suffering, and terror, and tears.

Now such a practice may be attended with many advantages, but it seems to be on the whole unwise. Aweing the pupils, by showing them the consequences of doing wrong, should be very seldom resorted to. It is far better to allure them by showing them the pleasures of doing right. Doing right is pleasant to every body, and no persons are so easily convinced of this, or rather so easily led to see it, as children. Now the true policy is, to let them experience the pleasure of doing their duty, and they will easily be allured to it.

In many cases where a fault has been publicly committed it seems at first view to be necessary that it should be publicly punished; but the end will, in most cases be answered, if it is *noticed* publicly, so that the pupils may know that it received attention, and then the ultimate disposal of the case may be made a private affair between the teacher and the individual concerned. If however every case of disobedience, or idleness, or disorder is brought out publicly before the school, so that all witness the teacher's displeasure, and feel the effects of it, (for to witness it, is to feel its most unpleasant effects,) the school becomes in a short time hardened to such scenes. Unpleasant associations become connected with the management of the school, and the scholars are prepared to do wrong with less reluctance since the consequence is only a repetition of what they are obliged to see every day.

Besides, if a boy does something wrong, and you severely reprove him in the presence of his class, you punish the class almost as much as you do him. In fact, in many cases you punish them more; for I believe it is almost invariably more unpleasant for a good boy to stand by and listen to rebukes, than for a bad boy to take them. Keep these things, therefore, as much as possible out of sight. Never bring forward cases of discipline, except on mature deliberation, and for a distinct and well-defined purpose.

3. Never bring forward a case of discipline of this kind, unless you are sure that public opinion will go in your favour. If a case comes up, in which the sympathy of the scholars is excited for the criminal in such a way as to be against yourself, it will always do more harm than good. Now this, unless there is a great caution, will often be the case. In fact, it is probable that a very large proportion of the punishments which are ordinarily inflicted in schools, only prepare the way for more offences.

It is however possible to bring forward individual cases in such a way, as to produce a very strong moral effect of the right kind. This is to be done by seizing upon those peculiar emergencies which will arise in the course of the administration of a school, and which each teacher must watch for, and discover himself. They cannot be pointed out. I may, however, give by an example, a clearer idea of what is meant by such emergencies. It is a case which actually occurred as here narrated.

In a school where nearly all the pupils were faithful

and docile, there were one or two boys who were determined to find amusement in those mischievous tricks so common in schools and colleges. There was one boy in particular, who was the life and soul of all these plans. Devoid of principle, idle as a scholar, morose and sullen in his manners, he was in every respect a true specimen of the whole class of mischief-makers, wherever they are to be found. His mischief consisted, as usual, in such exploits as stopping up the key-hole, upsetting the teacher's inkstand, or fixing something to his desk to make a noise, and interrupt the school.

It so happened that there was a standing feud between the boys of his neighbourhood, and those of another, situated a mile or two from it. By his malicious activity, he had stimulated this quarrel to a high pitch, and was very obnoxious to the boys of the other party. One day when taking a walk, the teacher observed a number of boys with excited looks, and armed with sticks and stones, standing around a shoemaker's shop, to which his poor pupil had gone for refuge from them. They had got him completely within their power, and were going to wait until he should be wearied with his confinement and come out, when they were going to inflict upon him the punishment they thought he deserved.

The teacher interfered, and by the united influence of authority, management, and persuasion, succeeded in effecting a rescue. The boy would probably have preferred to owe his safety to any one else than to the teacher, whom he had so often tried to tease; but he was glad to escape in any way. The teacher said nothing about the subject, and the boy soon supposed it was entirely forgotten.

But it was not forgotten. The teacher knew perfectly

well that the boy would before long be at his old tricks again, and was reserving this story as the means of turning the whole current of public opinion against such tricks, should they again occur.

One day he came to school in the afternoon, and found the room filled with smoke; the doors and windows were all closed, though as soon as he came in, some of the boys opened them. He knew by this circumstance that it was roguery, not accident, which caused the smoke. He appeared not to notice it, however, said he was sorry it smoked, and asked the mischievous boy, for he was sure to be always near in such a case, to help him fix the fire. The boy supposed it was understood to be accidental, and perhaps secretly laughed at the dullness of his master.

In the course of the afternoon, the teacher ascertained, by private inquiries, that his suspicions were correct as to the author of the mischief. At the close of school, when the studies were ended, and the books laid away, he told the scholars that he wanted to tell them a story.

He then with a pleasant tone and manner gave a very minute, and to the boys, a very interesting narrative of his adventure two or three weeks before, when he rescued this boy from his danger. He called him, however, simply *a boy*, without mentioning his name, or even hinting that he was a member of the school. No narrative could excite a stronger interest among an audience of school-boys, than such a one as this; and no act of kindness from a teacher would make as vivid an impression, as interfering to rescue a trembling captive from such a situation as the one this boy had been in.

'The scholars listened with profound interest and attention, and though the teacher said little about his share in the affair, and spoke of what he did, as if it were a matter of course, that he should thus befriend a boy in distress, an impression, very favourable to himself, must have been made. After he had finished his narrative, he said,

'Now should you like to know who this boy was?'

'Yes, sir;' 'Yes, sir;' said they, eagerly.

'It was a boy that you all know.'

The boys looked around upon one another. Who could it be?

'He is a member of this school.'

There was an expression of fixed, and eager, and increasing interest, on every face in the room.

'He is here now,' said the teacher, winding up the interest and curiosity of the scholars, by these words, to the highest pitch. 'But I cannot tell you his name; for what return do you think he made to me? To be sure it was no very great favour that I did him: I should have been unworthy the name of teacher, if I had not done it for him, or for any boy in my school. But at any rate, it showed my good wishes for him—it showed that I was his friend, and what return do you think he made me for it? Why, to-day he spent his time between schools in filling the room with smoke, that he might torment his companions here, and give me trouble, and anxiety and suffering, when I should come. If I should tell you his name, the whole school would turn against him for his ingratitude.' The business ended here, and it put a stop, a final stop to all malicious tricks in the school.

Now it is not very often that so fine an opportunity occurs, to kill, by a single blow, the disposition to do wilful, wanton injury, as this circumstance afforded; but the principle illustrated by it, bringing forward individual cases of transgression, in a public manner, only for the sake of the general effect, and so arranging what is said and done as to produce the desired effect upon the public mind, in the highest degree, may very frequently be acted upon. Cases are continually occurring, and if the teacher will keep it constantly in mind, that when a particular case comes before the whole school, the object is an influence upon the whole, and not the punishment or reform of the guilty individual, he will insensibly so shape his measures, as to produce the desired result.

(4.) There should be a great difference made between the *measures you take* to prevent wrong, and the *feelings of displeasure* against wrong, when it is done. The former should be strict, authoritative, unbending; the latter should be mild and gentle. Your measures, if uniform and systematic, will never give offence, however, powerfully you may restrain and controul. It is the morose look, the harsh expression, the tone of irritation and fretfulness, which is so unpopular in school. The sins of childhood, are by nine tenths of mankind enormously overrated, and perhaps none overrate them more extravagantly than teachers. We confound the trouble they give us, with their real moral turpitude, and measure the one by the other. Now if a fault prevails in a school, one teacher will scold and fret himself about it, day after day, until his scholars are tired both of school and of him: and yet he will *do* nothing effectual to remove it. Another will take efficient and decided measures, and yet say very little on the subject, and the whole evil will be removed, without suspending for a moment, the good humour and pleasant feeling, which should prevail in school.

The expression of your displeasure, on account of any thing that is wrong, will seldom or never do any good.

The scholars consider it scolding; it is scolding, and though it may, in many cases, contain many sound arguments and eloquent expostulations, it operates simply as a punishment. It is unpleasant to hear it. General instruction must indeed be given, but not general reproof.[1]

(5.) Feel that in the management of the school, *you* are under obligation as well as the scholars, and let this feeling appear in all that you do. Perhaps your boys wish you to dismiss them earlier than usual, on some particular occasion, or to allow them an extra holiday. Show by the manner in which you consider and speak of the question, that your main inquiry is what is *your duty*. Speak often of your responsibility to your employers, not formally, but incidentally and naturally as you will speak, if you feel this responsibility.

It will assist very much too, in securing cheerful good-humoured obedience to the regulations of the school, if you extend their authority over yourself. Not that the teacher is to have no liberty from which the scholars are debarred; this would be impossible. But the teacher should submit himself to every thing which he requires of his scholars, unless it is in cases where a different course is necessary.

Suppose for instance, a study card, like the one described in a preceding chapter, is made, so as to mark the time of recess and of study. The teacher near the close of recess, is sitting with a group of his pupils around him, telling them some story. They are all interested, and they see he is interested. He looks at

---

[1] I cannot admit that general reproof should not be occasionally given either to a class or to the whole school. Undoubtedly it ought to be measured and temperate, even more so than individual rebuke, but when properly administered, it is an important instrument of moral discipline.

his watch, and shows by his manner, that he is desirous of finishing what he is saying, but that he knows that the striking of the bell will cut short his story. Perhaps he says not a word about it, but his pupils see that he is submitting to the controul which is placed over them: and when the card goes up, and he stops instantly in the middle of his sentence, and rises with the rest, each one to go to his own place, to engage at once in their several duties, he teaches them a most important lesson, and in the most effectual way. Such a lesson of fidelity and obedience, and such an example of it, will have more influence, than a half hour's scolding about whispering without leave, or a dozen public punishments. At least so I find it, for I have tried both.

Show then continually, that you see and enjoy the beauty of system, and of strict discipline, and that you submit to it yourself, as well as require it of others.

(6.) Lead your pupils to see that they must share with you, the credit or the disgrace, which success or failure may bring. Lead them to feel this, not by telling them so, for there are very few things which can be impressed upon children by direct efforts to impress them; but by so speaking of the subject, from time to time, as to lead them to see that you understand it so.

Repeat, with judicious caution, what is said of the school, both for and against it; and thus endeavour to interest the scholars in its public reputation. This feeling of interest in the institution may very easily be awakened. It sometimes springs up spontaneously, and where it is not guided aright by the teacher, sometimes produces very bad effects upon the minds of the pupils, in rival institutions. When two schools are situated near each other, evil consequences will result from this feeling, unless the teacher manages it so as to deduce good consequences. I recollect, that in my boyish days, there was a standing quarrel between the boys of a town school and an academy, which were in the same village. We were all ready, at any time, when out of school, to fight for the honour of our respective institutions, but very few were ready to be diligent and faithful, when in it, though it would seem that that might have been a rather more effectual means of establishing the point. If the scholars are led to understand that the school is to a great extent their institution, that they must assist to sustain its character, and that they share the honour, if any honour is acquired, a feeling will prevail in the school, which may be turned to a most useful account.

(7.) In giving instruction on moral duty, the subject should be taken up generally, in reference to imaginary cases, or cases which are unknown to most of the scholars. If this is done, the pupils feel that the object of bringing up the subject is to do good; whereas, if questions of moral duty are only brought up, from time to time, when some prevailing or accidental fault in schools calls for it, the feeling will be that the teacher is only endeavouring to remove from his own path, a source of inconvenience and trouble. The most successful mode of giving general moral instruction that I have known, and which has been adopted in many schools, with occasional variations of form, is the following.

When the time has arrived a subject is assigned, and small papers are distributed to the whole school, that all may write something concerning it. These are then read and commented on by the teacher, and are made the occasion of any remarks, which he may wish to make. The interest is strongly excited to hear the papers read, and the instruction which the teacher may give, produces a deeper effect, when engrafted thus, upon something which originates in the minds of the pupils.

To take a particular case: a teacher addressed his scholars thus. 'The subject for the moral exercise to day, is *Prejudice*. Each boy may take one of the papers which have been distributed, and write upon them any thing relating to the subject. As many as have thought of any thing to write, may raise their hands.'

One or two only of the older scholars gave the signal.

' I will mention the kinds of communications you can make, and perhaps what I say will suggest something to you. As fast as you think of any thing, you may raise your hands, and as soon as I see a sufficient number up, I will give directions to begin. You can describe any case in which you have been prejudiced yourselves, either against persons or things.'

Here a number of the hands went up.

' You can mention any facts relating to antipathies of any kind, or any cases where you know other persons to be prejudiced. You can ask any questions in regard to the subject, questions about the nature of prejudice, or the causes for it, or the remedy of it.'

As he said this, many hands were successively raised, and at last, directions were given for them to begin to write. Five minutes were allowed, and at the end of that time, the papers were collected and read. The following specimens, transcribed verbatim from the originals, with the remarks made, as nearly as they could be remembered immediately after the exercise, will give an idea of the ordinary operation of this plan.

' I am very much prejudiced against spiders, and every insect in the known world, with scarcely an exception. There is a horrid sensation created by their ugly forms, that makes me wish them all to Jericho. The butterfly's wings are pretty, but he is dreadful ugly. There is no affectation in this, for my pride will not permit me to show this prejudice to any great degree, when I can help it. I do not fear the little wretches; but I do hate them.'—ANTI-SPIDER-SPARER.

'This is not expressed very well, the phrases, '*to Jericho*' and '*dreadful ugly*,' are vulgar, and in very bad taste. Such a dislike too is more commonly called an antipathy, than a prejudice, though perhaps it comes under the general head of prejudices.'

'How may we overcome prejudice? I think that when we are prejudiced against a person, it is the hardest thing in the world to overcome it.'

'A prejudice is usually founded on some unpleasant association, connected with the subject of it. To connect some pleasant association with it, is therefore, the best way to overcome the prejudice against it.

'For example, to take the case of the antipathy to the spider, alluded to in the last article. The reason why that young lady dislikes spiders, is undoubtedly because some unpleasant idea is associated with the thought of those insects, perhaps for example, the idea of their crawling upon her—which is certainly not a very pleasant one to any body. Now the way to correct such a prejudice, is to try to connect some pleasant thoughts with the sight of the animal.

'I once found a spider in an empty apartment, hanging in its web on the wall, with a large ball of eggs which it had suspended by its side. My companion and myself cautiously brought up a tumbler under the web, and pressed it suddenly against the wall, so as to enclose both spider and eggs within it. We then contrived to run in a pair of shears, so as to cut off the web, and let both the animal and its treasure fall down into the tumbler. We put a book over the top, and walked off with our prize to a table, to see what it would do.

'At first it tried to climb up the side of the tumbler, but its feet slipped from the smooth glass. We then inclined the glass, so as to favour its climbing and to enable it to reach the book at the top. As soon as it touched the book, it was safe. It could cling to the book easily, and we now placed the tumbler again upright, to watch its motions.

'It attached a thread to the book and let itself down by it to the bottom of the tumbler, and walked round and round the ball of eggs, apparently in great trouble. Presently it ascended by its thread, and then came down again. It attached a new thread to the ball, and then went up, drawing the ball with it. It hung the ball at a proper distance from the book, and bound it firmly in its place by threads running from it, in every direction, to the parts of the book which were near, and then the animal took its place, quietly by its side.

'Now I do not say, that if anybody had a strong antipathy to a spider, seeing one perform such a work as this would entirely remove it; but it would certainly soften it. It would *tend* to remove it. It would connect an interesting and pleasant association with the object. So if she should watch a spider in the fields making his web. You have all seen those beautiful, regular webs, in the morning dew, ('Yes, sir,' 'Yes, sir.') composed of concentric circles, and radii diverging in every direction. ('Yes, sir.') Well, watch a spider when making one of these, or observe his artful ingenuity and vigilance, when he is lying in wait for a fly. By thus connecting pleasant ideas, with the sight of the animal, you will destroy the unpleasant association which constitutes the prejudice. In the same manner, if I wished to create an antipathy to a spider, in a child, it would be very easily done. I would tie her hands behind her, and put three or four upon her, to crawl over her face.

'Thus you must destroy prejudices in all cases, by connecting pleasant thoughts and associations with the objects of them.'

'I am very often prejudiced against new scholars, without knowing why?'

'We sometimes hear a person talk in this way, 'I do not like such or such a person, at all.''

''Why?'

''Oh I don't know, I do not like her at all. I can't bear her.'

''But why not. What is your objection to her.'

''Oh I don't know, I have not any particular reason, but I never did like her.'

'Now whenever you hear any person talk so, you may be sure that her opinion, on any subject, is worth nothing at all. She forms opinions in one case, without grounds, and it depends merely upon accident, whether she does not, in other cases.'

'Why is it that so many of our countrymen *are*, or seem to be prejudiced against the unfortunate children of Africa? Almost every *large white* boy, who meets a *small black* boy, insults him, in some way or other.'

'It is so hard to *overcome* prejudices, that we ought to be careful how we *form* them.'

'When I see a new scholar enter this school and she does not happen to suit me exactly in her ways and manners, I very often get prejudiced against her, though sometimes I find her a valuable friend, after I get acquainted with her.'

'There is an inquiry I should like very much to make, though I suppose it would not be quite right to make it. I should like to ask all those, who have some particular friend in school, and who can recollect the impression which the individual made upon them, when they first saw her, to rise, and then I should like to inquire in how many cases, the first impression was favourable, and in how many unfavourable.'

'Yes, sir; yes, sir.'

'Do you mean you would like to have the inquiry made?'

'Yes, sir.'

'All, then, who have intimate friends, and can recollect the impression which they first made upon them, may rise.'

[About thirty rose; more than two thirds of which, voted that the first impression made by the persons, who had since become their particular friends, was unfavourable.]

'This shows how much dependance you can justly place on first impressions.'

'It was the next Monday morning, after I had attained the wise age of four years, that I was called up into my mother's room, and told that I was the next day going to school.

'I called forth all my reasoning powers, and with all the ability of a child of four years, I reasoned with my mother, but to no purpose. I told her that I *hated* the schoolmistress then; though I had never seen her. The very first day I tottered under the weight of the mighty fools-cap. I only attended her school two quarters; with prejudice I went, and with prejudice I came away.

'The old school-house is now torn down, and a large brick house takes the place of it. But I never pass by without remembering my teacher. I am prejudiced to [against] the very spot?

'Is it not right to allow prejudice, to have influence over our minds as far as this? If any thing comes to our knowledge, with which wrong seems to be connected, and one in whom we have always felt confidence is engaged in it, is it not right to allow our prejudice in favour of this individual to have so much influence over us, as to cause us to believe that all is really right, though every circumstance which has come to our knowledge is against such a conclusion? I felt this influence not many weeks since, in a very great degree.'

'No; it would not be prejudice in such a case. That is, a prejudice would not be a sufficient ground to justify witholding blame. Well-grounded confidence in such a person, if there was reason for it, ought to have such an effect, but not prejudice.'

The above may be considered as a fair specimen of the ordinary operation of such an exercise. It is taken as an illustration, not by selection from the large number of similar exercises which I have witnessed, but simply because it was an exercise occurring at the time when a description was to be written. Besides the articles quoted above, there were thirty or forty others, which were read and commented on. The above will, however, be sufficient to give the reader a clear idea of the exercise, and to show what is the nature of the moral effect it is calculated to produce.

The subjects which may be advantageously brought forward in such a way, are of course very numerous. They are such as the following. In connexion with each, give the suggestions as to the kind of articles to be written, which the pupils may receive at the time the subject is assigned.

1. DUTIES TO PARENTS. Anecdotes of good or bad conduct at home. Questions. Cases where it is most difficult to obey. Dialogues between parents and children. Excuses which are often made for disobedience.

2. SELFISHNESS. Cases of selfishness any of the pupils have observed. Dialogues they have heard exhibiting it. Questions about its nature. Indications of selfishness.

3. FAULTS OF THE SCHOOL. Any bad practices the scholars may have observed; in regard to general deportment, recitations, habits of study, or the scholars' treatment of each other. Each scholar may write what is his own greatest trouble in school, and whether he thinks any thing can be done to remove it. Any thing they think can be improved in the management of the school by the teacher. Unfavourable things they have heard said about it, out of school, though without names.

4. EXCELLENCES OF THE SCHOOL. Good practices, which ought to be persevered in. Any little incidents the scholars may have noticed illustrating good character. Cases which have occurred in which scholars have done right, in temptation, or when others around were doing wrong. Favourable reports in regard to the school, in the community around.

5. THE SABBATH. Any thing the scholars may have known to be done

on the Sabbath which they doubt whether right or wrong. Questions in regard to the subject. Various opinions they have heard expressed. Difficulties they have in regard to proper ways of spending the Sabbath.

(8.) We have one other method to describe, by which a favourable moral influence may be exerted in school. The method can, however, be put in full operation, only where there are several pupils who have made considerable advances in mental cultivation.

It is to provide a way by which teachers and pupils may write, anonymously, for the school. This may be done by having a place of deposit for such articles as may be written, where any person may leave what he wishes to have read, nominating, by a memorandum upon the article itself, the reader. If a proper feeling on the subject of good discipline, and the formation of good character, prevails in school, many articles, which will have a great deal of effect upon the pupils, will find their way through such a channel once opened. The teacher can himself often bring forward, in this way, his suggestions, with more effect than he otherwise could do. Such a plan is, in fact, like the plan of a newspaper for an ordinary community, where sentiments and opinions stand on their own basis, and influence the community, just in proportion to their intrinsic merits, unassisted by the authority of the writer's name, and unimpeded by any prejudice which may exist against him. In my own school, this practice has had a very powerful effect. I have myself often thus anonymously addressed my pupils, and I have derived great assistance from communications which many of the pupils have written. Sometimes we have had full discussions of proposed measures, and at others, criticisms of the management of the school, or of prevailing faults. Sometimes good humoured satires, and sometimes simple descriptions

It is true the practice is not steadily kept up. Often, for months together, there is not an article offered. Still the place of deposit remains, and, after a time, some striking communication is made, which awakens general attention, and calls out other pens, until the fifteen minutes, corresponding to the afternoon general exercise, in the plan provided in a preceding chapter,—which is all which is allowed to be devoted to such purposes, is not sufficient to read what is daily offered. Of course, in such a plan as this, the teacher must have the usual editorial powers, to comment upon what is written, or to alter or suppress it at pleasure.[1]

By means like these, it will not be difficult for any teacher to obtain an ascendency over the minds of his pupils, so far, as to secure an overwhelming majority in favour of good order, and co-operation with him in his plans for elevating the character of the school. But let it be distinctly understood, that this, and this only, has been the object of this chapter, thus far. The first point brought up, was the desirableness of making, at first a favourable impression,—the second, the necessity of taking general views of the condition of the school, and aiming to improve it in the mass, and not merely to rebuke or punish accidental faults,—and the third, the importance and the means of gaining a general influence and ascendancy over the minds of the pupils. But, though an overwhelming majority can be reached by such methods as these, all cannot. We must have the majority secured, however, in order to enable us to reach and to reduce the others. But to this work we must come at last.

4. I am therefore now to consider under a fourth general head, what course is to be taken with *individual*

---

[1] See Note A. Appendix.

offenders, whom the general influences of the school-room will not control.

(1.) The first point to be attended to, is to ascertain who they are. Not by appearing suspiciously to watch any individuals, for this would be almost sufficient to make them bad, if they were not so before. Observe, however; notice from day to day the conduct of individuals, not for the purpose of reproving or punishing their faults, but to enable you to understand their characters. This work will often require great adroitness, and very close scrutiny; and you will find as the results of it, a considerable variety of character, which the general influences above described will not be sufficient to control. The number of individuals will not be great, but the diversity of character comprised in it will be such as to call into exercise all your powers of vigilance and discrimination. On one seat you will find a coarse, rough looking boy, who will openly disobey your commands and oppose your wishes; on another, a more sly rogue, whose demure and submissive look is assumed, to conceal a mischief-making disposition. Here is one whose giddy spirit is always leading him into difficulty, but who is of so open and frank a disposition, that you will most easily lead him back to duty; but there is another, who, when reproved, will fly into a passion; and there, a third, who will stand sullen and silent before you when he has done wrong, and is neither to be touched by kindness, nor awed by authority.

Now all these characters must be studied. It is true that the caution given in a preceding part of this chapter, against devoting undue and disproportionate attention to such persons must not be forgotten. Still these individuals will require, and it is right that they should receive, a much greater degree of attention, so far as the moral administration of the school is concerned, than their mere numbers would appear to justify. This is the field in which the teacher is to study human nature, for here it shows itself without disguise. It is through this class, too, that a very powerful moral influence is to be exerted upon the rest of the school. The manner in which such individuals are managed; the tone the teacher assumes towards them; the gentleness with which he speaks of their faults, and the unbending decision with which he restrains them from wrong, will have a most powerful effect upon the rest of the school. That he may occupy this field therefore to the best advantage, it is necessary that he should first thoroughly explore it.

By understanding the dispositions and characters of such a class of pupils as I have described, I do not mean merely watching them with vigilance in school, so that none of their transgressions shall go unobserved and unpunished. I intend a far deeper and more thorough examination of character. Every boy has something or other which is good in his disposition and character which he is aware of, and on which he prides himself; find out what it is, for it may often be made the foundation on which you may build the superstructure of reform. Every one has his peculiar sources of enjoyment, and objects of pursuit, which are before his mind from day to day; find out what they are, that by taking an interest in what interests him, and perhaps sometimes assisting him in his plans, you can bind him to you. Every boy is, from the circumstances in which he is placed at home, exposed to temptations, which have, perhaps, had a far greater influence in the formation of his character, than any deliberate and intentional depravity of his own. Ascertain what these temptations are, that you may know where to pity him, and where to blame. The knowledge which such an examination of character will give you, will not be confined to making you acquainted with the individual. It will be the most valuable knowledge which a man can possess, both to assist him in the general administration of the school, and in his intercourse with mankind in the business of life. Men are but boys, only with somewhat loftier objects of pursuit. Their principles, motives, and ruling passions are essentially the same. Extended commercial speculations are, so far as the human heart is concerned, substantially what trading in jack-knives and toys is at school; and building a snow fort, to its own architects, the same as erecting a monument of marble.

(2.) After exploring the ground, the first thing to be done as a preparation for reforming individual character in school, is to secure the personal attachment of the individuals to be reformed. This must not be attempted by professions and affected smiles, and still less by that sort of obsequiousness common in such cases, which produces no effect but to make the bad boy suppose that his teacher is afraid of him; which, by the way, is in fact in such cases, usually true. Approach the pupil in a bold and manly, but frank and pleasant manner. Approach him as his superior, but still as his friend; as desirous to make him happy, not merely to obtain his good-will. And the best way to secure these appearances, is just to secure the reality. Actually be the boy's friend. Really desire to make him happy; happy, too, in his own way, not in yours. Feel that you are his superior, and that you must and will enforce obedience; but with this feel, that probably obedience will be rendered without any contest. If these are really the feelings which reign within you, the boy will see it, and they will exert a strong influence over him, but you cannot successfully counterfeit them.

A most effectual way to secure the good will of a scholar, is to ask him to assist you. The Creator has so formed the human heart, that doing good must be a source of pleasure, and he who tastes this pleasure once, will almost always wish to taste it again. To do good to any individual, creates or increases the desire to do it.

There is a boy in your school who is famous for his skill in making whistles from the green branches of the poplar. He is a bad boy, and likes to turn his ingenuity to purposes of mischief. You observe him some day in school, when he thinks your attention is engaged in another way, blowing softly upon one which he has concealed in his desk for the purpose of amusing his neighbours, without attracting the attention of the teacher. Now, there are two remedies. Will you try the physical one? Then call him out into the floor; inflict painful punishment, and send him smarting to his seat, with his heart full of anger and revenge, to plot some new and less dangerous scheme of annoyance. Will you try the moral one? Then wait till the recess, and while he is out at his play, send a message out by another boy, saying that you have heard he is very skilful in making whistles, and asking him to make one for you to carry home to a little child at your boarding-house. What would, in ordinary cases, be the effect? It would certainly be a very simple application; but its effect would be, to open an entirely new train of thought and feeling for the boy. 'What!' he would say to himself while at work on his task, 'give the master *pleasure* by making whistles! Who ever heard of such a thing? I never thought of any thing but giving him trouble and pain. I wonder who told him I could make whistles?' He would find too, that the new enjoyment was far higher and purer than the old, and would have little disposition to return to the latter.

I do not mean by this illustration, that such a measure as this would be the only notice that ought to be taken of such an act of wilful disturbance in school. Probably it would not. What measures in direct reference to the fault committed would be necessary, would depend upon the circumstances of the case. It is not necessary to our purpose that they should be described here.

The teacher can awaken in the hearts of his pupils a personal attachment to himself, by asking in various ways their assistance in school, and then appearing honestly gratified with the assistance rendered. Boys and girls are delighted to have what powers and attainments they possess brought out into action, especially where they can lead to useful results. They love to be of some consequence in the world, and will be especially gratified in being able to assist their teacher. Even if the studies of a turbulent boy are occasionally interrupted for half an hour, that he may help you arrange papers, or rule books, or cut the tops of quills, or distribute exercises, it will be time well spent. Get him to co-operate with you in anything, and he will feel how much pleasanter it is to co-operate, than to thwart and oppose; and by judicious measures of this kind, almost any boy may be brought over to your side.

Another means of securing the personal attachment of boys, is to notice them—to take an interest in their pursuits, and the qualities and powers which they value in one another. It is astonishing what an influence is exerted by such little circumstances as stopping at a play-ground a moment to notice with interest, though perhaps without saying a word, speed of running,—or exactness of aim,—the force with which a ball is struck, or the dexterity with which it is caught or thrown. The teacher must, indeed, in all his intercourse with his pupils, never forget his station, nor allow them to lay aside the respect, without which authority cannot be maintained. But he may be, notwithstanding this, on the most intimate and familiar footing with them all. He may take a strong and open interest in all their enjoyments, and thus awaken on their part a personal attachment to himself, which will exert over them a constant and powerful control.

(3.) The efforts described under the last head for gaining a personal influence over those who, from their disposition and character, are most in danger of doing wrong, will not be sufficient entirely to prevent transgression. Cases of deliberate, intentional wrong will occur, and the question will arise, What is the duty of the teacher in such an emergency? When such cases occur, the course to be taken is, first of all, to come to a distinct understanding on the subject with the guilty individual. Think of the case calmly, until you have obtained just and clear ideas of it. Endeavour to understand precisely in what the guilt of it consists. Notice every palliating circumstance, and take as favourable a view of the thing as you can, while at the same time you fix most firmly in your mind the determination to put a stop to it. Then go to the individual, and lay the subject before him, for the purpose of understanding distinctly from his own lips what he intends to do. I can however, as usual, explain more fully what I mean, by describing a particular case substantially true.

The teacher of a school observed himself, and learned from several quarters, that a certain boy was in the habit of causing disturbance during time of prayer at the opening and close of school, by whispering, playing, making gestures to the other boys, and throwing things about from seat to seat. The teacher's first step was, to speak of the subject generally before the whole school, not alluding, however, to any particular instance which had come under his notice. These general remarks produced, as he expected, but little effect.

He waited for some days, and the difficulty still continued. Had the irregularity been very great, it would have been necessary to have taken more immediate measures, but he thought the case admitted of a little delay. In the mean time, he took a little pains to cultivate the acquaintance of the boy, to discover and to show that he noticed what was good in his character and conduct, occasionally to get from him some little assistance,—and thus to gain some personal ascendancy over him.

One day when every thing had gone smoothly and pleasantly, the teacher told the boy at the close of the school, that he wanted to talk with him a little, and asked him to walk home with him. It was not uncommon for the teacher to associate thus with his pupils out of school, and this request, accordingly, attracted no special attention. On the walk the teacher thus accosted the criminal.

'Do you like frank open dealing, James?'

James hesitated a moment, and then answered faintly, 'Yes, sir.'

'Most boys do, and I do; and I supposed that you would prefer being treated in that way. Do you?'

'Yes, sir.'

'Well, I am going to tell you of one of your faults. I have asked you to walk with me, because I supposed it would be pleasanter for you to have me see you privately, than to bring it up in school.'

James said it would be pleasanter.

' Well, the fault is, being disorderly at prayer time. Now if you like frank and open dealing, and are willing to deal so with me, I should like to talk with you a little about it, but if you are not willing, I will dismiss the subject. I do not wish to talk with you now about it, unless you yourself desire it. But if we talk at all, we must both be open, and honest, and sincere. Now should you rather have me talk with you or not?'

' Yes, sir; I should rather have you talk with me now than in school.'

The teacher then described his conduct in a mild manner, using the style of simple narration,—admitting no harsh epithets,—no terms of reproach. The boy was surprised, for he supposed he had not been noticed. He thought, perhaps, he should have been punished if he had been observed. The teacher said in conclusion:

' Now, James, I do not suppose you have done this from any designed irreverence towards God, or deliberate intention of giving me trouble and pain. You have several times lately assisted me in various ways, and I know from the cheerful manner with which you comply with my wishes, that your prevailing desire is to give me pleasure, not pain. You have fallen into this practice through thoughtlessness; but that does not alter the character of the sin. To do so is a great sin against God, and a great offence against good order in school. You see yourself, that my duty to the school will require me to adopt the most decided measures to prevent the continuance and the spread of such a practice. I should be imperiously bound to do it, even if the individual was the very best friend I had in school, and if the measures necessary should bring upon him great disgrace and suffering. Do you not think it would be so?'

'Yes, sir,' said James, seriously, 'I suppose it would.'

'I want to remove the evil, however, in the pleasantest way. Do you remember my speaking on this subject in school the other day?'

'Yes, sir.'

'Well, my object in that, was almost entirely to persuade you to reform, without my having to speak to you directly. I thought it would be pleasanter to you to be reminded of your duty in that way. But I do not think it did you much good. Did it?'

'I don't think I have played so much since then.'

'Nor I. You have improved a little, but you have not decidedly and thoroughly reformed. So I was obliged to take the next step, which would be least unpleasant to you; that is, talking with you alone. Now you told me when we began, that you would deal honestly and sincerely with me, if I would with you. I have been honest and open. I have told you all about it, so far as I am concerned. Now I wish you to be honest, and tell me what you are going to do. If you think from this conversation that you have done wrong, and if you are fully determined to do so no more, and to break off at once and forever from this practice, I should like to have you tell me, and then the whole thing will be settled. On the other hand, if you feel about it pretty much as you have done, I should like to have you tell me that too, honestly and frankly, that we may have a distinct understanding, and that I may be considering what to do next. I shall not be offended with you for giving me either of these answers, but be sure that you are honest; you promised to be so.'

The boy looked up in his master's face, and said with great earnestness,

'Mr. T. I *will* do better. I *will not* trouble you any more.'

I have detailed this case thus particularly, because it exhibits clearly what I mean, by going directly and frankly to the individual, and coming at once to a full understanding. In nine cases out of ten, this course will be effectual. For four years, and with a very large school, I have found this sufficient in every case of discipline which has occurred, except in three or four instances, where something more was required. To make it successful, however, it must be done properly. Several things are necessary. It must be deliberate; generally better after a little delay. It must be indulgent, so far as the view which the teacher takes of the guilt of the pupil, is concerned; every palliating consideration must be felt. It must be firm and decided, in regard to the necessity of a change, and the determination of the teacher to effect it. It must also be open and frank; no insinuations, no hints, no surmises, but plain, honest, open dealing.

In many cases, the communication may be made most delicately, and most successfully, in writing. The more delicately you touch the feelings of your pupils, the more tender these feelings will become. Many a teacher hardens and stupifies the moral sense of his pupils, by the harsh and rough exposures to which he drags out the private feelings of the heart. A man may easily produce such a state of feeling in his schoolroom, that to address even the gentlest reproof to any individual in the hearing of the next, would be a most severe punishment; and on the other hand, he may so destroy that sensitiveness, that his vociferated reproaches will be as unheeded as the wind.

If now the teacher has taken the course recommended in this chapter; if he has, by his general influence in the school, done all in his power to bring the majority of his pupils to the side of order and discipline; if he has then studied attentively and impartially, the characters of those who cannot thus be led; if he has endeavoured to make them his friends, and to acquire by every means, a personal influence over them; if, finally, when they do wrong, he goes plainly, but in a gentle and delicate manner to them, and lays before them the whole case; if he has done all this, he has gone as far as moral influence will carry him. My opinion is, that this course, faithfully and judiciously pursued, will in almost all instances succeed; but it will not in all, and where it fails, there must be other and more vigorous and decided measures. What these measures of restraint or punishment shall be, must depend upon the circumstances of the case; but in resorting to them, the teacher must be decided and unbending.

The course above recommended, is not trying lax and inefficient measures for a long time, in hopes of their being ultimately successful, and then, when they are found not to be so, changing the policy. There should be, through the whole, the tone and manner of *authority*, not of *persuasion*. The teacher must be a *monarch*, and while he is gentle and forbearing, always looking on the favourable side of conduct, so far as guilt is concerned: he must have an eagle eye, and an efficient hand, so far as relates to arresting the evil and stopping the consequences. He may slowly and cautiously, and even tenderly approach a delinquent. He may be several days in gathering around him the circumstances of which he is ultimately to avail himself, in bringing him to submission; but, while he proceeds thus slowly and tenderly, he must come with the air of authority and power. The fact that the teacher bases all his plans on the idea of his ultimate authority in every case, may be perfectly evident to all the pupils, while he proceeds with moderation and gentleness in all his specific measures. Let it be seen, then, that the constitution of your school is a monarchy, absolute and unlimited,—but let it also be seen, that the one who holds the power, is himself under the control of moral principle in all that he does, and that he endeavours to make the same moral principle which guides him, go as far as it is possible to make it go, in the government of his subjects.

CHAPTER V.

RELIGIOUS INFLUENCE.

There are many teachers who profess to cherish the spirit, and to entertain the hopes of piety, who yet make no effort whatever, to extend its influence to the hearts of their pupils. Others appeal sometimes to religious truth, merely to assist them in the government of the school. They perhaps bring it before the minds of disobedient pupils, in a vain effort to make an impression upon the conscience of one who has done wrong, and who cannot by other means be brought to submission. But the pupil, in such cases, understands, or at least he believes, that the teacher applies to religious truth, only to eke out his own authority, and of course it produces no effect. Another teacher thinks he must, to discharge his duty, give a certain amount weekly, of what he considers religious instruction. He accordingly appropriates a regular portion of time to a formal lecture or exhortation, which he delivers without regard to the mental habits of thought and feeling, which prevail among his charge. He forgets that the heart must be led, not driven to piety, and that unless his efforts are adapted to the nature of the minds he is acting upon, and suited to influence them, he must as certainly fail of success, as when there is a want of fitness between the means and the end in any other undertaking whatever.

The arrangement which seems to me as well calculated as any for the religious exercises of a school, is this:

1. In the morning open the school with a very short prayer, resembling in its object and length, the opening prayer in the morning, at congregational churches. The posture, which from four years' experience I would recommend at this exercise, is, sitting with the heads reclined upon the desks. The prayer, besides being short, should be simple in its language, and specific in its petitions. A degree of particularity and familiarity which might be improper elsewhere, is not only allowable here, but necessary to the production of the proper effect. That the reader may understand to what extent I mean to be understood to recommend this, I will subjoin a form, such as in spirit, I suppose such a prayer ought to be.

'Our Father in heaven, who hast kindly preserved the pupils and the teacher of this school during the past night, come and grant us a continuance of thy protection and blessing during this day. We cannot spend the day prosperously and happily without thee. Come then, and be in this schoolroom during this day, and help us all to be faithful and successful in duty.

'Guide the teacher in all that he may do. Give him wisdom and patience and faithfulness. May he treat all his pupils with kindness; and if any of them should do any thing that is wrong, wilt thou help him, gently but firmly to endeavour to bring him back to duty. May he sympathise with the difficulties and trials of all, and promote the present happiness, as well as the intellectual progress of all who are committed to his care.

'Take care of the pupils too. May they spend the day pleasantly and happily together. Wilt Thou who didst originally give us all our powers, direct and assist us all this day, in the use and improvement of them. Remove difficulties from our path, and give us all fidelity and patience in every duty. Let no one of us destroy our peace and happiness this day, by breaking any of thy commands, or encouraging our companions, in sins—or neglecting, in any respect, our duty. We ask all in the name of our great Redeemer. Amen.'

Of course the prayer of each day will be varied, unless in special cases, the teacher prefers to read some form like the above. But let every one be *minute and particular*, relating especially to school, to school temptations, and trials, and difficulties. Let every one be filled with expressions relating to school, so that it will bear, upon every sentence, the impression, that it is the petition of a teacher and his pupils at the throne of grace.

2. If the pupils can sing, there may be a single verse, or sometimes two verses of some well-known hymn sung after the prayer, at the opening of the school. Teachers will find it much easier to introduce this practice, than it would at first be supposed. In almost every school there are enough who can sing to begin, especially if the first experiment is made in a recess, or before or after school; and the beginning once made, the difficulty is over. If but few tunes are sung, a very large proportion of the scholars will soon learn them.

3. Let there be no other regular exercise until the close of the afternoon school. When that hour has arrived, let the teacher devote a very short period, five minutes perhaps, to religious *instruction*, given in various ways. At one time he may explain and illustrate some important truth. At another, read and comment upon a very short portion of Scripture. At another, relate an anecdote or fact, which will tend to interest the scholars in the performance of duty. The teacher should be very careful not to imitate on these occasions, the formal style of exhortation from the pulpit. Let him use no cant and hackneyed phrases, and never approach the subject of personal piety,—i. e. such feelings as penitence for sin, trust in God, and love for the Saviour, unless his own heart is really at the time,

warmed by the emotions which he wishes to awaken in others. Children very easily detect hypocrisy. They know very well when a parent or teacher is talking to them on religious sbjects, merely as a matter of course, for the sake of effect; and such constrained and formal efforts never do any good.

Let then every thing which you do, in reference to this subject, be done with proper regard to the character and condition of the youthful mind, and in such a way as shall be calculated to *interest,* as well as to *instruct.* A cold and formal exhortation, or even an apparently earnest one, delivered in a tone of affected solemnity, will produce no good effect. Perhaps I ought not to say it will produce *no* good effect: for good does sometime result, as a sort of accidental consequence, from almost any thing; but I mean it will have no effectual *tendency* to do good. You must vary your method too, in order to interest your pupils. Watch their countenances when you are addressing them, and see if they look interested. If they do not, be assured that there is something wrong, or at least something ill-judged, or inefficient, in your manner of explaining the truths which you desire should produce an effect upon their minds.

That you may be prepared to bring moral and religious truths before their minds in the way I have described, your own mind must take a strong interest in this class of truths. You must habituate yourself to look at the moral and religious aspects and relations of all that you see and hear. When you are reading, notice such facts, and remember such narratives as you can turn to good account in this way. In the same way, treasure up in mind such occurrences as may come under your own personal observation, when travelling, or when mixing with society.

That the spirit and manner of these religious exercises, may be the more distinctly understood, I will give some examples.

Let us suppose then, that the hour for closing school has come. The books are laid aside; the room is still; the boys expect the few words which the teacher is accustomed to address to them, and looking up to him, they listen to hear what he has to say.

'You may take your Bibles.'

The boys, by a simultaneous movement, open their desks, and take from them their copies of the sacred volume.

'What is the first book of the New Testament?'

'Matthew,' they all answer at once.

'The second?' 'Mark.' 'The third?' 'Luke.' 'The next;' 'John.' 'The next?' 'The Acts.' 'The next?'

Many answer, 'Romans.'

'The next?'

A few voices say, faintly and with hesitation, 'First of Corinthians.'

'I perceive your answers become fainter and fainter. Do you know what is the last book of the New Testament?'

The boys answer promptly, 'Revelation.'

'Do you know what books are between the Acts and the book of the Revelation?'

Some say, 'No, sir;' some begin to enumerate such books as occur to them, and some perhaps begin to name them promptly, and in their regular order.

'I do not mean,' interrupts the teacher, 'the *names* of the books, but the *kinds* of books.'

The boys hesitate.

'They are epistles or letters. Do you know who wrote the letters?'

'Paul.' 'Peter,' answer many voices at once.

'Yes,' there were several writers. Now the point which I wish to bring before you, is this. Do you know in what order, I mean on what principles the books are arranged?'

'No sir,' is the universal reply.

'I will tell you. First come all Paul's epistles. If you turn over the leaves of the Testament, you will see that Paul's letters are all put together, after the book of the Acts; and what I wish you to notice is, that they are arranged in the *order* of *their length*. The longest comes first, and then the next, and so on to the shortest, which is the epistle to Philemon. This of course comes last—No; I am wrong in saying it is the last of Paul's Epistles, there is one more,—to the Hebrews; and this comes after all the others, for there has been a good deal of dispute whether it was really written by Paul. You will see that his name is not at the beginning of it, as it is in his other epistles: so it was put last.'

'Then comes the epistle of James. Will you see whether it is longer than any that comes after it?' The boys, after a minute's examination, answer, 'Yes, sir,' 'Yes, sir.'

'What comes next?'

'The epistles of Peter.'

'Yes; and you will see that the longest of Peter's epistles is next in length to that of James: and indeed all his are arranged in the order of their length.'

'Yes, sir.'

'What comes next?'

'John's.'

'Yes, and they are arranged in the order of their length. Do you now understand the principle of the arrangement of the epistles?'

'Yes, sir.'

'I should like to have any of you who are interested in it, try to express this principle in a few sentences, on paper, and lay it on my desk to-morrow, and I will read what you write. You will find it very difficult to express it. Now you may lay aside your books. It will be pleasanter for you if you do it silently.'

Intelligent children will be interested even in so simple a point as this; much more interested than a maturer mind, unacquainted with the peculiarities of children, would suppose. By bringing up, from time to time, some such literary inquiry as this, they will be led insensibly to regard the Bible as opening a field for interesting intellectual research, and will more easily be led to study it.

At another time, the teacher spends his five minutes in aiming to accomplish a very different object. I will suppose it to be one of those afternoons, when all has gone smoothly and pleasantly in school. There has been nothing to excite strong interest or emotion, and there has been, as every teacher knows there sometimes will be, without any assignable cause which he can perceive, a calm, and quiet, and happy spirit, diffused over the minds and countenances of the little assembly. His evening communications should accord with this feeling, and he should make it the occasion to promote those pure and hallowed emotions in which every immortal mind must find its happiness, if it is to enjoy any worth possessing.

When all is still, the teacher addresses his pupils as follows:

'I have nothing but a simple story to tell you to-night. It is true, and the fact interested me very much when I witnessed it, but I do not know that it will interest you now, merely to hear it repeated. It is this:—

'Last vacation, I was travelling in a remote and thinly settled country, among the mountains in another state; I was riding with a gentleman on an almost unfrequented road. Forests were all around us, and the houses were small and very few.

'At length as we were passing a humble and solitary dwelling, the gentleman said to me, "There is a young woman sick in this house; should you like to go in and see her?". "Yes. sir," said I, " very much. She can have very few visitors, I think, in this lonely place, and if you think she would like to see us, I should like to go.'"

'We turned our horses towards the door, and as we were riding up, I asked what was the matter with the young woman.

'"Consumption," the gentleman replied, " and I suppose she will not live long.'"

'At that moment, we dismounted and entered the house. It was a very pleasant summer's afternoon, and the door was open. We entered and were received by an elderly lady, who seemed glad to see us. In one corner of the room was a bed, on which was lying the patient whom we had come to visit. She was pale and thin in her countenance, but there was a very calm and happy expression beaming in her eye. I went up to her bed-side and asked her how she did.

'I talked with her some time, and found that she was a Christian. She did not seem to know whether she would get well again or not, and in fact, she did not seem to care much about it. She was evidently happy then, and believed she should continue so. She had been penitent for her sins, and sought and obtained forgiveness, and enjoyed, in her loneliness, not only the protection of God, but also his presence in her heart, diffusing peace, and happiness there. When I came into the house, I said to myself, "I pity, I am sure, a person who is confined by sickness in this lonely place, with nothing to interest or amuse her;" but when I came out, I said to myself, "I do not pity her at all."

Never destroy the effect of such a communication as this, by attempting to follow it up with an exhortation, or with general remarks, vainly attempting to strengthen the impression.

Never do I say? Perhaps there may be some exceptions. But children are not reached by formal exhortations; their hearts are touched and affected in other ways. Sometimes you must reprove, sometimes you must condemn. But indiscriminate and perpetual harangues about the guilt of impenitence, and earnest entreaties to begin a life of piety, only harden the hearts they are intended to soften, and consequently confirm those who hear them, in the habits of sin.

In the same way a multitude of other subjects, infinite in number and variety, may be brought before your pupils at stated seasons for religious instruction. It is unnecessary to give any more particular examples, but still it may not be amiss to suggest a few general principles, which ought to guide those who are addressing the young, on every subject, and especially on the subject of religion.

I. *Make no effort to simplify language.* Children always observe this, and are always displeased with it, unless they are very young; and it is not necessary. They can understand ordinary language well enough, if the *subject* is within their comprehension, and treated in a manner adapted to their powers. If you doubt whether children can understand language, tell such a story as this, with ardour of tone and proper gesticulation, to a child only two or three years old.

'I saw an enormous dog in the street the other day. He was sauntering along slowly, until he saw a huge piece of meat lying down on the ground. He grasped it instantly between his teeth and ran away with all speed, until he disappeared around a corner so that I could see him no more.'

In such a description, there is a large number of words which such a child would not understand if they stood alone, but the whole description would be perfectly intelligible. The reason is, the *subject* is simple; the facts are such as a very little child would be interested in;—and the connexion of each new word, in almost every instance, explains its meaning. That is the way by which children learn all language. They learn the meaning of words, not by definitions, but by their connexion in the sentences in which they hear them: and by long practice they acquire an astonishing facility of doing this. It is true they sometimes mistake, but not often; and the teacher of children of almost any age, need not be afraid that he shall not be understood. There is no danger from his using the *language* of men, if his subject, and the manner in which he treats it, and the form and structure of his sentences are what they ought to be. Of course there may be cases, in fact there often will be cases, where particular words will require special explanation, but they will be comparatively few, and instead of making efforts to avoid them, it will be better to let them come. The pupils will be interested and profited by the explanation.

Perhaps some may ask what harm it will do, to simplify language, when talking to children. 'It certainly can do no injury,' they may say, 'and it removes all possibility of being misunderstood.' It does injury in at least three ways.

(1.) It disgusts the young persons to whom it is addressed, and prevents their being interested in what is said. I once met two children twelve years of age, who had just returned from hearing a very able discourse, delivered before a number of sabbath schools, assembled on some public occasion. 'How did you like the discourse?' said I.

'Very well indeed,' they replied, 'only,' said one of them, smiling, 'he talked to us as if we were all little children.'

Girls and boys, however young, never consider themselves little children, for they can always look down upon some younger than themselves. They are mortified too at being treated as though they could not understand what is really within the reach of their faculties. They do not like to have their powers underrated; and they are right in this feeling. It is common to all, old and young.

(2.) Children are kept back in learning language, if their teacher makes an effort to *come down*, as it is called, to their comprehension in the use of words. Notice that I say, *in the use of words*, for as I shall show presently, it is absolutely necessary to come down to the comprehension of children in some other respects. If however, in the use of words, those who address children, confine themselves to such words as children already understand, how are they to make progress in that most important of all studies, the knowledge of language. Many a mother keeps back her child, in this way, to a degree that is hardly conceivable; thus doing all in her power to perpetuate in the child, an ignorance of its mother tongue.

Teachers ought to make constant efforts to increase their scholars' stock of words, by using new ones from time to time, taking care to explain them when the connexion does not do it for them. So that instead of *coming down* to the language of childhood, he ought rather to go as far away from it as he possibly can, without leaving his pupils behind him.

(3.) But perhaps the greatest evil of this practice is, it satisfies the teacher. He thinks he addresses his pupils in the right manner, and overlooks altogether, the real peculiarities, in which the power to interest the young depends. He talks to them in simple language, and wonders why they are not interested. He certainly is *plain* enough. He is vexed with them for not attending to what he says, attributing it to their dulness or regardlessness of all that is useful or good, instead of perceiving that the great difficulty is his own want of skill. These three evils are sufficient to deter the teacher from the practice.

II. Present your subject not in its *general views*, but in its *minute details*. This is the great secret of interesting the young. Present it in its details, and in its practical exemplifications; do this with any subject whatever, and children will always be interested.

To illustrate this, let us suppose two teachers, wishing to explain to their pupils the same subject, and taking the following opposite methods of doing it. One, at the close of school addresses his charge as follows:

' The moral character of any action, that is, whether it is right or wrong, depends upon the *motives* with which it is performed. Men look only at the outward conduct, but God looks at the heart. In order now that any action should be pleasing to God, it is necessary that it should be performed from the motive of a desire to please him.

'Now there are a great many other motives of action which prevail among mankind, besides this right one. There is love of praise, love of money, affection for friends, &c.'

By the time the teacher has proceeded thus far, he finds, as he looks around the room, that the countenances of his pupils are assuming a listless and inattentive air. One is restless in his seat, evidently paying no attention. Another has reclined his head upon his desk, lost in a reverie, and others are looking round the room, at one another, or at the door, restless and impatient, hoping the dull lecture will soon be over.

The other teacher says:

'I have thought of an experiment I might try, which would illustrate to you a very important subject. Suppose I should call one of the boys, A. to me, and should say to him; 'I want you to go to your seat and transcribe for me a piece of poetry, as handsomely as you can. If it is written as well as you can possibly write it, I will give you 25 cents.' Suppose I say this to him privately, so that none of the rest of the boys can hear, and he goes to take his seat, and begins to work. You perceive that I have presented to him a motive to exertion.'

'Yes, sir,' say the boys, all looking with interest at the teacher, wondering how this experiment is going to end.

'Well, what would that motive be?'

'Money.' 'The quarter of a dollar.' 'Love of money,' or perhaps other answers are heard, from the various parts of the room.

'Yes, love of money, it is called. Now suppose I should call another boy, one with whom I was particularly acquainted, and, who, I should know would make an effort to please me, and should say to him, 'For a particular reason, I want you to copy this poetry'—giving him the same—' I wish you to copy it handsomely, for I wish to send it away, and have not time to copy it myself. Can you do it as well as not?'

'Suppose the boy should say he could, and should take it to his seat, and begin ; neither of the boys knowing what the other was doing. I should now have offered to this second boy a motive. Would it be the same with the other!'

' No, sir.'

' What was the other ?'

' Love of money.'

' What is this ?'

The boys hesitate.

' It might be called,' continues the teacher, ' friendship. It is the motive of a vast number of the actions which are performed in this world.'

' Do you think of any other common motive of action, besides love of money, and friendship?'

' Love of honour,' says one ; ' fear,' says another.

' Yes,' continues the teacher, ' both these are common motives. I might in order to exhibit them, call two more boys, one after the other, and say to the one, I will thank you to go and copy this piece of poetry as well as you can ; I want to send it to the school committee as a specimen of improvement made in this school.'

' To the other, I might say; you have been a careless boy to-day ; you have not got your lessons well. Now take your seat, and copy this poetry. Do it carefully.

Unless you take pains, and do it as well as you possibly can, I shall punish you severely, before you go home.'

'How many motives have I got now? Four, I believe.'

'Yes, sir,' say the boys.

'Love of money, friendship, love of honour, and fear. We called the first boy A; let us call the others B C and D; no, we shall remember better to call them by the name of their motives. We will call the first M, for money; the second F, for friendship; the third H, for honour: and the last F,—we have got an F. already: what shall we do? On the whole, it is of no consequence, we will have two F.'s, we shall remember not to confound them.

'But there are a great many other motives entirely distinct from these. For example, suppose I should say to a fifth boy, 'Will you copy this piece of poetry? it belongs to one of the little boys in school: he wants a copy of it, and I told him I would try to get some one to copy it for him.' This motive now would be benevolence; that is, if the boy who was asked to copy it, was not particularly acquainted with the other, and did it chiefly to oblige him. We will call this boy B, for benevolence.'

'Now suppose I call a sixth boy, and say to him, 'I have set four or five boys to work, copying this piece of poetry: now I want you to sit down and see if you cannot do it better than any of them. No one of them knows that any other is writing, except you, but after the others are all done, I will compare them and see if yours is not the best.' This would be trying to excite *emulation*. We must call this boy then, E.—But the time I intended to devote to talking with you on this subject for to-day, is expired. Perhaps, to-morrow, I will take up the subject again.'

The reader now will observe that the grand peculiarity of the instructions given by this last teacher, as distinguished from those of the first, consists in this; that the parts of the subject are presented *in detail*, and in *particular exemplification*. In the first case, the whole subject was despatched in a single, general, and comprehensive description; in the latter, it is examined minutely, one point being brought forward at a time. The discussions enlivened too, by meeting and removing such little difficulties, as will naturally come up, in such an investigation. Boys and girls will take an interest in such a lecture; they will regret to have it come to a conclusion, and will give their attention when the subject is again brought forward, on the following day. Let us suppose the time for continuing the exercise to have arrived. The teacher resumes the discussion thus.

'I was talking to you yesterday about the motives of action; how many had I made?'

Some say, 'Four,' some 'Five,' some 'Six.'

'Can you name any of them?'

The boys attempt to recollect them, and they give the names in the order, in which they accidentally occur to the various individuals. Of course, the words Fear, Emulation, Honour, Friendship, and others, come in confused and irregular sounds from every part of the school-room.

'You do not recollect the order,' says the teacher, 'and it is of no consequence, for the order I named was only accidental. Now to go on with my account; suppose all these boys to sit down, and go to writing, each one acting under the impulse of the motive, which had been presented to him individually. But in order to make the supposition answer my purpose, I must add two other cases. I will imagine that one of these boys is called away a few minutes, and leaves his paper on his desk, and that another boy, of an ill-natured and morose disposition, happening to pass by and see his paper, thinks he will sit down and write upon it a few lines, just to plague and vex the one who was called away. We will also suppose that I call another boy to me, whom, I have reason to believe to be a sincere Christian, and say to him, ' Here is a new duty for you to perform this afternoon. This piece of poetry is to be copied; now do it carefully and faithfully. You know that this morning you committed yourself to God's care during the day ; now remember he has been watching you all the time, thus far, and he will be noticing you all the time you are doing this ; he will be pleased if you do your duty faithfully.''

'The boys thus all go to writing. Now suppose a stranger should come in, and seeing them all busy, should say to me,

' " What are all these boys doing ! " '

' " They are writing." '

' " What are they writing? " '

' " They are writing a piece of poetry." '

' " They seem to be very busy ; they are very industrious, good boys." '

' " Oh no ! it is not by any means certain that they are *good* boys." '

' " I mean that they are good boys *now*; that they are doing right at *this time*." '

' " *That* is not certain; some of them are doing right and some are doing very wrong; though they are all writing the same piece of poetry." '

'The stranger would perhaps look surprised while I said this, and would ask an explanation, and I might properly reply as follows.'

'" Whether the boys are, at this moment, doing right or wrong, depends not so much upon what they are doing, as upon the feeling of the heart, with which they are doing it. I acknowledge that they are all doing the same thing outwardly,—they are all writing the same extract, and they are all doing it attentively and carefully, but they are thinking of very different things."'

'" What are they thinking of?"'

'" Do you see that boy?" I might say, pointing to one of them, "His name is M." He is writing for money. He is saying to himself all the time, " I hope I shall get the quarter of a dollar.' He is calculating what he shall buy with it, and every good or bad letter that he makes, he is considering the chance whether he shall succeed or fail in obtaining it."'

'" What is the next boy to him thinking of?"'

'" His name is B. He is copying to oblige a little fellow, whom he scarcely knows, and is trying to make his copy handsome so as to give him pleasure. He is thinking how gratified his schoolmate will be when he receives it, and is forming plans to get acquainted with him."'

'" Do you see that boy in the back seat. He has maliciously taken another boy's place just to spoil his work. He knows too that he is breaking the rules of the school, in being out of his place, but he stays, notwithstanding, and is delighting himself with thinking how disappointed and sad his schoolmate will be, when he comes in and finds his work spoiled, because he was depending on doing it all himself."'

'"I see,' the stranger might say by this time, 'that there is a great difference among these boys; have you told me about them all?'"

'"No,' I might reply, 'there are several others. I will only mention one more. He sits in the middle of the second desk. He is writing carefully, simply because he wishes to do his duty, and please God. He thinks that God is present and loves him, and takes care of him, and he is obedient and grateful in return. I do not mean that he is all the time thinking of God, but love to Him is his motive of effort.'"

'Do you see now, boys, what I mean to teach you by this long supposition?'

'Yes sir.'

'I presume you do. Perhaps it would be difficult for you to express it in words, I can express it in general terms, thus,

'*Our characters depend not only on what we do, but on the spirit and motive with which we do it.* What I have been saying, throws light upon one important verse in the Bible, which I should like to have read. James, have you a Bible in your desk?'

'Yes sir.'

'Will you turn to 1 Samuel xvi. 7, and then rise, and read it. Read it loud, so that all the school can hear.'

James reads as follows.

"MAN LOOKETH ON THE OUTWARD APPEARANCE, BUT THE LORD LOOKETH ON THE HEART."

This is the way to reach the intellect and the heart of the young. *Go into detail.* Explain truth and duty, not in an abstract form, but exhibit it, in *actual and living examples.*

III. Be very cautious how you bring in the awful

sanctions of religion, to assist you directly, in the discipline of your school. You will derive a most powerful indirect assistance, from the influence of religion in the little community which you govern. But this will be, through the prevalence of its spirit in the hearts of your pupils, and not from any assistance which you can usually derive from it, in managing particular cases of transgression. Many teachers may make great mistakes in this respect. A bad boy, who has done something openly and directly subversive of the good order of the school, or the rights of his companions, is called before the master, who thinks that the most powerful weapon to wield against him is the Bible. So while the trembling culprit stands before him, he administers to him a reproof, which consists of an almost ludicrous mixture of scolding, entreaty, religious instruction, and threatening of punishment. But such an occasion as this is no time to touch a bad boy's heart. He is steeled, at such a moment, against any thing but mortification, and the desire to get out of the hands of the master; and he has an impression, that the teacher appeals to religious principles, only to assist him to sustain his own authority. Of course, religious truth, at such a time, can make no good impression. There may be exceptions to this rule. There doubtless are. I have found some; and every successful teacher who reads this will probably call some to mind, some which have occurred in the course of his own experience. I am only speaking of what ought to be the general rule, which is, to reserve religious truths for moments of a different character altogether. Bring the principles of the Bible forward, when the mind is calm, when the emotions are quieted, and all within is at rest; and in exhibiting them, be actuated not by a desire to make your duties of government easier, but to promote the real and permanent happiness of your charge.

IV. Do not be eager to draw from your pupils, an expression of their personal interest in religious truth. Lay before them, and enforce, by all the means in your power, the principles of Christian duty, but do not converse with them for the purpose of gratifying your curiosity in regard to their piety, or your spiritual pride by counting up the numbers of those who have been led to piety by your influence. Beginning to act from christian principles, is the beginning of a new life, and it may be an interesting subject of inquiry to you, to ascertain how many of your pupils have experienced the change. But, in many cases, it would merely gratify curiosity to know. There is no question too, that in very many instances, the faint glimmering of religious interest, which would have kindled into a bright flame, is extinguished at once and perhaps forever, by the rough inquiries of a religious friend. Besides if you make inquiries, and form a definite opinion of your pupils, they will know that this is your practice, and many a one will repose in the belief that you consider him or her a Christian, and you will thus increase the number, already unfortunately too large, of those who maintain the form and pretences of piety, without its power; whose hearts are filled with self-sufficiency and spiritual pride, and perhaps zeal for the truths and external duties of religion, while the real spirit of piety has no place there. They trust to some imaginary change, long since passed by, and which has proved to be spurious by its failing of its fruits. The best way, in fact the only way, to guard against this danger, especially with the young, is to show, by your manner of speaking and acting on this subject, at all times, that you regard a truly religious life, as the only evidence of piety; and that consequently, however much interest your pupils may apparently take in religious instruction, they cannot know, and you cannot know, whether Christian principle reigns within them, in any other way than by following them through life and observing how, and with what spirit, the various duties of it are performed.

There are very many fallacious indications of piety; so fallacious and so plausible, that there are very few, even among intelligent Christians, who are not often greatly deceived. "By their fruits ye shall know them," said the Saviour, a direction sufficiently plain one would think, and pointing to a test, sufficiently easy to be applied. But it is slow and tedious work to wait for fruits; and we accordingly seek a criterion which will help us quicker to a result. You see your pupil serious and thoughtful. It is well: but it is no proof of piety. You see him deeply interested when you speak of his obligations to his Maker, and the duties he owes to him. This is well; but it is no proof of piety. You know he reads his Bible daily, and offers his morning and evening prayers. When you speak to him of God's goodness, and of his past ingratitude, his bosom heaves with emotion, and the tear stands in his eye. It is all well. You may hope that he is going to devote his life to the service of God. But you cannot know; you cannot even believe with any great confidence. These appearances are not piety. They are not conclusive evidences of it. They are only in the young, faint grounds of hope, that the genuine fruits of piety will appear.

I am aware that there are many persons so habituated to judging with confidence of the piety of others from some such indications as I have described, that they will think I carry my cautions to the extreme. Perhaps I do; but the Saviour said, "By their fruits ye shall know them," and it is safest to follow his direction.

By the word "fruits," however, our Saviour unquestionably does not mean the mere moral virtues of this life. The fruits to be looked for, are the fruits of *piety*, that is, indications of permanent attachment to the Creator, and a desire to obey his commands. We must look for these.

There is no objection to your giving particular individuals special instruction adapted to their wants and circumstances. You may do this by writing, or in other ways; but do not lead them to make up their minds fully that they are Christians, in such a sense as to induce them to feel that the work is done. Let them understand that becoming a Christian is *beginning* a work, not *finishing* it. Be cautious how you form an opinion even yourself on the question of the genuineness of their piety. Be content not to know. You will be more faithful and watchful if you consider it uncertain, and they will be more faithful and watchful too.

V. Bring very fully and frequently before your pupils, the practical duties of religion in all their details, especially their duties at home to their parents, and to their brothers and sisters. Do not, however, allow them to mistake Morality for Religion. Shew them clearly what piety is in its essence, and this you can do most successfully by exhibiting its effects.

VI. Finally, let me insert as the key-stone of all that I have been saying in this chapter:—be sincere, and ardent, and consistent, in your own piety. The whole structure which I have been attempting to build, will tumble into ruins without this. Be constantly watchful and careful, not only to maintain intimate communion with God, and to renew it daily in your seasons of retirement, but guard your conduct. Let piety animate, controul, and regulate it. Show your pupils that it makes you amiable, patient, forbearing, benevolent in little things, as well as in great things, and your example will co-operate with your instructions, and allure your pupils to walk in the paths which you tread. But no clearness and faithfulness in religious teaching will atone for the injury which a bad example will effect. Conduct speaks louder than words, and no persons are more shrewd than the young, to discover the hollowness of empty professions, and the heartlessness of mere pretended interest in their good.

I am aware that this book may fall into the hands of some who may take little interest in the subject of this chapter. To such I may perhaps owe an apology for having thus fully discussed a topic, in which only a part of my readers can be supposed to be interested. My apology is this. It is obvious and unquestionable that we all owe allegiance to the Supreme. It is so obvious and unquestionable, as to be entirely beyond the necessity of proof, for it is plain that nothing but such a bond of union can keep the peace among the millions of distinct intelligences with which the creation is filled. It is therefore the plain duty of every man to establish that connexion between himself and his Maker which the Bible requires, and to do what he can to bring others to the peace and happiness of piety. These truths are so plain, that they admit of no discussion and no denial, and it seems to me highly unsafe for any man to neglect or to postpone the performance of the duty which arises from them. A still greater hazard is incurred when such a man having forty or fifty fellow beings almost entirely under his influence, leads them by his example away from their Maker, or widens the breach that separates them from Him. With these views I could not, when writing on the duties of a teacher of the young, refrain from bringing distinctly to view, this, which has so imperious a claim.

CHAPTER VI.

THE MOUNT VERNON SCHOOL.

There is perhaps no way by which teachers can, in a given time, do more to acquire a knowledge of their art, and an interest in it, than by visiting each others' schools.

It is not always the case, that any thing is observed by the visitor, which he can directly and wholly introduce into his own school,—but what he sees, suggests to him modifications or changes,—and it gives him at any rate, renewed strength and resolution in his work, to see how similar objects are accomplished, or similar difficulties removed by others. I have often thought that there ought on this account to be far greater freedom and frequency in the interchange of visits than there is.

Next, however, to a visit to a school, comes the reading of a vivid description of it. I do not mean a cold, theoretical exposition of the general principles of its management and instruction; for these are essentially the same in all good schools. I mean a minute account of the plans and arrangements by which these general principles are applied. Suppose twenty of the most successful teachers in New England would write such a description, each of his own school, how valuable would be the volume which should contain them!

With these views I have concluded to devote one chapter to a description of the school, which has been for four years under my care. The account was originally prepared and *printed*, but not published, for the purpose of distribution among the scholars, simply because this seemed to be the easiest and surest method of making them on their admission to the school, acquainted with its arrangements and plans. It is addressed, therefore, throughout to a pupil, and I preserve its original form, as by its being addressed to pupils, and intended to influence them, it is an example of the mode of address, and the kind of influence recommended in this work. It was chiefly designed for new scholars; a copy of it was presented to each on the day of her admission to the school, and it was made her first duty to read it attentively.

The system which it describes is one which gradually grew up in the institution under the writer's care. The school was commenced with a small number of pupils, and without any system or plan whatever, and the one here described was formed insensibly, and by slow degrees, through the influence of various and accidental circumstances. I have no idea that it is superior to the plans of government and instruction adopted in many other schools. It is true that there must necessarily be some system in every large school; but different instructers will fall upon different principles of organization, which will naturally be such as are adapted to the habits of thought, and manner of instruction of their respective authors, and consequently each will be best for its own place. While, therefore, some system,— some methodical arrangement is necessary in all schools, it is not necessary that it should be the same in all. It is not even desirable that it should be. I consider this plan as only one among a multitude of others, each of which will be successful, not by the power of its intrinsic qualities, but just in proportion to the ability and faithfulness with which it is carried into effect.

There may be features of this plan, which teachers who read it, will be inclined to adopt. In other cases suggestions may occur to the mind of the reader, which will modify in some degree his present plans. Others may merely be interested in seeing how others effect what they, by easy methods, are equally successful in effecting.

It is in these, and similar ways, that I have often myself been highly benefitted in visiting schools, and in reading descriptions of them; and it is for such purposes that I insert the account here.

TO A NEW SCHOLAR ON HER ADMISSION TO THE MOUNT VERNON SCHOOL.

As a large school is necessarily somewhat complicated in its plan, and as new scholars usually find that it requires some time, and gives them no little trouble to understand the arrangements they find in operation here, I have concluded to write a brief description of these arrangements, by help of which, you will, I hope the sooner feel at home in your new place of duty. That I may be more distinct and specific, I shall class what I have to say under separate heads.

I.—YOUR PERSONAL DUTY.

Your first anxiety as you come into the school-room,

and take your seat among the busy multitude, if you are conscientiously desirous of doing your duty, will be, lest, ignorant as you are of the whole plan, and of all the regulations of the institution, you should inadvertently do what will be considered wrong. I wish first then to put you at rest on this score. There is but one rule of this school; and that you can easily keep.

You will observe on one side of my desk a clock upon the wall, and upon the other a piece of apparatus, that is probably new to you. It is a metallic plate, upon which are marked in gilded letters, the words, '*Study Hours.*'

Now when this '*Study Card,*'[1] as the scholars call it, is *up*, so that the words 'STUDY HOURS' are presented to the view of the school, it is the signal for silence and study. THERE IS THEN TO BE NO COMMUNICATION, AND NO LEAVING OF SEATS, EXCEPT AT THE DIRECTION OF TEACHERS. When it is *half-down*, each scholar may leave her seat and whisper, but she must do nothing which will disturb others. When it is *down*, all the duties of the school are suspended, and scholars are left entirely at liberty.

As this is the only rule of the school, it deserves a little more full explanation; for not only your progress in study, but your influence in promoting the welfare of the school, and consequently your peace and happiness while you are a member of it, will depend upon the strictness with which you observe it.

Whenever, then, the study card goes up, and you hear the sound of its little bell, immediately and instantaneously stop, whatever you are saying. If you are away from your seat go directly to it, and there remain,

---

[1] This apparatus has been previously described. See p. 37.

and forget in your own silent and solitary studies, so far as you can, all that are around you. You will remember that all *communication* is forbidden. Whispering, making signs, writing upon paper or a slate, bowing to any one,—and in fact, *every* possible way by which one person may have any sort of mental intercourse with another, is wrong. A large number of the scholars take a pride and pleasure in carrying this rule into as perfect an observance as possible. They say, that as this is the only rule with which I trouble them, they ought certainly to observe this faithfully. I myself, however, put it upon other ground. I am satisfied that it is better and pleasanter for you to observe it most rigidly, if it is attempted to be enforced at all.

You will ask, 'Cannot we obtain permission of you or of the teachers to leave our seats, or to whisper, if it is necessary?' The answer is, 'No.' You must never ask permission of me or of the teachers. You can leave seats, or speak at the *direction* of the teachers; i. e. when they of their own accord tell you to do it, but you are never to ask their permission. If you should, and if any teachers should give you permission, it would be of no avail. I have never given them authority to grant any permissions of the kind.

You will then say, are we never on any occasion whatever, to leave our seats in study hours? Yes, you are. There are two ways.

1. *At the direction of teachers.* Going to and from recitations is considered as *at the direction of teachers.* So, if a person is requested by a teacher to transact any business, or is elected to a public office, or appointed upon a committee,—leaving seats, or speaking, so far as is really necessary for the accomplishing such a purpose, is considered as *at the direction of teachers,* and is

consequently right. In the same manner, if a teacher should ask you individually, or give general notice to the members of a class to come to her seat for private instruction, or to go to any part of the school-room for her, it would be right to do it. The distinction, you observe, is this. The teacher may *of her own accord*, direct any leaving of seats which she may think necessary to accomplish the objects of the school. She must not, however, *at the request of an individual* for the sake of her mere private convenience, give her permission to speak or to leave her seat. If for example, a teacher should say to you in your class, ' As soon as you have performed a certain work you may bring it to me,'—you would in bringing it, be acting under her *direction*, and would consequently do right. If, however, you should want a pencil, and should ask her to give you leave to borrow it, even if she should give you leave, you would do wrong to go, for you would not be acting at her *direction*, but simply by her *consent*, and she has no authority to grant consent.

2. The second case in which you may leave your seat is, when some very uncommon occurrence takes place, which is sufficient reason for suspending all rules. If your neighbour is faint, you may speak to her, and if necessary, lead her out. If your mother, or some other friend should come into the school-room, you can go and sit with her upon the sofa, and talk about the school:—and so in many other similar cases. Be very careful not to abuse this privilege, and make slight causes the grounds of your exceptions. It ought to be a very clear case. If a young lady is unwell in a trifling degree, so as to need no assistance, you would evidently do wrong to talk to her. The rule, in fact, is very similar to that which all well-bred people observe

at church. They never speak or leave their seats unless some really important cause, such as sickness, requires them to break through all rules and go out. You have in the same manner, in really important cases, such as serious sickness in your own case, or in that of your companions, or the coming in of a stranger,—or something else equally extraordinary, power to lay aside any rule, and to act as the emergency may require. In using this discretion, however, be sure to be on the safe side; in such cases never ask permission. You must act on your own responsibility.

Reasons for this rule. When the school was first established, there was no absolute prohibition of whispering. Each scholar was allowed to whisper in relation to her studies. They were often, very often, enjoined to be conscientious and faithful, but as might have been anticipated, the experiment failed. It was almost universally the practice to whisper more or less about subjects entirely foreign to the business of the school. This they all repeatedly acknowledged; and the scholars almost unanimously admitted, that the good of the school required the prohibition of all communication during certain hours. I gave them their choice, either always to ask permission when they wished to speak, or to have a certain time allowed for the purpose, during which, free inter-communication might be allowed to all the school, with the understanding, however, that out of this time, no permission should ever be asked or granted. They very wisely chose the latter plan, and the *Study Card* was constructed and put up to mark the times of free communication, and of silent study. The card was at first down every half hour for one or two minutes. The scholars, afterwards thinking that their intellectual habits would be improved, and the welfare of the school promoted by their having a longer time for uninterrupted study, of their own accord, without any influence from me, proposed that the card should be down only once an hour. This plan was adopted by them by vote. I wish it to be understood, that it was not *my* plan, but *theirs*, and that I am at any time willing to have the study card down once in half an hour, whenever a majority of the scholars, voting by ballot, desire it.

You will find that this system of having a distinct time for whispering, when all may whisper freely, all communication being entirely excluded at other times, will at first give you some trouble. It will be hard for you, if you are not accustomed to it, to learn conscientiously and faithfully to comply. Besides, at first, you will often need some little information, or an article which you might obtain in a moment, but which you cannot innocently ask for till the card is down, and this might keep you waiting an hour. You will, however, after a few such instances, soon learn to make your preparations before-hand, and if you are a girl of enlarged views and elevated feelings, you will good-humouredly acquiesce in suffering a little inconvenience yourself, for the sake of helping to preserve those *distinct* and well-*defined* lines, by which all boundaries must be marked in a large establishment, if order and system are to be preserved at all.

Though at first you may experience a little inconvenience, you will soon take pleasure in the scientific strictness of the plan. It will gratify you to observe the profound stillness of the room where a hundred are studying. You will take pleasure in observing the sudden transition from the silence of study hours, to the joyful sounds and the animating activity of recess, when the study card goes down; and then, when it rises again at the close of the recess, you will be gratified to observe how suddenly the sounds which have filled the air and made the room so lively a scene, are hushed into silence by the single and almost inaudible touch of that little bell. You will take pleasure in this, for young and old always take pleasure in the strict and rigid operation of *system*, rather than in laxity and disorder. I am convinced also that the scholars do like the operation of this plan, for I am not obliged to make any efforts to sustain it. With the exception that occasionally, (usually not oftener than once in several months) I allude to the subject, and that chiefly on account of a few careless and unfaithful individuals, I have little to say or to do to maintain the authority of the study card. Most of the scholars obey it of their own accord, implicitly and cordially. And I believe they consider this faithful monitor, not only one of the most useful, but one of the most agreeable friends they have. We should not only regret its services, but miss its company, if it should be taken away.

This regulation then, viz. to abstain from all communication with one another, and from all leaving of seats, at certain times which are marked by the position of the study card, is the only one which can properly be called a *rule* of the school. There are a great many arrangements and plans relating to the *instruction* of the pupils, but no other specific *rules* relating to *their conduct*. You are, of course, while in the school, under the same moral obligations which rest upon you elsewhere. You must be kind to one another, respectful to superiors, and quiet and orderly in your deportment. You must do nothing to encroach upon another's rights, or to interrupt and disturb your companions in their pursuits.

You must not produce disorder, or be wasteful of the public property, or do any thing else which you might know is in itself wrong. But you are to avoid these things, not because there are any rules in this school against them, for there are none; but because they are in *themselves wrong;* in all places and under all circumstances, wrong. The universal and unchangeable principles of duty are the same here as elsewhere. I do not make rules pointing them out, but expect that you will, through your own conscience and moral principle, discover and obey them.

Such a case as this, for example, once occurred. A number of little girls began to amuse themselves in recess with running about among the desks, in pursuit of one another, and they told me, in excuse for it, that they did not know that it was '*against the rule.*'

'It is not against the rule;' said I, 'I have never made any rule against running about among the desks.'

'Then,' asked they, 'did we do wrong?'

'Do you think it would be a good plan,' I inquired, 'to have it a common amusement in the recess, for the girls to hunt each other among the desks?'

'No sir,' they replied simultaneously.

'Why not? There are some reasons. I do not know, however, whether you will have the ingenuity to think of them.'

'We may start the desks from their places,' said one.

'Yes,' said I, 'they are fastened down very slightly, that I may easily alter their position.'

'We might upset the inkstands,' said another.

'Sometimes,' added a third, 'we run against the scholars who are sitting in their seats.'

'It seems then you have ingenuity enough to discover

the reasons. Why did not these reasons prevent your doing it.'

'We did not think of them before.'

'True; that is the exact state of the case. Now when persons are so eager to promote their own enjoyment, as to forget the rights and the comforts of others, it is *selfishness*. Now is there any rule in this school against selfishness.'

'No, sir.'

'You are right. There is not. But selfishness is wrong,—very wrong, in whatever form it appears,— here, and every where else; and that, whether I make any rules against it or not.'

You will see from this anecdote that though there is but one rule of the school, I by no means intend to say that there is only *one way of doing wrong here*. That would be very absurd. You *must not do anything which you may know, by proper reflection, to be in itself wrong*. This however is an universal principle of duty, not a *rule* of the Mount Vernon School. If I should attempt to make rules which would specify and prohibit every possible way by which you might do wrong, my laws would be innumerable. And even then I should fail of securing my object, unless you had the disposition to do your duty. No legislation can enact laws as fast as a perverted ingenuity can find means to evade them.

You will perhaps ask what will be the consequence if we transgress,—either the single rule of the school, or any of the great principles of duty. In other words what are the punishments which are resorted to in the Mount Vernon School? The answer is, there are no punishments. I do not say that I should not, in case all other means should fail, resort to the most decisive measures to secure obedience and subordination. Most certainly, I should do so, as it would plainly be my duty to do it. If you should at any time be so unhappy as to violate your obligations to yourself, to your companions, or to me,—should you misemploy your time, or exhibit an unkind or a selfish spirit, or be disrespectful or insubordinate to your teachers,—I should go frankly and openly, but kindly to you, and endeavour to convince you of your fault. I should very probably do this by addressing a note to you, as I suppose this would be less unpleasant to you than a conversation. In such a case, I shall hope that you will as frankly and openly reply; telling me whether you admit your fault and are determined to amend, or else informing me of the contrary. I shall wish you to be *sincere*, and then I shall know what course to take next. But as to the consequences which may result to you if you should persist in what is wrong, it is not necessary that you should know them before hand. They who wander from duty, always plunge themselves into troubles they do not anticipate; and if you do what, at the time you are doing it, you know to be wrong, it will not be unjust that you should suffer the consequences, even if they were not before-hand understood and expected. This will be the case with you all through life, and it will be the case here.

I say it *will* be the case here; I ought rather to say that it *would be* the case, should you be so unhappy as to do wrong and to persist in it. Such cases however never occur. At least they occur so seldom, and at intervals so great, that every thing of the nature of punishment, that is, the depriving a pupil of any enjoyment, or subjecting her to any disgrace, or giving her pain in any way in consequence of her faults, except the simple pain of awakening conscience in her bosom is almost entirely unknown. I hope that you will always be ready to confess and forsake your faults, and endeavour while you remain in the school, to improve in character, and attain as far as possible, every moral excellence.

I ought to remark before dismissing this topic, that I place very great confidence in the scholars in regard to their moral conduct and deportment, and they fully deserve it. I have no care and no trouble in what is commonly called *the government of the school*. Neither myself nor any one else is employed in any way in watching the scholars, or keeping any sort of account of them. I should not at any time hesitate to call all the teachers in an adjoining room, leaving the school alone for half an hour, and I should be confident, that at such a time, order and stillness and attention to study would prevail as much as ever. The scholars would not look to see whether I was in my desk, but whether the Study Card was up. The school was left in this way, half an hour every day, during a quarter, that we might have a teachers' meeting, and the school went on, generally quite as well, to say the least, as when the teachers were present. One or two instances of irregular conduct occurred. I do not now recollect precisely what they were. They were however, fully acknowleged and not repeated, and I believe the scholars were generally more scrupulous and faithful then than at other times. They would not betray the confidence reposed in them. This plan was continued until it was found more convenient to have the teachers' meeting in the afternoon.

When any thing wrong is done in school, I generally state the case and request the individuals who have done it to let me know who they are. They do it sometimes by notes and sometimes in conversation,—but they always do it. The plan *always* succeeds. The scholars all know that there is nothing to be feared from confessing faults to me; but that on the other hand, it is a most direct and certain way to secure returning peace and happiness.

I can illustrate this, by describing a case which actually occurred. Though the description is not to be considered so much an accurate account of what occurred in a particular case, as an illustration of the *general spirit and manner* in which such cases are disposed of. I accidentally understood, that some of the younger scholars were in the habit, during recesses and after school, of ringing the door bell and then running away, to amuse themselves with the perplexity of their companions, who should go to the door and find no one there. I explained in a few words, one day, to the school, that this was wrong.

'How many,' I then asked, 'have ever been put to the trouble to go to the door, when the bell has thus been rung? They may rise.'

A very large number of scholars stood up. Those who had done the mischief were evidently surprised at the extent of the trouble they had occasioned.

'Now,' I continued, 'I think all will be convinced that the trouble which this practice has occasioned to the fifty or sixty young ladies, who cannot be expected to find amusement in such a way, is far greater than the pleasure it can have given to the few who are young enough to have enjoyed it. Therefore it was wrong. Do you think the girls who rang the bell might have known this, by proper reflection?'

'Yes, sir,' the school generally answered.

'I do not mean,' said I, 'if they had set themselves formally at work to think about the subject; but with such a degree of reflection as ought reasonably to be expected of little girls, in the hilarity of recess and of play.

'Yes, sir,' was still the reply, but fainter than before.

'There is one way by which I might ascertain whether you were old enough to know that this was wrong, and that is by asking those who have refrained from doing this, because they supposed it would be wrong, to rise. Then if some of the youngest scholars in school should stand up, as I have no doubt they would, it would prove that all might have known, if they had been equally conscientious. But if I ask those to rise who have *not* rung the bell, I shall make it known to the whole school, who they are that have done it, and I wish that the exposure of faults should be private, unless it is *necessary* that it should be public. I will therefore not do it. I have myself however, no doubt that all might have known that it was wrong.'

'There is,' continued I, 'another injury which must grow out of such a practice. This I should not have expected the little girls could think of. In fact, I doubt whether any in school will think of it. Can any one tell what it is?'

No one replied.

'I should suppose that it would lead you to disregard the bell when it rings, and that consequently a gentleman or lady might sometimes ring in vain; the scholars near the door saying, "Oh, it is only the little girls."'

'Yes, sir,' was heard from all parts of the room.

I found from farther inquiry that this had been the case, and I closed by saying,

'I am satisfied, that those who have inadvertently fallen into this practice are sorry for it, and that if I should leave it here, no more cases of it would occur, and this is all I wish. At the same time, they who have done this, will feel more effectually relieved from the pain which having done wrong must necessarily give them, if they individually acknowledge it to me. I wish therefore that all who have done so, would write me notes stating the facts. If any one does not do it, she will punish herself severely, for she will feel for many days to come, that while her companions were willing to acknowledge their faults, she wished to conceal and cover hers. Conscience will reproach her bitterly for her insincerity and whenever she hears the sound of the door-bell, it will remind her not only of her fault, but of what is far worse *her willingness to appear innocent when she was really guilty.*'

Before the close of the school I had eight or ten notes acknowledging the fault, describing the circumstances of each case, and expressing promises to do so no more.

It is by such methods as this, rather than by threatening and punishment that I manage the cases of discipline, which from time to time occur, but even such as this, slight as it is, occur very seldom. Weeks and weeks sometimes elapse without one. When they do occur, they are always easily settled by confession and reform. Sometimes I am asked to *forgive* the offence. But I never forgive. I have no power to forgive. God must forgive you when you do wrong, or the burden must remain. My duty is to take measures to prevent future transgression, and to lead those who have been guilty of it, to God for pardon. If they do not go to him, though they may satisfy me, as Principal of a school, by not repeating the offence—they must remain *unforgiven.* I can *forget* and I do forget. For example, in this last case, I have not the slightest recollection of any individual who was engaged in it. The evil was entirely removed, and had it not afforded me a convenient illustration here, perhaps I should never have thought of it again—still it may not yet be *forgiven*. It may seem strange to some that I should speak so seriously of God's forgiveness for such a trifle as that. 'Does he notice a child's ringing a door bell in play?' He notices when a child is willing to yield to temptation, to do what she knows to be wrong, and to act, even in the slightest trifle, from a selfish disregard for the convenience of others. This spirit he always notices, and though I may stop any particular form of its exhibition, it is for Him alone to forgive it and to purify the heart from its power. But I shall speak more particularly on this subject under the head of Religious Instruction.

II.—ORDER OF DAILY EXERCISES.

There will be given you when you enter the school a blank schedule in which the divisions of each forenoon for one week are marked, and in which your own employments for every half hour are to be written. A copy of this is inserted on the adjoining page.

This schedule, when filled up, forms a sort of a map of the week, in which you can readily find what are your duties for any particular time. The following description will enable you better to understand it.

OPENING OF THE SCHOOL.

The first thing which will call your attention as the hour for the commencement of the school approaches in the morning, is the ringing of a bell, five minutes before the time arrives, by the regulator, who sits at the curtained desk before the Study Card. One minute before the time, the bell is rung again, which is the signal for all to take their seats and prepare for the opening of the school. When the precise moment arrives, the Study Card is drawn up, and at the sound of its little bell, all the scholars recline their heads upon their desks and unite with me in a very short prayer for God's protection and blessing during the day. I adopted the plan of allowing the scholars to sit, because I thought it would be pleasanter for them, and they have in return been generally, so far as I know, faithful in complying with my wish that they would all assume the posture proposed, so that the school may present the uniform and serious aspect which is proper, when we are engaged in so solemn a duty. If you move your chair back a little, you will find the posture not inconvenient; but the only reward you will have for faithfully complying with the general custom is the pleasure of doing your duty, for no one watches you, and you would not be called to account should you neglect to conform.

After the prayer, we sing one or two verses of a hymn. The music is led by the piano, and we wish all to join in it who can sing. The exercises which follow are exhibited to the eye by the following diagram.

MOUNT VERNON SCHOOL.

Schedule of Studies.

Miss _____

1834.

	First Hour.	Second Hour.			Third Hour.			Fourth Hour.
	Evening Lessons.	Languages.	G.	R.	Mathematics.	G.	R.	Sections.
Monday								
Tuesday								
Wednesday								
Thursday								
Friday								
Saturday								

FIRST HOUR.—EVENING LESSONS.

(See plan; page 213.)

We then, as you will see by the schedule, commence the first hour of the day. It is marked evening lessons, because most, though not all, of the studies are intended to be prepared out of school. These studies are miscellaneous in their character, comprising Geography, History, Natural and Intellectual Philosophy and Natural History. This hour, like all the other hours for study, is divided into two equal parts, some classes reciting in the first part, and others in the second. A bell is always rung *five minutes before the time* for closing the recitation, to give the teachers notice, that their time is nearly expired, and then again *at the time*, to give notice to new classes to take their places. Thus you will observe that five minutes before the half hour expires, the bell will ring—soon after which, the classes in recitation will take their seats. Precisely at the end of the half hour, it will ring again, when new classes will take their places. In the same manner, notice is given five minutes before the second half of the hour expires, and so in all the other three hours.

At the end of the first hour, the Study Card will be let half down, five minutes, and you will perceive that the sound of its bell will immediately produce a decided change in the whole aspect of the room. It is the signal, as has been before explained, for universal permission to whisper, and to leave seats, though not for loud talking or play, so that those who wish to continue their studies may do so without interruption. When the five minutes have expired, the Card goes up again, and its sound immediately restores silence and order.

SECOND HOUR.—LANGUAGES.

(See plan.)

We then commence the second hour of the school. This is devoted to the study of the Languages. The Latin, French, and English classes recite at this time. By English classes I mean those studying the English *as a language*, i. e. classes in Grammar, Rhetoric and Composition. The hour is divided as the first hour is, and the bell is rung in the same way, i. e. at the close of each half hour, and also five minutes before the close, to give the classes notice that the time for recitation is about to expire.

FIRST GENERAL EXERCISE.

(See plan.)

You will observe then, that there follows upon the schedule, a quarter of an hour marked G. That initial stands for General Exercise, and when it arrives, each pupil is to lay aside her work, and attend to any exercise which may be proposed. This quarter of an hour is appropriated to a great variety of purposes. Sometimes I give a short and familiar lecture on some useful subject connected with science or art, or the principles of duty. Sometimes we have a general reading lesson. Sometimes we turn the school into a Bible class, and again the time is occupied in attending to some general *business* of the school. The bell is rung one minute before the close of the time, and when the period appropriated to this purpose has actually expired, the Study Card, for the first time in the morning, is let entirely down, and the room is at once suddenly transformed into a scene of life and motion and gaiety.

FIRST RECESS.

(See plan.)

The time for the recess is a quarter of an hour, and as you will see, it is marked R. on the schedule. We have various modes of amusing ourselves and finding exercise and recreation in recesses. Sometimes the girls bring their battledores to school. Sometimes they have had a large number of soft balls, with which they amuse themselves. A more common amusement is marching to the music of the piano. For this purpose, a set of signals by the whistle, has been devised, by which commands are communicated to the school.

In these and similar amusements, the recess passes away, and one minute before it expires, the bell is rung, to give notice of the approach of study hours.

At this signal, the scholars begin to prepare for a return to the ordinary duties of school, and when at the full expiration of the recess, the Study Card again goes up, silence and attention and order is to be immediately restored.

THIRD HOUR.—MATHEMATICS.

(See plan.)

There follows next, as you will see by reference to the schedule, an hour marked Mathematics. It is the time for studying and reciting arithmetic, algebra, geometry, and similar studies. It is divided as the previous hours were, into two equal parts, and the bell is rung as has been described, five minutes before the close, and precisely at the close of each half hour.

SECOND GENERAL EXERCISE.—BUSINESS.

(See plan.)

Then follow two quarter hours, appropriated like those before described, the first to a General Exercise, the second to a Recess. At the first of these, the general business of the school is transacted. As this business will probably appear new to you, and will attract your attention, I will describe its nature and design.

At first you will observe a young lady rise at the secretary's desk, to read a journal of what was done the day before. The notices which I gave,—the arrangements I made,—the subjects discussed and decided, and in fact every thing important and interesting in the business or occurrences of the preceding day—is recorded by the secretary of the school, and read at this time. This journal ought not to be a mere dry record of votes and business, but as far as possible, an interesting description in a narrative style, of the occurrences of the day. The Secretary must keep a memorandum, and ascertain that every thing important really finds a place in the record, but she may employ any good writer in school to prepare, from her minutes, the full account.

After the record is read, you will observe me take from a little red morocco wrapper, which has been brought to my desk, a number of narrow slips of paper, which I am to read aloud. In most assemblies it is customary for any person wishing it, to rise in his place, and propose any plan, or as it is called, 'make any motion' that he pleases. It would be unpleasant for a young lady to do this, in presence of a hundred companions, and we have consequently resorted to another plan. The red wrapper is placed in a part of the room, accessible to all, and any one who pleases, writes upon a narrow slip of paper any thing she wishes to lay before the school, and deposits it there, and at the appointed time, the whole are brought to me. These propositions are of various kinds. I can perhaps best give you an idea of them by specimens such as occur to me.

'A. B. resigns her office of copyist, as she is about to leave the school.'

'Proposed, that a class in Botany be formed. There are many who would like to join it.'

'When will the vacation commence?'

'Proposed, That a music committee be appointed, so that we can have some marching in recess.'

'Proposed, That school begin at nine o'clock.'

'Mr. Abbott. Will you have the goodness to explain to us what is meant by the Veto Message?'

'Proposed, That we have locks upon our desks.'

You see that the variety is very great, and there are usually from four or five to ten or fifteen of such papers daily. You will be at liberty to make in this way, any suggestion or inquiry, or to propose any change you please in any part of the instruction or administration of the school. If any thing dissatisfies you, you ought not to murmur at it in private, or complain of it to your companions, thus injuring, to no purpose, both your own peace and happiness and theirs,—but you ought immediately to bring up the subject in the way above described, that the evil may be removed. I receive some of the most valuable suggestions in this way, from the older and more reflecting pupils. These suggestions are read. Sometimes I decide myself. Sometimes I say the pupils may decide. Sometimes I ask their opinion and wishes, and then after taking them into consideration, come to a conclusion.

For example, I will insert a few of these propositions, as these papers are called, describing the way in which they would be disposed of. Most of them are real cases.

'Mr. Abbott. The first class in geography is so large that we have not room in the recitation seats. Cannot we have another place?'

After reading this, I should perhaps say,

'The class in geography may rise and be counted.'

They rise. Those in each division are counted by the proper officer, as will hereafter be explained; and the numbers are reported aloud to me. It is all done in a moment.

'How many of you think you need better accommodations?'

If a majority of hands are raised, I say,

'I wish the teacher of that class would ascertain whether any other place of recitation is vacant, or occupied by a smaller class at that time, and report the case to me.'

'Proposed, That we be allowed to walk upon the common in the recesses.'

'I should like to have some plan formed, by which you can walk on the common in recesses, but there are difficulties. If all should go out together, it is probable that some would be rude and noisy, and that others would come back tardy and out of breath. Besides as the recess is short, so many would be in haste, to prepare to go out, that there would be a great crowd, and much confusion in the ante-room and passage ways. I do not mention these as insuperable objections, but only as difficulties which there must be some plan to avoid. Perhaps, however, they cannot be avoided. Do any of you think of any plan?'

I see perhaps two or three hands raised, and call upon the individuals by name, and they express their opinions. One says that a part can go out at a time.

Another proposes that those who are tardy one day should not go out again, &c.

'I think it possible that a plan can be formed on these or some such principles. If you will appoint a committee who will prepare a plan, and mature its details, and take charge of the execution of it, you may try the experiment. I will allow it to go on as long as you avoid the evils I have above alluded to.'

A committee is then raised to report in writing at the business hour of the following day.

'Proposed that the Study Card be down every half hour.'

'You may decide this question yourselves. That you may vote more freely, I wish you to vote by ballot. The boxes will be open during the next recess. The Vote Receivers will write the question, and place it upon the boxes. All who feel interested in the subject may carry in their votes, Aye or Nay. When the result is reported to me, I will read it to the school.'

In this and similar ways the various business brought up, is disposed of. This custom is useful to the scholars, for it exercises and strengthens their judgment and their reflecting powers more than almost any thing besides; so that if interesting them in this way in the management of the school were of no benefit to me, I should retain the practice as most valuable to them. But it is most useful to me and to the school. I think nothing has contributed more to its prosperity than the active interest which the scholars have always taken in its concerns, and the assistance they have rendered me in carrying my plans into effect.

You will observe, that in transacting this business, very little is actually done by myself, except making the ultimate decision. All the details of business are assigned to teachers, or to officers and committees appointed for the purpose. By this means we dispatch business very rapidly. The system of offices will be explained in another place; but I may say here, that all appointments and elections are made in this quarter hour, and by means of the assistance of these officers, the transaction of business is so facilitated, that much more can sometimes be accomplished than you would suppose possible. I consider this period as one the most important in the whole morning.

SECOND RECESS.

(See plan.)

After the expiration of the quarter hour above described, the study card is dropped, and a recess succeeds.

FOURTH HOUR.—SECTIONS.

(See plan.)

In all the former part of the day, the scholars are divided into *classes*, according to their proficiency in particular branches of study, and they resort to their *recitations* for *instruction*. They now are divided into six *sections* as we call them, and placed under the care of *superintendents*, not for instruction, but for what may be called supervision. *Teaching* a pupil is not all that is necessary to be done for her in school. There are many other things, such as supplying her with the various articles necessary for her use, seeing that her desk is convenient,—that her time is well arranged,—that she has not too much to do, nor too little,— and that no difficulty which can be removed, obstructs her progress in study, or her happiness in school. The last hour is appropriated to this purpose with the understanding, however, that such a portion of it as is not wanted by the superintendent, is to be spent in study. You will see then, when the last hour arrives, that all the scholars go in various directions to the meetings of their respective sections. Here they remain as long as the superintendent retains them. Sometimes they adjourn almost immediately; perhaps after having simply attended to the distribution of pens for the next day; at other times they remain during the hour, attending to such exercises as the superintendent may plan. The design, however, and nature of this whole arrangement, I shall explain more fully in another place. I only mean here to say, that it occupies this hour.

CLOSE OF THE SCHOOL.

As the end of the hour approaches, five minutes notice is given by the bell; and when the time arrives, the study card is half dropped for a moment before the closing exercises. When it rises again, the room is restored to silence and order. We then sing a verse or two of a hymn, and commend ourselves to God's protection in a short prayer. As the scholars raise their heads from the posture of reverence they have assumed, they pause a moment till the regulator lets down the study card, and the sound of its bell is the signal that our duties at school are ended for the day.

III.—INSTRUCTION AND SUPERVISION OF PUPILS.

For the instruction of the pupils, the school is divided into *classes*, and for their general supervision, into *sections*, as has been intimated in the preceding chapter. The head of a *class* is called a *Teacher*, and the head of a *section* a *Superintendent*. The same individual may be both the Teacher of a class, and the Superintendent of a section. The two offices are, however, entirely distinct in their nature and design. As you will perceive by recalling to mind the daily order of exercises; the classes meet and recite during the first three hours of the school, and the sections assemble on the fourth and last. We shall give each a separate description.

1.—CLASSES.

The object of the division into classes is *instruction*. Whenever it is desirable that several individuals should pursue a particular study, a list of their names is made out, a book selected, a time for recitation assigned, a teacher appointed, and the exercises begin. In this way a large number of classes have been formed, and the wishes of parents or the opinion of the principal, and in many cases that of the pupil, determines how many and what shall be assigned to each individual. A list of these classes, with the average age of the members, the name of the teacher, and the time of recitation, is posted in a conspicuous place, and public notice is given whenever a new class is formed. You will therefore have the opportunity of knowing all the arrangements of the school in this respect, and I wish you to exercise your own judgment and discretion a great deal, in regard to your studies. I do not mean, I expect you to *decide*, but to *reflect* upon them. Look at the list, and consider what are most useful for you. Propose to me or to your parents, changes, whenever you think any are necessary; and when you finish one study, reflect carefully yourself on the question what you shall next commence.

The scholars prepare their lessons when they please. They are expected to be present and prepared at the time of recitation, but they make the preparation when it is most convenient. The more methodical and systematic of the young ladies mark the times of *study* as well as of *recitation* upon their schedules, so that the employment of their whole time at school is regulated by a systematic plan. You will observe too, that by this plan of having a great many classes reciting through the first three hours of the morning, every pupil can be employed as much, or as little as her parents please. In a case of ill-health, she may, as has often been done in such cases, at the request of parents, join one or two classes only, and occupy the whole forenoon in preparing for them, and be entirely free from school duties at home. Or she may, as is much more frequently the case, choose to join a great many classes, so as to fill up, perhaps, her whole schedule with recitations, in which case she must prepare all her lessons at home. It is the duty of teachers to take care, however, when a pupil pleads want of time as a reason for being unprepared in any lesson, that the case is fully examined, that it may be ascertained whether the individual has joined too many classes, in which case some one should be dropped, and thus the time and the employments of each individual should be so adjusted as to give her constant occupation *in school*, and as much more as her parents may desire. By this plan of the classes, each scholar goes on just as rapidly in her studies, as her time, and talents, and health will allow. No one is kept back by the rest. Each class goes on regularly and systematically, all its members keeping exactly together in that study, but the various members of it will have joined a greater or less number of other classes, according to their age or abilities or progress in study, so that all will or may have full employment for their time.

When you first enter the school, you will, for a day or two, be assigned to but few classes, for your mind will be distracted by the excitement of new scenes and pursuits, and the intellectual effort necessary for *joining* a class is greater than that requisite for *going on* with it, after being once under way. After a few days you will come to me and say, perhaps, for this is ordinarily the process:—

'Mr. Abbott, I think I have time for some more studies.'

'I will thank you to bring me your schedule,' I say in reply, ' so that I can see what you have now to do.'

By glancing my eye over the schedule in such a case, I see in a moment what duties have been already assigned you, and from my general schedule, containing all the studies of the school, I select what would be most suitable for you, after conferring with you about your past pursuits, and your own wishes or those of your parents in regard to your future course. Additions are thus made, until your time is fully occupied.

The manner of recitation in the classes, is almost boundlessly varied. The design is not to have you commit to memory what the book contains, but to understand and digest it,—to incorporate it fully into your own mind, that it may come up in future life, in such a form as you wish it, for use. Do not then, in ordinary cases, endeavour to fix *words*, but *ideas* in your minds. Conceive clearly,—paint distinctly to your imagination what is described,—contemplate facts in all their bearings and relations, and thus endeavour to exercise the judgment, and the thinking and reasoning powers, rather than the mere memory, upon the subjects which will come before you.

2.—SECTIONS.

In describing the order of daily exercises, I alluded to the *sections* which assemble in the last hour of the school. It is necessary that I should fully describe the system of sections, as it constitutes a very important part of the plan of the school.

Besides giving the scholars the necessary intellectual instruction, there are, as I have already remarked, a great many other points which must receive attention, in order to promote their progress, and to secure the regular operation and general welfare of the school. These various points have something common in their nature, but it is difficult to give them a common name. They are such as supplying the pupils with pens and paper, and stationary of other kinds,—becoming acquainted with each individual, ascertaining that she has enough, and not too much to do,—arranging her work so that no one of her duties shall interfere with another, —assisting her to discover and to correct her faults, and removing any sources of difficulty, or causes of discontent, which may gradually come in her way. These, and a multitude of similar points, constituting what may be called the general *administration* of the school, become, when the number of pupils is large, a most important branch of the teacher's duty.

To accomplish these objects more effectually, the school is divided into SIX SECTIONS, arranged not according to proficiency in particular studies, as the several CLASSES are, but according to *age and general maturity of mind*. Each one of these sections is assigned to the care of a superintendent. These superintendents, it is true, during most of school hours are also teachers:

their duties however as *teachers*, and as *superintendents*, are entirely distinct. I shall briefly enumerate the duties which devolve upon her in the latter capacity.

1. A superintendent ought to prepare an exact list of the members of her section, and to become intimately acquainted with them, so as to be as far as possible their friend and confidant, and to feel a stronger interest in their progress in study and their happiness in school, and a greater personal attachment to them than to any other scholars.

2. She is to superintend the preparation of their schedules,—to see that each one has enough and not too much to do, by making known to me the necessity of a change, where such necessity exists;—to see that the schedules are submitted to the parents, and that their opinion, or suggestions, if they wish to make any, are reported to me.

3. She is to take care that all the daily wants of her sections are supplied,—that all have pens and paper, and desks of suitable height. If any are new scholars, she ought to interest herself in assisting them to become acquainted in the school,—if they are friendless and alone, to find companions for them, and to endeavour in every way, to make their time pass pleasantly and happily.

4. To watch the characters of the members of her section. To inquire of their several teachers as to the progress they make in study, and the faithfulness and punctuality with which they prepare their lessons. She ought to ascertain whether they are punctual at school, and regular in their habits; whether their desks are neat and well arranged, and their exercises carefully executed. She ought to correct, through her own influence, any evils of this kind she may find, or else

immediately to refer the cases where this cannot be done, to me.

The better and the more pleasantly to accomplish the object of exerting a favourable influence upon the characters of the members of their sections, the superintendents ought often to bring up subjects connected with moral and religious duty in section meetings. This may be done in the form of subjects assigned for composition, or proposed for free discussion in writing or conversation, or the superintendents may write themselves, and read to the section the instructions they wish to give.

5. Though the superintendents as such, have necessarily speaking, no *teaching* to do, still they ought particularly to secure the progress of every pupil in what may be called the *essential* studies, such as reading, writing, and spelling. For this purpose they either see that their pupils are going on successfully in classes in school, in these branches, or they may attend to them in the section, provided that they never allow such instruction to interfere with their more appropriate and important duties.

In a word, the superintendents are to consider the members of their sections as pupils confided to their care, and they are not merely to discharge mechanically any mere routine of duty, such as can be here pointed out, but to exert all their powers, their ingenuity, their knowledge of human character, their judgment and discretion in every way, to secure for each of those committed to their care, the highest benefits which the institution to which they belong can afford. They are to keep a careful and faithful record of their plans, and of the history of their respective sections, and to endeavour, as faithfully and as diligently, to advance the interests of the members of them, as if the sections were separate and independent schools of their own.

A great responsibility is thus evidently intrusted to them, but not a great deal of *power*. They ought not to make changes, except in very plain cases, without referring the subject to me. They ought not to make rash experiments, or even to try many new plans without first obtaining my approval of them. They ought to refer all cases which they cannot easily manage, to my care. They ought to understand the distinction between *seeing that a thing is done*, and *doing it*. For example, if a superintendent thinks that one of her section is in too high a class in Arithmetic, her duty is not to undertake, by her own authority, to remove her to a lower one, for, as superintendent, she has no authority over Arithmetic classes; nor should she go to the opposite extreme of saying, 'I have no authority over Arithmetic classes, and therefore I have nothing to do with this case.' She ought to go to the teacher of the class to which her pupil had been unwisely assigned, converse with her, obtain her opinion, then find some other class more suited to her attainments, and after fully ascertaining all the facts in the case, bring them to me, that I may make the change. This is *superintendence; looking over* the condition and progress of the scholar. The superintendents have thus great responsibility, and yet comparatively little power. They accomplish a great deal of good, and in its ordinary course, it is by their direct personal efforts; but in making changes and remedying defects and evils, they act generally in a different way.

The last hour of school is devoted to the Sections. No classes recite then, but the Sections meet, if the Superintendents wish, and attend to such exercises as they provide. Each section has its own organization, its own officers and plans. These arrangements of course, vary in their character according to the ingenuity and enterprize of the superintendents, and more especially according to the talents and intellectual ardour of the members of the section.

The two upper sections are called Senior, the next two Middle, and the two younger Junior. The senior sections are distinguished by using paper for section purposes, with a light blue tinge. To the middle sections is assigned a light straw colour, and to the junior, pink. These colours are used for the schedules of the members, and for the records, and other documents of the section.

This account, though it is brief, will be sufficient to explain to you, the general principles of the plan. You will soon become acquainted with the exercises and arrangements of the particular section to which you will be assigned; and by taking an active interest in them, and endeavouring to co-operate with the superintendent, in all her measures, and to comply with her wishes, you will very materially add to her happiness, and do your part towards elevating the character of the circle to which you will belong.

IV.—OFFICERS.

In consequence of the disposition early manifested by the scholars, to render me every assistance in their power in carrying into effect the plans of the school, and promoting its prosperity, I gradually adopted the plan of assigning to various officers and committees, a number of specific duties, relating to the general business of the school. These offices have gradually multiplied, as the school has increased, and as business has accumulated. The system has, from time to time, been revised, condensed, and simplified, and at the present time it is thus arranged. The particular duties of each officer are minutely described to the individuals themselves at the time of their election; all I intend here, is to give a general view of the plan, such as is necessary for the scholars at large.

There are then, *five departments* of business entrusted to officers of the school, the names of the officers, and a brief exposition of their duties are as follows.

[I omit the particular explanation of the duties of the officers, as the arrangement must vary in the different schools, and the details of any one plan can only be useful in the school-room to which it belongs. It will be sufficient to name the officers of each department with their duties in general terms.]

1. REGULATORS. To assist in the ordinary routine of business in school; ringing the bells: managing the study card; distributing and collecting papers, counting votes, &c.

2. SECRETARIES. Keeping the records and executing writing of various kinds.

3. ACCOUNTANTS. Keeping a register of the scholars, and various other duties connected with the accounts.

4. LIBRARIANS. To take charge of books and stationary.

5. CURATORS. To secure neatness and good order, in the apartments.

The Secretaries and Accountants are appointed by the Principal, and will generally be chosen from the teachers. The first in each of the other departments are chosen by ballot, by the scholars. Each one thus chosen, nominates the second in her department, and they two, the assistants. These nominations must be approved at a teachers' meeting; for if a scholar is inattentive to her studies, disorderly in her desk, or careless and troublesome in her manners, she evidently ought not to be appointed to public office. No person can hold an office in two of these departments at once. She can, if she pleases, however, resign one to accept another. Each of these departments ought often to assemble, and consult together, and form plans for carrying into effect with greater efficiency, the objects entrusted to them. They are to keep a record of all their proceedings, the head of the department acting as secretary for this purpose.

The following may be given as an example of the manner in which business is transacted by means of these officers. On the day that the above description of their duties was written, I wished for a sort of directory, to assist the collector employed to receive payments for the bills; and to obtain it, I took the following steps.

At the business quarter hour, I issued the following order.

'Before the close of school I wish the distributors to leave upon each of the desks, a piece of paper, (the size I described.) It is for a purpose which I shall then explain.'

Accordingly at any leisure moment, before the close of school, each one, went with her box to the stationary shelves, which you will see in the corners of the room, where a supply of paper, of all the various sizes, used in school, is kept, and taking out a sufficient number, they supplied all the desks in their respective divisions.

When the time for closing school arrived, I requested each young lady to write the name of her parent or guardian upon the paper, and opposite to it his place of business. This was done in a minute or two.

'All those whose parent's or guardian's name begins with a letter above *m.* may rise.'

They rose.

'The distributors may collect the papers.'

The officers then passed round in regular order, each through her own division, and collected the papers.

'Deliver them at the Accountant's desk.'

They were accordingly carried there, and received by the Accountants.

In the same manner the others were collected and received by the Accountants, but kept separate.

'I wish now the second Accountant would copy these into a little book I have prepared for the purpose, arranging them alphabetically, referring all doubtful cases again to me.'

The second Accountant then arranged the papers, and prepared them to go into the book, and the writer who belongs to the department copied them fairly.

I describe this case, because it was one which occurred at the time I was writing the above description, and not because there is any thing otherwise peculiar in it. Such cases are continually taking place, and by the division of labour above illustrated, I am very much assisted in a great many of the duties, which would otherwise consume a great portion of my time.

Any of the scholars may, at any time, make suggestions in writing, to any of these officers, or to the whole school. And if an officer should be partial, or unfaithful, or negligent in her duty, any scholar may propose her impeachment. After hearing what she chooses to write in her defence, a vote is taken on sustaining the impeachment. If it is sustained, she is deprived of the office, and another appointed to fill her place.

V.—THE COURT.

I have already described how all serious cases of doing wrong, or neglect of duty are managed in the school. I manage them myself, by coming as directly and as openly as I can, to the heart and conscience of the offender. There are, however, a number of little transgressions, too small to be individually worthy of serious attention, but which are yet troublesome to the community, when frequently repeated. These relate chiefly to *order in the school rooms*. These misdemeanors are tried, half in jest, and half in earnest, by a sort of *court*, whose forms of process might make a legal gentleman smile. They however fully answer our purpose. I can best give you an idea of the court, by describing an actual trial. I ought however first to say, that any young lady, who chooses to be free from the jurisdiction of the court, can signify that wish to me, and she is safe from it. This however is never done. They all see the useful influence of it, and wish to sustain it.

Near the close of school, I find perhaps on my desk, a paper of which the following may be considered a copy. It is called the indictment.

We accuse Miss A. B. of having waste papers in the aisle opposite her desk, at 11 o'clock, on Friday, Oct. 12.

C. D.
E. F. } Witnesses.

I give notice after school that a case is to be tried. Those interested, twenty or thirty perhaps, gather round my desk, while the sheriff goes to summon the accused and the witnesses. A certain space is marked off, as the precincts of the court, within which no one must enter, in the slightest degree, on pain of imprisonment, i. e. confinement to her seat until the court adjourns.

'Miss A. B, you are accused of having an untidy floor about your desk. Have you any objection to the indictment?'

While she is looking over the indictment, to discover a mis-spelt word, or an error in the date, or some other latent flaw, I appoint any two of the bystanders jury. The jury come forward to listen to the cause.

The accused returns the indictment, saying, she has no objection, and the witnesses are called upon to present their testimony.

Perhaps the prisoner alleges in defence that the papers were out *in the aisle*, not *under her desk*, or that she did not put them there, or that they were too few, or small, to deserve attention.

My charge to the jury would be somewhat as follows.

'You are to consider and decide whether she was guilty of disorder; taking into view the testimony of the witnesses, and also her defence. It is considered here that each young lady is responsible not only for the appearance of the carpet, *under the desk*, but also for *the aisle opposite to it*, so that her first ground of defence must be abandoned. So also with the second, that she did not put them there. She ought not to have them there. Each scholar must keep her own place in a proper condition;—so that if disorder is found there, no matter who made it, she is responsible, if she only had time to remove it. As to the third, you must judge whether enough has been proved by the witnesses to make out real disorder.' The jury write *guilty* or *not guilty* upon the verdict, and it is returned to me. If sentence is pronounced it is usually confinement to the seat, during a recess, or part of a recess, or something that requires slight effort or sacrifice, for the public good. The sentence is always something *real*, though always *slight*, and the court has a great deal of influence in a double way; making amusement, and preserving order.

The cases tried are very various, but none of the serious business of the school is entrusted to it. Its sessions are always held out of school hours, and in fact is hardly considered by the scholars as a constituent part of the arrangements of the school. So much so, that I hesitated much about inserting an account of it in this description.

VI.—RELIGIOUS INSTRUCTION.

In giving you this account, brief as it is, I ought not to omit to speak of one feature of our plan, which we have always intended should be one of the most prominent and distinctive characteristics of the school. The gentlemen who originally interested themselves in its establishment, had mainly in view the exertion, by the Principal, of a decided moral and religious influence over the hearts of the pupils. Knowing, as they did, how much more dutiful and affectionate at home you would be, how much more successful in your studies at school, how much happier in your intercourse with each other, and in your prospects for the future, both here and hereafter, if your hearts could be brought under the influence of Christian principles, they were strongly desirous that the school should be so conducted, that its religious influence, though gentle and alluring in its character, should be frank, and open, and decided. I need not say that I myself entered very cordially into these views. It has been my constant effort, and one of the greatest sources of my enjoyment, to try to win my pupils to piety, and to create such an atmosphere in the school, that conscience, and moral principle and affection for the unseen Jehovah, should reign here. You can easily see how much pleasanter it is for me to have the school controlled by such an influence, than if it were necessary for me to hire you to diligence in duty, by prizes or rewards, or to deter you from neglect or from transgression, by reproaches and threatenings and punishments.

The influence which the school has thus exerted, has always been cordially welcomed by my pupils, and approved, so far as I have known, by their parents, though four or five denominations, and fifteen or twenty different congregations have been, from time to time, represented in the school. There are few parents who would not like to have their children *Christians;* sincerely and practically so; for every thing which a parent can desire in a child, is promoted, just in proportion as she opens her heart to the influence of the spirit of piety. But that you may understand what course is taken, I shall describe, first what I wish to effect in the hearts of my pupils, and then what means I take to accomplish the object.

1. A large number of young persons of your age, and in circumstances similar to those in which you are placed, perform with some fidelity, their various outward duties, *but maintain no habitual and daily communion with God.* It is very wrong for them to live thus without God, but they do not see—or rather do not feel the guilt of it. They only think of their accountability to *human beings* like themselves, for example their parents, teachers, brothers, and sisters, and friends. Conse-

quently they think most of their *external* conduct, which is all that human beings can see. Their *hearts* are neglected and become very impure—full of evil thoughts and desires and passions, which are not repented of, and consequently not forgiven. Now what I wish to accomplish in regard to all my pupils is, that they should begin to *feel their accountability to God*, and to act according to it. That they should explore their *hearts* and ask God's forgiveness for all their past sins, through Jesus Christ, who died for them that they might be forgiven; and that they should from this time, try to live *near to God*, feel his presence, and to enjoy that solid peace and happiness which flows from a sense of his protection. When such a change takes place, it relieves the mind from that constant and irritating uneasiness which the great mass of mankind feel, as a constant burden; the ceaseless forebodings of a troubled conscience, reproaching them for their past accumulated guilt, and warning them of a judgment to come. The change which I endeavour to promote, relieves the heart both of the present suffering and of the future danger.

After endeavouring to induce you to begin to act from Christian principle, I wish to explain to you, your various duties to yourselves, your parents, and to God.

2. The measures to which I resort to accomplish these objects are three.

First. *Religious Exercises in School.* We open and close the school with a very short prayer, and one or two verses of a hymn. Sometimes I occupy ten or fifteen minutes at one of the general exercises, or at the close of the school, in giving instruction upon practical religious duty. The subjects are sometimes suggested by a passage of scripture, read for the purpose, but more commonly in another way.

You will observe often at the close of the school or at an appointed general exercise, a scholar will bring to my desk, a dark-coloured morocco wrapper, containing several small strips of paper upon which questions relating to moral or religious duty, or subjects for remarks from me, or anecdotes, or short statements of facts, giving rise to inquiries of various kinds, are written. This wrapper is deposited in a place accessible to all the scholars, and any one who pleases, deposits in it any question or suggestion on religious subjects which may occur to her. You can, at any time, do this yourself, thus presenting any doubt, or difficulty, or inquiry, which may at any time occur to you.

Second. *Religious Exercise on Saturday afternoon.* In order to bring up more distinctly and systematically the subject of religious duty, I established a long time ago, a religious meeting on Saturday afternoon. It is intended for those who feel interested in receiving such instruction, and who can conveniently attend at that time. If you have no other engagements, and if your parents approve of it, I should be happy to have you attend. There will be very little to interest you except the subject itself; for I make all the instructions which I give there as plain, direct, and practical as is in my power. A considerable number of the scholars usually attend, and frequently bring with them many of their female friends. You can at any time invite any one whom you please, to come to the meeting. It commences at half past three and continues about half an hour.

Third. *Personal religious instruction.* In consequence of the large number of my pupils, and the constant occupation of my time in school, I have scarcely any opportunity of religious conversation with them, even with those who particularly desire it. The practice has therefore arisen, and gradually extended itself almost universally in school, of writing to me on the subject. These communications are usually brief notes, expressing the writer's interest in the duties of piety,—or bringing forward her own peculiar practical difficulties, or making specific inquiries, or asking particular instruction in regard to some branch of religious duty. I answer in a similar way,—very briefly and concisely however,—for the number of notes of this kind which I receive, is very large, and the time which I can devote to such a correspondence necessarily limited. I should like to receive such communications from all my pupils; for advice or instruction communicated in reply, being directly personal, is far more likely to produce effect. Besides, my remarks being in writing, can be read a second time, and be more attentively considered and re-considered, than when words are merely spoken. These communications must always be begun by the pupil. I never (unless there may be occasional exceptions in some few very peculiar cases) commence. I am prevented from doing this both by unwillingness to obtrude such a subject personally upon those who might not welcome it, and by want of time. I have scarcely time to write to all those who are willing first to write to me. Many cases have occurred where individuals have strongly desired some private communication with me, but have hesitated long, and shrunk reluctantly from the first step. I hope it will not be so with you. Should you ever wish to receive from me any direct religious instruction, I hope you will write immediately and freely. I shall very probably not even notice that it is the first time I have received such a communication from you. So numerous and so frequent are these communications that I seldom observe, when I receive one from any individual for the first time, that it comes from one who has not written to me before.

Such are the means to which I resort in endeavouring to lead my pupils to God and to duty. And you will observe that the whole design of them is to win and to allure, not to compel. The regular devotional exercises of school, are all which you will *necessarily* witness. These are very short, occupying much less time than many of the pupils think desirable. The rest is all private and voluntary. I never make any effort to urge any one to attend the Saturday meeting, nor do I, except in a few rare and peculiar cases, ever address any one personally, unless she desires to be so addressed. You will be left therefore in this school unmolested,— to choose your own way. If you should choose to neglect religious duty, and to wander away from God, I shall still do all in my power to make you happy in school, and to secure for you in future life, such a measure of enjoyment, as can fall to the share of one, over whose prospects in another world there hangs so gloomy a cloud. I shall never reproach you, and perhaps may not even know what your choice is. Should you on the other hand prefer the peace and happiness of piety, and be willing to begin to walk in its paths, you will find many both among the teachers and pupils of the Mount Vernon School to sympathise with you, and to encourage and help you on your way.

CHAPTER VII.

SCHEMING.

The best teachers in our country, or rather those who might be the best, lose a great deal of their time, and endanger, or perhaps entirely destroy their hopes of success, by a scheming spirit, which is always reaching forward to something new. One has in his mind, some new school-book, by which arithmetic, grammar or geography are to be taught with unexampled rapidity,—and his own purse to be filled in a much more easy way, than by waiting for the rewards of patient industry. Another has the plan of a school, bringing into operation new principles of management or instruction, which he is to establish on some favoured spot, and which is to become in a few years a second Hofwyl. Another has some royal road to learning, and though he is trammelled and held down by what he calls the ignorance and stupidity of his Trustees or his School Committee, yet if he could fairly put his principles and methods to the test, he is certain of advancing the science of education half a century at least, at a single leap.

Ingenuity in devising new ways, and enterprise in following them, are among the happiest characteristics of a new country rapidly filling with a thriving population. Without these qualities there could be no advance; society must be stationary, and from a stationary to a retrograde condition, the progress is inevitable. The disposition to make improvements and changes may however be too great. If so, it must be checked. On the other hand a slavish attachment to old established practices may prevail. Then the spirit of enterprise and experiment must be awakened and encouraged. Which of these two is to be the duty of a writer at any time, will of course depend upon the situation of the community at the time he writes, and of the class of readers for which he takes up his pen. Now at the present time, it is undoubtedly true, that, while among the great mass of teachers there may be too little originality and enterprise, there is still among many a spirit of innovation and change, to which a caution ought to be addressed. But before I proceed, let me protect myself from misconception by one or two remarks.

1. There are a few individuals in various parts of our country, who, by ingenuity and enterprise, have made real and important improvements in many departments of our science, and are still making them. The science is to be carried forward by such men. Let them not therefore understand that any thing which I am going to say, applies at all to those real improvements which are from time to time, brought before the public. As examples of this, there might easily be mentioned, were it necessary, several new modes of study, and new text books, and literary institutions on new plans, which have been brought forward within a few years, and proved, on actual trial, to be of real and permanent value.

These are, or rather they were, when first conceived by the original projectors, new schemes; and the result has proved that they were good ones. Every teacher, too, must hope that such improvements will continue to be made. Let nothing therefore which shall be said on the subject of scheming in this chapter, be interpreted as intended to condemn real improvements of this kind, or to check those which may now be in progress by men of age or experience, or of sound judgment, who are capable of distinguishing between a real improvement and a whimsical innovation, which can never live any longer than it is sustained by the enthusiasm of the original inventor.

2. There are a great many teachers in our country, who make their business a mere dull and formal routine, through which they plod on, month after month, and year after year, without variety or change, and who are inclined to stigmatize with the appellation of idle scheming, all plans of whatever kind, to give variety or interest to the exercises of the school. Now whatever may be said in this chapter against unnecessary innovation and change, does not apply to efforts to secure variety in the details of daily study, while the great leading objects are steadily pursued. This subject has already been discussed in the chapter on Instruction, where it has been shown that every wise teacher, while he pursues the same great object, and adopts in substance the same leading measures at all times, will exercise all the ingenuity he possesses, and bring all his inventive powers into requisition to give variety and interest to the minute details.

To explain now what is meant by such scheming, as is to be condemned, let us suppose a case which is not very uncommon. A young man, while preparing for college, takes a school. When he first enters upon the duties of his office, he is diffident and timid, and walks cautiously in the steps which precedent has marked out for him. Distrusting himself, he seeks guidance in the example which others have set for him; and very probably he imitates precisely, though it may be insensibly and involuntarily, the manners and the plans of his own last teacher. This servitude soon however, if he is a man of natural abilities, passes away: he learns to try one experiment after another, until he insensibly finds that a plan may succeed, even if it was not pursued by his former teacher. So far it is well. He throws greater interest into his school, and into all its exercises, by the spirit with which he conducts them. He is successful. After the period of his services has expired, he returns to the pursuit of his studies, encouraged by his success, and anticipating further triumphs in his subsequent attempts.

He goes on through college we will suppose, teaching from time to time in the vacations, as opportunity occurs, taking more and more interest in the employment, and meeting with greater and greater success. This success is owing, in a very great degree, to the *freedom* of his practice, that is, to his escape from the thraldom of imitation. So long as he leaves the great objects of the school untouched, and the great features of its organization unchanged, his many plans for accomplishing these objects in new and various ways, awaken interest and spirit both in himself and in his scholars, and all goes on well.

Now in such a case as this, a young teacher philosophizing upon his success and the causes of it, will almost invariably make this mistake: viz. he will attribute it to something essentially excellent in his plans, the success which, in fact, results from the novelty of them.

When he proposes something new to a class, they all

take an interest in it, because it is *new*. He takes, too, a special interest in it, because it is an experiment which he is trying, and he feels a sort of pride and pleasure in securing its success. The new method which he adopts, may not be, *in itself*, in the least degree better than old methods. Yet it may succeed vastly better in his hands, than any old method he had tried before. And why? Why because it is new. It awakens interest in his class, because it offers them variety, and it awakens interest in him, because it is a plan which he has devised, and for whose success therefore he feels that his credit is at stake. Either of these circumstances is abundantly sufficient to account for its success. Either of these would secure success, unless the plan was a very bad one indeed.

This may easily be illustrated, by supposing a particular case. The teacher has, we will imagine, been accustomed to teach spelling in the usual way, by assigning a lesson in the spelling book, which the scholars have studied in their seats, and then they have recited, by having the words put to them individually in the class. After some time, he finds that one class has lost its interest in this study. He can *make* them get the lesson, it is true, but he perceives perhaps, that it is a weary task to them. Of course they proceed with less alacrity, and consequently, with less rapidity and success. He thinks, very justly, that it is highly desirable to secure cheerful, not forced, reluctant efforts from his pupils, and he thinks of trying some new plan. Accordingly he says to them,

' Boys, I am going to try a new plan for this class.'

The mere annunciation of a new plan awakens universal attention. The boys all look up, wondering what it is to be.

'Instead of having you study your lessons in your seats as heretofore, I am going to let you all go together into one corner of the room, and choose some one to read the lesson to you, spelling all the words aloud. You will all listen and endeavour to remember how the difficult ones are spelt. Do you think you can remember?'

'Yes, Sir,' say the boys. Children always think they *can* do every thing which is proposed to them as a new plan or experiment, though they are very often inclined to think they *cannot* do what is required of them as a task.

'You may have,' continues the teacher, ' the words read to you once, or twice, just as you please. Only if you have them read but once, you must take a shorter lesson.'

He pauses and looks round upon the class. Some say ' once,' some ' twice.'

'I am willing that you should decide this question. How many are in favour of having shorter lessons, and having them read but once? How many prefer longer lessons, and having them read twice?'

After comparing the numbers, it is decided according to the majority, and the teacher assigns, or allows them to assign a lesson.

'Now,' he proceeds, ' I am not only going to have you study in a different way, but recite in a different way too. You may take your slates with you, and after you have had time to hear the lesson read slowly and carefully twice, I shall come and dictate to you the words aloud, and you will all write them from my dictation. Then I shall examine your slates, and see how many mistakes are made.'

Any class of boys now would be exceedingly interested in such a proposal as this, especially if the master's ordinary principles of government and instruction had been such, as to interest the pupils in the welfare of the school, and in their own progress in study. They will come together in the place assigned, and listen to the one who is appointed to read the words to them, with every faculty aroused, and their whole souls engrossed in the new duties assigned them. The teacher, too, feels a special interest in his experiment. Whatever else he may be employed about, his eye turns instinctively to this group, with an intensity of interest which an experienced teacher who has long been in the field, and who has tried experiments of this sort a hundred times, can scarcely conceive. For let it be remembered that I am describing the acts and feelings of a new beginner; of one who is commencing his work with a feeble and trembling step, and perhaps this is his first step from the beaten path in which he has been accustomed to walk.

This new plan is continued, we will suppose, a week; during which time, the interest of the pupils continues. They get longer lessons, and make fewer mistakes than they did by the old method. Now in speculating on this subject, the teacher reasons very justly, that it is of no consequence whether the pupil receives his knowledge through the eye, or through the ear; whether they study in solitude or in company. The point is to secure their progress in learning to spell the words of the English language; and as this point is secured far more rapidly and effectually by his new method, the inference is to his mind very obvious, that he has made a great improvement,—one of real and permanent value. Perhaps he will consider it an extraordinary discovery.

But the truth is, that in almost all such cases as this, the secret of the success is, not that the teacher has discovered a *better* method than the ordinary ones, but that he has discovered a *new* one. The experiment will succeed in producing more successful results, just as long as the novelty of it continues to excite unusual interest and attention in the class, or the thought that it is a plan of the teacher's own invention, leads him to take a peculiar interest in it. And this may be a month, or perhaps a quarter, and precisely the same effects would have been produced if the whole had been reversed, that is, if the plan of dictation had been the old one, which in process of time had, in this supposed school, lost its interest, and the teacher by his ingenuity and enterprize had discovered and introduced what is now the common mode.

'Very well,' perhaps my reader will reply, 'it is surely something gained to awaken and continue interest in a dull study, for a quarter, or even a month. The experiment is worth something as a pleasant and useful change, even if it is not permanently superior to the other.'

It is indeed worth something. It is worth a great deal; and the teacher who can devise and execute such plans *understanding their real place and value, and adhering steadily through them all, to the great object which ought to engage his attention,* is in the almost certain road to success as an instructor. What I wish is, not to discourage such efforts; they ought to be encouraged to the utmost, but to have their real nature and design, and the real secret of their success fully understood, and to have the teacher, above all, take good care that all his new plans are made, not the substitutes for the great objects which he ought to keep steadily in view, but only the means by which he may carry them into more full and complete effect.

In the case we are supposing, however, we will imagine that the teacher does not do this. He fancies that he has made an important discovery, and begins to inquire whether the *principle* as he calls it, cannot be applied to some other studies. He goes to philosophizing upon it, and can find many reasons why knowledge received through the ear makes a more ready and lasting impression than when it comes through the eye. He tries to apply the method to Arithmetic and Geography, and in a short time is forming plans for the complete metamorphosis of his school. When engaged in hearing a recitation, his mind is distracted with his schemes and plans; and instead of devoting his attention fully to the work he may have in hand, his thoughts are wandering continually to new schemes and fancied improvements, which agitate and perplex him, and which elude his efforts to give them a distinct and definite form. He thinks he must, however, carry out his *principle*. He thinks of its applicability to a thousand other cases. He revolves over and over again in his mind, plans for changing the whole arrangement of his school. He is again and again lost in perplexity, his mind is engrossed and distracted, and his present duties are performed with no interest, and consequently with little spirit or success.

Now his error is in allowing a new idea, which ought only to have suggested to him an agreeable change for a time, in one of his classes, to swell itself into undue and exaggerated importance, and to draw off his mind from what ought to be the objects of his steady pursuit.

Perhaps some teacher of steady intellectual habits, and a well balanced mind may think that this picture is fanciful, and that there is little danger that such consequences will ever actually result from such a cause.

But far from having exaggerated the results, I am of opinion that I might have gone much farther. There is no doubt that a great many instances have occurred, in which some simple idea like the one I have alluded to, has lead the unlucky conceiver of it, in his eager pursuit, far deeper into the difficulty than I have here supposed. He gets into a contention with the school committee,—that formidable foe to the projects of all scheming teachers; and it would not be very difficult to find many actual cases, where the individual has, in consequence of some such idea, quietly planned and taken measures to establish some new institution, where he can carry on unmolested, his plans, and let the world see the full results of his wonderful discoveries.

[1] We have in our country a very complete system of literary institutions, so far as external organization will go, and the prospect of success is far more favourable in efforts to carry these institutions into more complete and prosperous operation, than in plans for changing them, or substituting others in their stead. Were it not that such a course would be unjust to individuals, a long and melancholy catalogue might easily be made out of abortive plans which have sprung up in the minds of young men, in the manner I have described, and which after, perhaps, temporary success, have resulted in partial, or total failure. These failures are of every kind. Some are school-books on a new plan, which succeed in the inventor's hand, chiefly on account of the spirit which carried it into effect; but which in ordinary hands, and under ordinary circumstances, and especially after long continued use, have failed of exhibiting any superiority. Others are institutions com-

---

[1] With whatever truth this may be said of the United States, it does not as yet apply to this country.

menced with great zeal by the projectors, and which succeed just as long as that zeal continues. Zeal will make anything succeed for a time. Others are new plans of instruction or government, generally founded on some good principle carried to an extreme, or made to grow into exaggerated and disproportionate importance. Examples almost innumerable of these things might be particularized if it were proper, and it would be found upon examination, that the amount of ingenuity and labour wasted upon such attempts, would have been sufficient, if properly expended, to have elevated very considerably the standard of education, and to have placed existing institutions in a far more prosperous and thriving state than they now exhibit.

The reader will, perhaps ask, shall we make no efforts at improvement? Must everything in education go on uniform and monotonous, and while all else is advancing, shall our cause alone stand still? By no means. It must advance; but let it advance mainly by the industry and fidelity of those who are employed in it, by changes slowly and cautiously made; not by great efforts to reach forward to brilliant discoveries, which will draw off the attention from essential duties, and after leading the projector through perplexities and difficulties without number, end in mortification and failure.

Were I to give a few concise and summary directions in regard to this subject to a young teacher, they would be the following:

1. Examine thoroughly the system of public and private schools as now constituted in New England, until you fully understand it, and appreciate its excellences and its completeness; see how fully it provides for the wants of the various classes of our population.

By this I mean to refer only to the completeness of the *System,* as a system of organization. I do not refer at all to the internal management of these institutions: this last is, of course, a field for immediate and universal effort at progress and improvement.

2. If after fully understanding this system as it now exists, you are of opinion that something more is necessary; if you think some classes of the community are not fully provided for, or that some of our institutions may be advantageously exchanged for others, whose plan you have in mind; consider whether your age and experience and standing as an instructor are such as to enable you to place confidence in your opinion.

I do not mean by this, that a young man may not make a useful discovery, but only that he may be led away by the ardour of early life, to fancy that essential and important, which is really not so. It is important that each one should determine whether this is not the case with himself, if his mind is revolving some new plan.

3. Perhaps you are contemplating only a single new institution, which is to depend for its success, on yourself and some coadjutors, whom you have in mind, and whom you well know. If this is the case, consider whether the establishment you are contemplating can be carried on, after you shall have left it, by such men, as can ordinarily be obtained. If the plan is founded on some peculiar notions of your own, which would enable you to succeed in it, when others, also interested in such a scheme, would probably fail, consider whether there may be danger that your plan may be imitated by others, who cannot carry it into successful operation, so that it may be the indirect means of doing injury. A man is, in some degree, responsible for his example, and for the

consequences which may indirectly flow from his course, as well as for the immediate results which he produces.[1] The Fellenberg school at Hofwyl has perhaps, by its direct results, been as successful for a given time, as perhaps any other institution in the world; but there is a great offset to the good which it has thus done, to be found in the history of the thousand wretched imitations of it, which have been started only to linger a little while and die, and in which a vast amount of time and talent and money have been wasted.

4. Consider the influence you may have upon the other institutions of our country, by attaching yourself to some one under the existing organization. If you take an academy or a private school, constituted and organized like other similar institutions, success in your own will give you influence over others. A successful teacher of an academy, raises the standard of academic instruction. A college professor, if he brings extraordinary talents to bear upon the regular duties of that office, throws light, universally, upon the whole science of college discipline and instruction. By going, however, to some new field, establishing some new and fanciful institution, you take yourself from such a sphere;—you exert no influence over others, except upon feeble imitators, who fail in

---

[1] Only if these results were reasonably to be anticipated. If M. de Fellenberg has produced beneficial consequences by immediate operation of his own institutions, he cannot surely be answerable for the evil resulting from injudicious application of his views. I have never been able to see any thing in the system pursued at Hofwyl, which rendered it peculiarly difficult of extension. If M. de Fellenberg's plans have succeeded, their success has been in spite of continual changes in the subordinate agents he employed. There is no mystery in his principles. The failure of his imitators must have been owing to their attempting a more complicated plan than they had skill to work out, instead of taking such parts as they could manage; or of their neglecting to accommodate general principles to the particular circumstances in which they were placed. How can M. de Fellenberg be answerable for this?

their attempts, and bring discredit upon your plans by the awkwardness with which they attempt to adopt them. How much more service to the cause of education, have Professors Cleaveland and Silliman rendered by falling in with the regularly organized institutions of the country, and elevating them, than if in early life, they had given themselves to some magnificent project of an establishment, to which their talents would unquestionably have given temporary success, but which would have taken them away from the community of teachers, and confined the results of their labours to the more immediate effects which their daily duties might produce.

5. Perhaps, however, your plan is not the establishment of some new institution, but the introduction of some new study or pursuit into the one with which you are connected. Before, however, you interrupt the regular plans of your school to make such a change, consider carefully what is the real and appropriate object of your institution. Every thing is not to be done in school. The principles of division of labour, apply with peculiar force to this employment; so that you must not only consider whether the branch, which you are now disposed to introduce, is important, but whether it is really such an one as it is, on the whole, best to include among the objects to be pursued in such an institution. Many teachers seem to imagine, that if any thing is in itself important, and especially if it is an important branch of education, the question is settled of its being a proper object of attention in school. But this is very far from being the case. The whole work of education can never be intrusted to the teacher. Much must of course remain in the hands of the parent;—it ought so to remain. The object of a school is not to take children out of the parental hands, substituting

the watch and guardianship of a stranger, for the natural care of father and mother. Far from it. It is only the association of the children for those purposes which can be more successfully accomplished by association. It is an union for few, specific, and limited objects, for the accomplishment of that part, and it is comparatively a small part of the general objects of education, which can be most successfully affected by public institutions, and in assemblies of the young.

6. If the branch which you are desiring to introduce, appears to you to be an important part of education, and if it seems to you that it can be most successfully attended to in schools, then consider whether the introduction of it, *and of all the other branches having equal claims*, will, or will not give to the common schools too great a complexity. Consider whether it will succeed in the hands of ordinary teachers. Consider whether it will require so much time and effort, as will draw off, in any considerable degree, the attention of the teacher from the more essential parts of his duty. All will admit that it is highly important that every school should be simple in its plan,—as simple as its size and general circumstances will permit, and especially, that the public schools in every town and village of our country should never lose sight of what is, and must be, after all, their great design—*teaching the whole population to read, write, and calculate.*

7. If it is a school-book, which you are wishing to introduce, consider well before you waste your time and your spirits in preparing it, in the vexatious work of getting it through the press, whether it is, *for general use*, so superior to those already published, as to induce teachers to make a change in favour of yours. I have italicised the words *for general use*, for no delusion is

more common than for a teacher to suppose, that because a text-book which he has prepared and uses in manuscript, is better for *him* than any other work which he can obtain, it will therefore be better for *general circulation*. Every man, if he has any originality of mind, has of course some peculiar method of his own, and he can of course prepare a text-book which will be better adapted to this method, than those ordinarily in use. The history of a vast multitude of text-books, arithmetics, geographies, and grammars, is this. A man of a somewhat ingenious mind, adopts some peculiar mode of instruction in one of these branches, and is quite successful, not because the method has any very peculiar excellence, but simply because he takes a greater interest in it, both on account of its novelty and also from the fact that it is his own invention. He conceives the plan of writing a text-book, to develope and illustrate this method. He hurries through the work. By some means or other, he gets it printed. In due time it is regularly advertised. The annals of education gives notice of it, the author sends a few copies to his friends, and that is the end of it. Perhaps a few schools may make a trial of it, and if, for any reason, the teachers who try it are interested in the work, perhaps in their hands, it succeeds. But it does not succeed so well as to attract general attention, and consequently does not get into general circulation. The author loses his time and his patience. The publisher, unless unfortunately it was published on the author's account, loses his paper. And in a few months, scarcely any body knows that such a book ever saw the light.

It is in this way, that the great multitude of school-books which are now constantly issuing from the press, take their origin. Far be it from me to discourage the preparation of good school-books. This department of our literature offers a fine field for the efforts of learning and genius. What I contend against, is the endless multiplicity of useless works, hastily conceived and carelessly executed, and which serve no purpose, but to employ uselessly, talents, which if properly applied, might greatly benefit both the community and the possessor.

8. If however, after mature deliberation you conclude that you have the plan of a school-book which you ought to try to mature and execute, be slow and cautious about it. Remember that so great is now the competition in this branch, that nothing but superior excellence will secure the favourable reception of a work. Examine all that your predecessors have done before you. Obtain, whatever may be the trouble and expense, all other text books on the subject, and examine them thoroughly. If you see that you can make a very decided advance on all that has been done, and that the public will probably submit to the inconvenience and expense of a change, to secure the result of your labours, go forward slowly, and thoroughly in your work. No matter how much investigation, how much time and labour it may require. The more difficulty you may find in gaining the eminence, the less likely will you be to be followed by successful competitors.

9. Consider in forming your text book, not merely the whole subject on which you are to write, but also look extensively and thoroughly at the institutions throughout the country, and consider carefully the character of the teachers by whom you expect it to be used. Sometimes a man publishes a text book, and when it fails on trial, he says, ' It is because they did not know how to use it. The book in itself was good. The whole

fault was in the awkwardness and ignorance of the teacher.' How absurd! As if to make a good text book, it was not as necessary to adapt it to teachers as to scholars. *A good text book which the teachers for whom it was intended did not know how to use!!* i. e. a good contrivance but entirely unfit for the purpose for which it was intended.

10. Lastly, in every new plan, consider carefully whether its success in your hands, after you have tried it, and found it successful, be owing to its novelty, and to your own special interest, or to its own innate and intrinsic superiority. If the former, use it so long as it will last, simply to give variety and interest to your plans. Recommend it in conversation or in other ways to teachers with whom you are acquainted; not as a wonderful discovery, which is going to change the whole science of education, but as one method among others, which may be introduced from time to time, to relieve the monotony of the teacher's labours.

In a word do not go away from the established institutions of our country, or deviate from the great objects which are at present, and ought to be pursued by them, without great caution, circumspection, and deliberate inquiry. But within these limits, exercise ingenuity and invention as much as you will. Pursue steadily the great objects which demand the teacher's attention; they are simple and few. Never lost sight of them, nor turn to the right or to the left to follow any ignis fatuus which may endeavour to allure you away; but exercise as much ingenuity and enterprise as you please, in giving variety and interest to the modes by which these objects are pursued.

If planning and scheming are confined within these limits, and conducted on these principles, the teacher will save all the agitating perplexity and care which will otherwise be his continual portion. He can go forward peaceably and quietly, and while his own success is greatly increased, he may be of essential service to the cause in which he is engaged, by making known his various experiments and plans to others. For this purpose it seems to me highly desirable that every teacher should KEEP A JOURNAL of all his plans. In these should be carefully entered all his experiments: the new methods he adopts; the course he takes in regard to difficulties which may arise; and any interesting incidents which may occur, which it would be useful for him to refer to, at some future time. These or the most interesting of them should be made known to other teachers. This may be done in several ways.

(1.) By publishing them in periodicals devoted to education. Such contributions, furnished by judicious men, would be among the most valuable articles in such a work. They would be far more valuable than any general speculations, however well conceived or expressed.

(2.) In newspapers intended for general circulation. There are very few editors, whose papers circulate in families, who would not gladly receive articles of this kind, to fill a teacher's department in their columns. If properly written they would be read with interest and profit by multitudes of parents, and would throw much light on family government and instruction.

(3.) By reading them in teachers' meetings. If half a dozen teachers who are associated in the same vicinity, would meet once a fortnight, simply to hear each other's journals, they would be amply repaid for their time and labour. Teacher's meetings will be interesting and useful, when those who come forward in them, will give up the prevailing practice of delivering orations, and come down at once to the scenes and to the business of the school-room.

There is one topic connected with the subject of this chapter, which deserves a few paragraphs. I refer to the rights of the Committee, or the Trustees, or Patrons, in the control of the school. The right to such control, when claimed at all, is usually claimed in reference to the teacher's new plans, which renders it proper to allude to the subject here; and it ought not to be omitted, for a great many cases occur, in which teachers have difficulties with the trustees or committee of their school. Sometimes these difficulties have amounted to an open rupture; at other times, only to a slight and temporary misunderstanding, arising from what the teacher calls an unwise and unwarrantable interference on the part of the committee or the trustees, in the arrangements of the school. Difficulties of some sort very often arise. In fact, a right understanding of this subject, is, in most cases, absolutely essential to the harmony and co-operation of the teacher, and the representatives of his patrons.

There are then, it must be recollected, three different parties connected with every establishment for education; the parents of the scholars, the teacher, and the pupils themselves. Sometimes, as for example, in a common private school, the parents are not organized, and whatever influence they exert, they must exert in their individual capacity. At other times, as in a common district or town school, they are by law organized, and the school committee chosen for this purpose, are their legal representatives. In other instances, a board of trustees are constituted by the appointment of the founders of the institution, or by the legislature of a state, to whom is committed the oversight of its concerns, and who are consequently the representatives of the founders and patrons of the school.

There are differences between these various modes of organization which I shall not now stop to examine, as it will be sufficiently correct for my purpose to consider them all as only various ways of organizing the *employers*, in the contract, by which the teacher is employed. The teacher is the agent; the patrons, represented in these several ways, are the principals. When, therefore, in the following paragraphs, I use the word *employers*, I mean to be understood to speak of the committee, or the trustees, or the visitors, or the parents themselves, as the case, in each particular institution, may be: that is, the persons, for whose purpose, and at whose expense, the institution is maintained; or their representatives.[1]

[1] The national character and the social relations of the United States, probably render the cautions which the author addresses to teachers peculiarly necessary. Nor are they without their application in this country, particularly in such institutions as Infant Schools, where the routine is not so definite and determined, as is the case in the generality of our public institutions for the children of the working classes. But for the most part there is as much danger in this country of undue, fickle, and vexatious interference in the part of Committees, as of too great independence on the part of the teacher. Many a promising institution has been dandled to death by an over-zealous committee, anxious to arrive at the end of education, but only partially acquainted with the means. Many a man of talent and ability has retired in disgust, from an institution which he loved; wearied out, not with the pupils, but with the governors. Show me a school well-regulated, and carried on with spirit, and I will show you a committee reposing confidence in the principal agent it employs, and scrupulously leaving the internal management of the school as much as possible in his hands. Indeed, if we desire a man of character to act with energy, we must take care how we lessen the sense of his own responsibility. But the more fully his plans are sanctioned, and the greater deference is paid to his suggestions, the stronger will become that sense of responsibility, and the more deeply will he feel himself committed in all the arrangements of the institution. One plan may be somewhat better or somewhat worse than another, but no accuracy in our theory of teaching, no wisdom in the combination of our ideas, can be put in competition with energy and devotedness in the

Now there is a very reasonable, and almost universally established rule, which teachers are very frequently prone to forget, viz. *the employed ought always to be responsible to the employers, and to be under their direction.* So obviously reasonable is this rule, and in fact, so absolutely indispensable in the transaction of all the business of life, that it would be idle to attempt to establish and illustrate it here. It has, however, limitations, and it is applicable to a much greater extent, in some departments of human labour, than in others. It is *applicable* to the business of teaching; and though, I confess, that it is somewhat less absolute and imperious here, still, it is obligatory, I believe, to far greater extent, than teachers have been generally willing to admit.

A young lady, I will imagine, wishes to introduce the study of botany into her school. The parents or the committee object; they say, that they wish the children to confine their attention exclusively to the elementary branches of education. 'It will do them no good,' says the chairman of the committee, 'to learn by heart some dozen or two of learned names. We want them to read well, to write well, and to calculate well, and not to waste their time in studying about pistils and stamens and nonsense.'

Now what is the duty of the teacher in such a case? Why, very plainly her duty is the same as that of the governor of a state, where the people, through their representatives regularly chosen, negative a proposal which he considers calculated to promote the public good. It is his duty to submit to the public will, and though he may properly do all in his power to present

---

master. But where shall we find sustained energy and devotedness in a moral and intellectual agent, without a certain measure of liberty and independence?

the subject to his employers in such a light, as to lead them to regard it as he does, he must still, until they do so regard it, bow to their authority; and every magistrate, who takes an enlarged and comprehensive view of his duties as the executive of a republican community, will do this without any humiliating feelings of submission to unauthorized interference with his plans. He will, on the other hand, enjoy the satisfaction of feeling that he confines himself to his proper sphere, and leave to others the full possession of rights which properly pertain to them.

It is so with every case where the relation of employer and employed subsists. You engage a carpenter to erect a house for you, and you present your plan; instead of going to work and executing your orders according to your wishes, he goes to criticising and condemning it: he finds fault with this, and ridicules that, and tells you you ought to make such and such an alteration in it. It is perfectly right for him to give his opinion, in the tone and spirit of *recommendation or suggestion*, with a distinct understanding, that with his employer rests the power and the right to decide. But how many teachers take possession of their school room, as though it was an empire in which they were supreme, who resist every interference of their employers, as they would an attack upon their personal freedom, and who feel, that in regard to every thing connected with the school, they have really no actual responsibility!

In most cases, the employers, knowing how sensitive teachers very frequently are on this point, acquiesce in it, and leave them to themselves. Whenever in any case, they think that the state of the school requires their interference, they come cautiously and fearfully to the teacher, as if they were encroaching upon his rights, instead of advancing with the confidence and directness with which employers have always a right to approach the employed: and the teacher, with the view he has insensibly taken of the subject, being, perhaps, confirmed by the tone and manner which his employers use, makes the conversation quite as often, an occasion of resentment and offence, as of improvement. He is silent, perhaps; but in his heart he accuses his committee or his trustees of improper interference in *his* concerns, as though it was no part of *their* business to look after work which is going forward for their advantage, and for which they pay.

Perhaps some individuals, who have had some collision with their trustees or committee, will ask me if I mean, that a teacher ought to be entirely and immediately under the supervision and control of the trustees, just as a mechanic is when employed by another man. By no means. There are various circumstances connected with the nature of this employment; the impossibility of the employers fully understanding it in all its details; and the character and the standing of the teacher himself, which always will, in matter of fact, prevent this. The employers always will, in a great many respects, place more confidence in the teacher and in his views, than they will in their own. But still, the ultimate power is theirs. Even if they err, if they wish to have a course pursued, which is manifestly inexpedient and wrong, *they still have a right to decide.* It is their work: it is going on at their instance, and at their expence, and the power of ultimate decision, on all disputed questions, must, from the very nature of the case, rest with them. The teacher may, it is true, have his option, either to comply with their wishes, or to seek employment in another sphere: but while he remains in the employ of any persons, whether in teaching or in any other service, he is bound to yield to the wishes of his employers, when they insist upon it, and to submit pleasantly to their direction, when they shall claim their undoubted right to direct.

This is to be done, it must be remembered, when they are wrong, as well as when they are right. The obligation of the teacher is not founded upon *the superior wisdom* of his employers, in reference to the business for which they have engaged him, for they are very probably his inferiors in this respect; but *upon their right as employers* to determine, *how their own work shall be done.* A gardener, we will suppose, is engaged by a gentleman to lay out his grounds. The gardener goes to work, and after a few hours, the gentleman comes out to see how he goes on, and to give directions. He proposes something which the gardener, who, to make the case stronger, we will suppose knows better than the proprietor of the grounds, considers ridiculous and absurd; nay, we will suppose, *it is* ridiculous and absurd. Now what can the gardener do? There are, obviously, two courses. He can say to the proprietor, after a vain attempt to convince him he is wrong, ' Well, sir, I will do just as you say. The grounds are yours, I have no interest in it, or responsibility, except to accomplish your wishes.' This would be right. Or he might say, ' Sir, you have a right to direct upon your own grounds, and I do not wish to interfere with your plans; but I must ask you to obtain another gardener. I have a reputation at stake, and this work, if I do it even at your direction, will be considered as a specimen of my taste, and of my planning, so that I must, in justice to myself, decline remaining in your employment.' This too, would be right, though probably, both in the business of gardening and of teaching, the case ought to be a strong one, to render it expedient.

But it would not be right for him, after his employer should have gone away, to say to himself, with a feeling of resentment at the imaginary *interference;* 'I shall not follow any such directions; I understand my own trade, and shall receive no instructions in it from him;' and then disobeying all directions, go on and do the work contrary to the orders of his employer, who alone has a right to decide.

And yet a great many teachers take a course as absurd and unjustifiable as this would be. Whenever the parents, or the committee, or the trustees express, however mildly and properly, their wishes in regard to the manner in which they desire to have their own work performed, their pride is at once aroused. They seem to feel it an indignity, to act in any other way, than just in accordance with their own will and pleasure; and they absolutely refuse to comply, resenting the interference as an insult. Or else, if they apparently yield, it is with mere cold civility, and entirely without any honest desires to carry the wishes thus expressed, into actual effect.

Parents may, indeed, often misjudge. A good teacher will, however, soon secure their confidence, and they will acquiesce in his opinion. But they ought to be watchful; and the teacher ought to feel and acknowledge their authority, on all questions connected with the education of their children. They have originally entire power in regard to the course which is to be pursued with them. Providence has made the parents responsible and wholly responsible for the manner in which their children are prepared for the duties of this life, and it is interesting to observe, how very cautious the laws of society are, about interfering with the parent's wishes, in regard to the education of the child. There are many cases in which enlightened governments might make arrangements which would be better than those made by the parents, if they are left to themselves. But they will not do it; they ought not to do it. God has placed the responsibility in the hands of the father and mother, and unless the manner in which it is exercised is calculated to endanger or to injure the community, there can rightfully be no interference, except that of argument and persuasion.

It ought also to be considered, that upon the parents will come the consequences of the good or bad education of their children, and not upon the teacher, and consequently it is right that they should direct. The teacher remains, perhaps, a few months with his charge, and then goes to other places, and perhaps hears of them no more. He has thus very little at stake. The parent has every thing at stake, and it is manifestly unjust to give one man the power of deciding, while he escapes all the consequences of his mistakes, if he makes any; and to take away all the *power* from those, upon whose heads, all the suffering, which will follow an abuse of the power, must descend.

CHAPTER VIII.

REPORTS OF CASES.

THERE is, perhaps, no way by which a writer can more effectually explain his views on the subject of education, than by presenting a great variety of actual cases, whether real or imaginary, and describing particularly the course of treatment he would recommend in each. This method of communicating knowledge is very extensively resorted to in the medical profession, where writers detail particular cases, and report the symptoms and the treatment for each succeeding day, so that the reader may almost fancy himself actually a visitor at the sick bed, and the nature and effects of the various prescriptions become fixed in the mind, with almost as much distinctness and permanency as actual experience would give.

This principle has been kept in view, the reader may perhaps think, too closely, in all the chapters of this volume; almost every point brought up having been illustrated by anecdotes and narratives. I propose, however, devoting one chapter now, to presenting a number of miscellaneous cases, without any attempt to arrange them. Sometimes the case will be merely stated, the reader being left to draw the inference; at others, such remarks will be added as the case suggests. All will, however, be intended to answer some useful purpose, either to exhibit good or bad management and its consequences, or to bring to view some trait of human nature, as it exhibits itself in children, which it may be desirable for the teacher to know. Let it be understood, however, that these cases are not selected with reference to their being strange or extraordinary. They are rather chosen, because they are common, i. e. these cases, or similar ones, will be constantly occurring to the teacher. Reading such a chapter will therefore be the best substitute for experience, which the teacher can have. Some are descriptions of literary exercises, or plans which the reader can adopt in classes, or with a whole school; others are cases of discipline—good or bad management, which the teacher can imitate or avoid. The stories are from various sources, and are the results of the experience of several individuals.

1. HATS AND BONNETS. The master of a district school happened to be looking out of the window one day, and he saw one of the boys throwing stones at a hat, which was put up for that purpose upon the fence. He said nothing about it at the time, but made a memorandum of the occurrence, that he might bring it before the school at the proper time. When the hour set apart for attending to the general business of the school had arrived, and all were still, he said,

'I saw one of the boys throwing stones at a hat to-day, did he do right or wrong?'

There were one or two faint murmurs which sounded like '*Wrong*,' but the boys generally made no answer.

'Perhaps it depends a little upon the question whose hat it was. Do you think it does depend upon that?'

'Yes, sir.'

'Well, suppose then it was not his own hat, and he was throwing stones at it without the owner's consent, would it be plain in that case, whether he was doing right or wrong?'

'Yes, sir; wrong,' was the universal reply.

'Suppose it was his own hat, would he have been right? Has a boy a right to do what he pleases with his own hat?'

'Yes, sir.' 'Yes, sir.' 'No, sir.' 'No, sir,' answered the boys confusedly.

'I do not know whose hat it was. If the boy who did it is willing to rise and tell me, it will help us to decide this question.'

The boy knowing that a severe punishment was not in such a case to be anticipated, and in fact, apparently pleased with the idea of exonerating himself from the blame of wilfully injuring the property of another, rose and said,

'I suppose it was I, sir, who did it, and it was my own hat?'

'Well, said the master, 'I am glad you are willing to tell frankly how it was; but let us look at this case. There are two senses in which a hat may be said to belong to any person. It may belong to him, because he bought it and paid for it; or it may belong to him, because it fits him, and he wears it. In other words, a person may have a hat as his property, or he may have it only as a part of his dress. Now you see, that according to the first of these senses, all the hats in this school belong to your fathers. There is not, in fact, a single boy in this school who has a hat of his own.'

The boys laughed.

'Is not this the fact?'

'Yes, sir.'

'It certainly is so, though I suppose James did not consider it. Your fathers bought your hats. They worked for them, and paid for them. You are only the wearers, and consequently every generous boy, and in fact every honest boy will be careful of the property which is intrusted to him, but which, strictly speaking, is not his own.'

2. MISTAKES. A wide difference must always be made between mistakes arising from carelessness, and those resulting from circumstances beyond control; such as want of sufficient data, &c. The former are always censurable; the latter, never; for they may be the result of correct reasoning from insufficient data, and it is the reasoning only for which the child is responsible.

'What do you suppose a prophet is?' said an instructor to a class of little boys. The word occurred in their reading lesson.

The scholars all hesitated, at last one ventured to reply.

'If a man should sell a yoke of oxen, and get more for them than they are worth, he would be a prophet.'

'Yes, said the instructor, 'that is right,' that is one kind of *profit*, but this is another, and a little different:' and he proceeded to explain the word, and the difference of the spelling.

This child had, without doubt, heard of some transaction of the kind which he described, and had observed that the word *profit* was applied to it. Now the care which he had exercised in attending to it at the time, and remembering it when the same word (for the difference in the spelling he of course knew nothing about,) occurred again, was really commendable. The fact, which is a mere accident, that we affix very different significations to the same sound, was unknown. The fault, if any where, was in the language, and not in him; for he reasoned correctly from the data he possessed, and he deserved credit for it.[1]

3. TARDINESS. 'My duty to this school,' said a teacher to his pupils, 'demands, as I suppose you all admit, that I should require you all to be here punctually at the time appointed for the commencement of the school. I have done nothing on this subject yet, for I wished to see whether you would not come early, on principle. I wish now, however, to inquire in regard to this subject, and to ascertain how many have been tardy, and to consider what must be done hereafter.'

He made the inquiries, and ascertained pretty nearly how many had been tardy, and how often within a week.

The number was found to be so great, that the scholars admitted that something ought to be done.

'What shall I do?' asked he. 'Can any one propose a plan which will remedy the difficulty?'

There was no answer.

'The easiest and pleasantest way to secure punctuality is, for the scholars to come early of their own accord, upon principle. It is evident from the reports, that many of you do so; but some do not. Now, there is only one plan which will not be attended with very serious difficulty, but I am willing to adopt that which will be pleasantest to yourselves, if it will be likely to accomplish the object. Has any one any plan to propose?'

There was a pause.

'It would evidently,' continued the teacher, 'be the

---

[1] The above, and one or two of the succeeding articles have been before published in periodicals.

easiest for me to leave this subject, and do nothing about it. It is of no personal consequence to me, whether you come early or not, but as long as I hold this office, I must be faithful; and I have no doubt the school committee, if they knew how many of you were tardy, would think I ought to do something to diminish the evil.'

'The best plan I can think of is, that all who are tardy should lose their recess.'

The boys looked rather anxiously at one another, but continued silent.

'There is a great objection to this plan, from the fact that a boy is sometimes necessarily absent, and by this rule he will lose his recess with the rest, so that the innocent will be punished with the guilty.'

'I should think, sir,' said William, 'that those who are *necessarily* tardy, might be excused.'

'Yes, I should be very glad to excuse them, if I could find out who they are.'

The boys seemed to be surprised at this remark, as if they thought it would not be a difficult matter to decide.

'How can I tell?' asked the master.

'You can hear their excuses, and then decide.'

'Yes,' said the teacher, 'but here are fifteen or twenty boys tardy this morning; now, how long would it take me to hear their excuses, and understand each case thoroughly, so that I could really tell whether they were tardy from good reasons or not.'

No answer.

'Should you not think it would take a minute apiece?'

'Yes, sir.'

'It would undoubtedly, and even then I could not in many cases tell. It would take fifteen minutes at least.

I cannot do this in school-hours, for I have not time, and if I do it in recess, it will consume the whole of every recess. Now, I need the rest of a recess as well as you, and it does not seem to me to be just that I should lose the whole of mine every day, and spend it in a most unpleasant business, when I take pains myself to come punctually every morning. Would it be just?'

'No, sir.'

'I think it would be less unjust to deprive all of their recess who are tardy; for then the loss of a recess by a boy who had not been to blame, would not be very common, and the evil would be divided among the whole; but in the plan of my hearing the excuses, it would all come upon one.'

After a short pause, one of the boys said, that they might be required to bring written excuses.

'Yes, that is another plan,' said the teacher, 'but there are objections to it. Can any of you think what they are? I suppose you have all been, either at this school, or at some other, required to bring written excuses, so that you have seen the plan tried; now, have you never noticed any objection to it?'

One boy said that it gave the parents a great deal of trouble at home.

'Yes,' said the teacher, 'this is a great objection; it is often very inconvenient to write. But that is not the greatest difficulty; can any of you think of any other?'

There was a pause.

'Do you think that these written excuses are, after all, a fair test of the real reasons for tardiness? I understand that sometimes boys will teaze their fathers or mothers for an excuse, when they do not deserve it: ('Yes, sir,') and sometimes they will loiter about when sent of an errand before school, knowing that they can get a written excuse, when they might easily have been punctual.'

' Yes, sir,' ' Yes, sir,' said the boys.

' Well, now if we adopt this plan, some unprincipled boy would always contrive to have an excuse, whether necessarily tardy or not; and besides, each parent would have a different principle, and a different opinion as to what was a reasonable excuse, so that there would be no uniformity, and consequently no justice in the operation of the system.'

The boys admitted the truth of this, and as no other plan was presented, the rule was adopted of requiring all those who are tardy to remain in their seats during the recess, whether they were necessarily tardy or not. The plan very soon diminished the number of loiterers.

4. HELEN'S LESSON. The possibility of being inflexibly firm in measures, and at the same time gentle and mild in manners and language, is happily illustrated in the following description, which is based on an incident narrated by Mrs. Sherwood.

' Mrs. M. had observed even during the few days that Helen had been under her care, that she was totally unaccustomed to habits of diligence and application. After making all due allowance for long indulged habits of indolence and inattention, she one morning assigned an easy lesson to her pupil, informing her at the same time, that she should hear it immediately before dinner. Helen made no objections to the plan, but she silently resolved not to perform the required task. Being in some measure a stranger, she thought her aunt would not insist upon perfect obedience, and besides, in her estimation, she was too old to be treated like a child.

' During the whole morning, Helen exerted herself to

be mild and obliging; her conduct towards her aunt was uncommonly affectionate. By these and various other artifices, she endeavoured to gain her first victory. Meanwhile, Mrs. M. quietly pursued her various avocations, without apparently noticing Helen's conduct. At length dinner hour arrived: the lesson was called for, and found unprepared. Mrs. M. told Helen she was sorry she had not got the lesson; and went on to explain one or two sentences more fully, and concluded, by saying that she hoped it would be learned before tea time.

Helen, finding she was not to come to the table, began to be a little alarmed. She was acquainted in some measure with the character of her aunt, still she hoped to be allowed to partake of the desert as she had been accustomed to on similar occasions at home, and soon regained her wonted composure. But the dinner cloth was removed, and there sat Helen, suffering not a little from hunger; still she would not complain; she meant to convince her aunt that she was not moved by trifles.

' A walk had been proposed for the afternoon, and as the hour drew near, Helen made preparations to accompany the party. Mrs. M. reminded her of her lesson, but she just noticed the remark by a toss of the head, and was soon in the green fields, apparently the gayest of the gay. After her return from the excursion, she complained of a head-ache, which in fact she had; she threw herself languidly on the sofa, sighed deeply, and took up her history.

' Tea was now on the table, and most tempting looked the white loaf. Mrs. M. again heard the pupil recite, but was sorry to find the lesson still imperfectly prepared. She left her, saying she thought an half hour's study would conquer all the difficulties she found in the lesson.

'During all this time, Mrs. M. appeared so perfectly calm, composed, and even kind, and so regardless of sighs and doleful exclamations, that Helen entirely lost her equanimity and let her tears flow freely and abundantly. Her mother was always moved by her tears, and would not her aunt relent? No. Mrs. M. quietly performed the duties of the table, and ordered the tea-equipage to be removed. This latter movement brought Helen to reflection. It is useless to resist, thought she, indeed why should I wish to do so. Nothing too much has been required of me. How ridiculous I have made myself appear, in the eyes of my aunt, and even of the domestics.

'In less than an hour, she had the satisfaction of reciting her lesson perfectly; her aunt made no comments on the occasion, but assigned her the next lesson, and went on sewing. Helen did not expect this; she had anticipated a refreshing cup of tea, after the long siege. She had expected even something nicer than usual to compensate her for past sufferings. At length worn out by long-continued watching and fasting, she went to the closet, provided herself with a cracker, and retired to bed to muse deliberately on the strange character of her aunt.

'Teachers not unfrequently threaten their pupils with some proper punishment; but when obliged to put the threat into execution, contrive in some indirect way, to abate its rigour and thus destroy all its effects. For example, a mother was in the habit, when her little boy ran beyond his prescribed play-ground, of putting him into solitary confinement. On such occasions, she was very careful to have some amusing book, or diverting play-thing in a conspicuous part of the room, and not unfrequently a piece of gingerbread was given to solace the runaway. The mother thought it very strange her little boy should so often transgress, when he knew what to expect from such a course of conduct. The boy was wiser than the mother; he knew perfectly well how to manage. He could play with the boys beyond the garden gate, and if detected, to be sure he was obliged to spend a quiet hour in the pleasant parlour. But this was not intolerable as long as he could expect a paper of sugar-plums, a cake, or at least something to compensate him amply for the loss of a game at marbles.'

5. COMPLAINTS OF LONG LESSONS. A college officer assigned lessons which the idle and ignorant members of the class thought too long. They murmured for a time, and at last openly complained. The other members of the class could say nothing in behalf of the professor, awed by the greatest of all fears to a collegian, the fear of being called a '*fisher*,' or a '*blueskin*.' The professor paid no attention to the petitions and complaints which were poured in upon him, and which, though originated by the idle, all were compelled to vote for. He coldly, and with uncompromising dignity, went on: the excitement in the class increased, and what is called a college rebellion, with all its disastrous consequences to the infatuated rebels, ensued.

Another professor had the dexterity to manage in a different way. After hearing that there was dissatisfaction, he brought up the subject as follows:—

'I understand, gentlemen, that you consider your lessons too long. Perhaps I have overrated the abilities of the class, but I have not intended to assign you more than you can accomplish. I feel no other interest in the subject, than the pride and pleasure it would give me, to have my class stand high, in respect to the amount of ground it has gone over, when you come to examination. I propose, therefore, that you appoint a committee in whose abilities and judgment you can confide, and let them examine this subject and report. They might ascertain how much other classes have done, and how much is expedient for this class to attempt; and then, by estimating the number of recitations assigned to this study, they can easily determine what should be the length of the lessons.'

The plan was adopted, and the report put an end to the difficulty.

6. ENGLISH COMPOSITION. The great prevailing fault of writers in this country, is an affectation of eloquence. It is almost universally the fashion to aim not at striking thoughts, simply and clearly expressed,—but at splendid language, glowing imagery, and magnificent periods. It arises, perhaps, from the fact that public speaking is the almost universal object of ambition, and consequently, both at school and at college, nothing is thought of but oratory. Vain attempts at oratory, result in nine cases out of ten, in grandiloquence, and empty verbiage; common thoughts expressed in pompous periods.

The teacher should guard against this, and assign to children such subjects as are within the field of childish observation. A little skill on his part will soon determine the question which kind of writing shall prevail in his school. The following specimens, both written with some skill, will illustrate the two kinds of writing alluded to. Both were written by pupils of the same age, twelve; one a boy, the other a girl. The subjects were assigned by the teacher. I need not say that the following was the writer's first attempt at composition, and that it is printed without alteration.

THE PAINS OF A SAILOR'S LIFE.

The joyful sailor embarks on board of his ship, the sails are spread to catch the playful gale, swift as an arrow he cuts the rolling wave. A few days thus sporting on the briny wave, when suddenly the sky is overspread with clouds, the rain descends in torrents, the sails are lowered, the gale begins, the vessel is carried with great velocity, and the shrouds unable to support the tottering mast, give way to the furious tempest; the vessel is drove among the rocks, is sprung aleak, the sailor works at the pumps, till, faint and weary, is heard from below, six feet of water in the hold; the boats are got ready, but before they are into them, the vessel dashed against a reef of rocks, some in despair throw themselves into the sea, others get on the rocks without any clothes or provisions, and linger a few days, perhaps weeks or months, living on shell fish or perhaps taken up by some ship, others get on pieces of the wreck, and perhaps be cast on some foreign country, where perhaps he may be taken by the natives, and sold into slavery where he never more returns.

In regard to the following specimen, it should be stated that when the subject was assigned, the pupil was directed to see how precisely she could imitate the language and conversation which two little children really lost in the woods would use. While writing, therefore, her mind was in pursuit of the natural, and the simple, not of the eloquent.

TWO CHILDREN LOST IN THE WOODS.

Emily. Look here! see how many berries I've got. I don't believe you've got so many.

Charles. Yes, I'm sure I have. My basket's 'most full; and if we hurry, we shall get ever so many before we go home. So pick away as fast as you can, Emily.

Emily. There, mine is full. Now we'll go and find some flowers for mother. You know somebody told us there were some red ones, close to that rock.

Charles. Well, so we will. We'll leave our baskets here, and come back and get them.

Emily. But if we can't find our way back, what shall we do?

Charles. Poh! I can find the way back. I only want a quarter to seven years old, and I shan't lose myself, I know.

Emily. Well! we've got flowers enough, and now I'm tired and want to go home.

Charles. I don't, but if you are tired we'll go and find our baskets.

Emily. Where do you think they are? We've been looking a great while for them. I know we are lost, for when we went after the flowers, we only turned once, and coming back, we have turned three times.

Charles. Have we? Well, never mind, I guess we shall find them.

Emily. I'm afraid we shan't. Do let's run.

Charles. Well, do so. Oh, Emily! here's a brook, and I am sure we didn't pass any brook going.

Emily. Oh, dear! we must be lost. Hark! Charles! didn't you hear that dreadful noise just now? Wasn't it a bear?

Charles. Poh! I should love to see a bear here. I guess if he should come near me, I would give him one good slap that would make him feel pretty bad. I could kill him at the first hit.

Emily. I should like to see you taking hold of a bear. Why didn't you know bears were stronger than men? But only see how dark it grows; we shan't see Ma' to night, I'm afraid.

Charles. So am I: do let's run some more.

Emily. O Charles, do you believe we shall ever find the way out of this dreadful long wood?

Charles. Let's scream, and see if somebody wont come.

Emily. Well, (screaming) Ma'! Ma'!

Charles. (Screaming also) Pa'! Pa'!

Emily. Oh, dear! there's the sun setting. It will be dreadfully dark by and by, won't it!

We have given enough for a specimen. The composition, though faulty in many respects, illustrates the point we had in view.

7. INSINCERE CONFESSION. An assistant in a school informed the principal that she had some difficulty in preserving order in a certain class, composed of small children. The principal accordingly went into the class, and something like the following dialogue ensued.

'Your teacher informs me,' said the principal, ' that there is not perfect order in this class. Now if you are satisfied that there has not been order, and wish to help me to discover and correct the fault, we can do it very easily. If, on the other hand, you do not wish to co-operate with me, it will be a little more difficult for me to correct it, and I must take a different course. Now I wish to know, at the outset, whether you do or do not wish to help me.'

A faint 'Yes, sir;' was murmured through the class.

'I do not wish you to assist me, unless you really and honestly desire it yourselves; and if you undertake to do it, you must do it honestly. The first thing which will be necessary, will be an open and thorough exposure of all which has been wrong, and this you know will be unpleasant. But I will put the question to the vote, by asking how many are willing that I should know, entirely and fully, all that they have done in this class, that has been wrong.'

Very nearly all the hands were raised at once, promptly, and the others were gradually brought up, though with more or less of hesitation.

'Are you willing, not only to tell me yourselves what you have done, but also, in case any one has forgotten something which she has done, that others should tell me of it?'

The hands were all raised.

After obtaining thus from the class a distinct and universal expression of willingness that all the facts should be made known, the principal called upon all those who had any thing to state, to raise their hands, and those who raised them, had opportunity to say what they wished. A great number of very trifling incidents were mentioned, such as could not have produced any difficulty in the class, and consequently could not have been the real instances of disorder alluded to. Or at least, it was evident if they were, that in the statement, they must have been so palliated and softened, that a really honest confession had not been made. This result might in such a case, have been expected. Such is human nature, that in nine cases out of ten, unless such a result had been particularly guarded against, it would have inevitably followed.

Not only will such a result follow in individual cases like this, but unless the teacher watches and guards against it, it will grow into a habit. I mean boys will get a sort of an idea that it is a fine thing to confess their faults, and by a show of humility and frankness, will deceive their teacher, and perhaps themselves, by a sort of acknowledgment, which in fact exposes nothing of the guilt which the transgressor professes to expose. A great many cases occur, where teachers are pleased with the confession of faults, and scholars perceive it, and the latter get into the habit of coming to the teacher, when they have done something which they think may get them into difficulty, and make a sort of half confession, which, by bringing forward every palliating circumstance, and suppressing every thing of different character, keeps entirely out of view all the real guilt of the transgression. The criminal is praised by the teacher for the frankness and honesty of the confession, and his fault is freely forgiven. He goes away therefore well satisfied with himself, when in fact he has been only submitting to a little mortification, voluntarily, to avoid the danger of a greater; much in the same spirit with that which leads a man to receive the small-pox by inoculation, to avoid the danger of taking it in the natural way.

The teacher who accustoms his pupils to confess their faults, voluntarily, ought to guard carefully against this danger. When such a case as the one just described occurs, it will afford a favourable opportunity of showing distinctly to pupils the difference between an honest and an hypocritical confession. In this instance, the teacher proceeded thus:

'Now I wish to ask you one more question, which I wish you all to answer by your votes, honestly. It is this. Do you think that the real disorder which has been in this class, that is, the real cases which you referred to, when you stated to me, that you thought that the class was not in good order, have been now really exposed, so that I honestly and fully understand the case? How many suppose so?

Not a single hand was raised.

'How many of you think, and are willing to avow your opinion, that I have *not* been fully informed of the case?'

A large proportion held up their hands.

'Now it seems, the class pretended to be willing that I should know all the affair. You pretended to be willing to tell me the whole, but when I call upon you for the information, instead of telling me honestly, you attempt to amuse me by little trifles, which, in reality, made no disturbance, and you omit the things which you know were the real objects of my inquiries. Am I right in my supposition?'

They were silent. After a moment's pause, one perhaps raised her hand, and began now to confess something, which she had before concealed.

The teacher however interrupted her, by saying,

'I do not wish to have the confession made now. I gave you all time to do that, and now I should rather not hear any more about the disorder. I gave an opportunity to have it acknowledged, but it was not honestly improved, and now I would rather not hear. I shall probably never know.

'I wished to see whether this class would be honest, —really honest, or whether they would have the insincerity to pretend to be confessing, when they were not doing so honestly, so as to get the credit of being frank and sincere, when in reality they are not so.

Now am I not compelled to conclude that this latter is the case?'

Such an example will make a deep and lasting impression. It will show that the teacher is upon his guard; and there are very few, so hardened in deception, that they would not wish that they had been really sincere, rather than rest under such an imputation.

8. COURT. A pupil, quite young, (says a teacher,) came to me one day with a complaint that one of her companions had got her seat. There had been some changes in the seats by my permission, and probably from some inconsistency in the promises which I had made, there were two claimants for the same desk. The complainant came to me, and appealed to my recollection of the circumstance.

'I do not recollect anything about it,' said I.

'Why! Mr. B.' replied she, with astonishment.

'No.' said I, 'you forget that I have, every day, arrangements almost without number, of such a kind to make, and as soon as I have made one, I immediately forget all about it.'

'Why, don't you remember that you got me a new baize?'

'No; I ordered a dozen new baizes at that time, but I do not remember who they were for.'

There was a pause; the disappointed complainant seemed not to know what to do.

'I will tell you what to do. Bring the case into court and I will try it, regularly.'

Why, Mr. B.! I do not like to do any thing like that, about it; besides, I do not know how to write an indictment.'

'Oh!' I replied, 'they will like to have a good trial. It will make a new sort of case. All our cases thus far have been for *offences*, that is what they call criminal cases, and this will be only an examination of the conflicting claims of two individuals to the same property, and it will excite a good deal of interest. I think you had better bring it into court.'

She went slowly and thoughtfully to her seat, and presently returned with an indictment.

'Mr. B. is this right?'

It was as follows:—

I accuse Miss A. B. of coming to take away my seat, the one Mr. B. gave me.

Witnesses, { C. D.
E. T.

'Why, ——— ——— yes,—that will do; and yet it is not exactly right. You see this is what they call a *civil* case.'

'I don't think it is very *civil*.'

'No, I don't mean it was civil to take your seat. But this is not a case where a person is prosecuted for having done any thing wrong.'

The plaintive looked a little perplexed, as if she could not understand how it could be otherwise than wrong, for a girl to usurp her seat.

'I mean, you do not bring it into court, as a case of wrong. You do not want her to be punished; do you?'

'No; I only want her to give me up my seat; I don't want her to be punished.'

'Well, then, you see, that although she may have done wrong to take your seat, it is not in that point of view, that you bring it into court. It is a question about the right of property, and the lawyers call such cases *civil cases*, to distinguish them from cases where persons are tried for the purpose of being punished for doing wrong. These are called criminal cases.'

The aggrieved party still looked perplexed. 'Well, Mr. B.' she continued, ' what shall I do? How shall I write it? I cannot say any thing about *civil* in it, can I?'

A form was given to her, which would be proper for the purpose, and the case was brought forward, and the evidence on both sides examined. The irritation of the quarrel, was soon dissipated, in the amusement of a semi-serious trial, and both parties good humouredly acquiesced in the decision.

9. TEACHERS' PERSONAL CHARACTER. Much has been said within a few years, by writers on the subject of education, in this country, on the desirableness of raising the business of teaching to the rank of a learned profession. There is but one way of doing this, and that is, raising the personal characters and attainments of teachers themselves. Whether an employment is elevated or otherwise in public estimation, depends altogether on the associations connected with it in the public mind ; and these depend altogether on the characters of the individuals who are engaged in it. Franklin, by the simple fact that he was a printer himself, has done more towards giving dignity and respectability to the employment of printing, than a hundred orations on the intrinsic excellence of the art. In fact all mechanical employments have, within a few years risen in rank, in this country, not through the influence of efforts to impress the community directly with a sense of their importance, but simply because mechanics themselves have risen in intellectual and moral character. In the same manner the employment of the teacher will be raised most effectually in the estimation of the public, not by the individual who writes the most eloquent oration on the intrinsic dignity of the

art, but upon the one who goes forward most successfully in the exercise of it, and who by his general attainments, and public character, stands out most fully to the view of the public, as a well-informed, liberal minded, and useful man.

If this is so, and it cannot well be denied, it furnishes to every teacher a strong motive to exertion, for the improvement of his own personal character. But there is a stronger motive still, in the results which flow directly to himself, from such efforts. No man ought to engage in any business which, as mere business, will engross all his time and attention. The Creator has bestowed upon every one a mind, upon the cultivation of which our rank, among intelligent beings, our happiness, our moral and intellectual power, every thing valuable to us, depend. And after all the cultivation which we can bestow, in this life, upon this mysterious principle, it will still be in embryo. The progress which it is capable of making is entirely indefinite. If by ten years of cultivation, we can secure a certain degree of knowledge and power, by ten more, we can double, or more than double it, and every succeeding year of effort, is attended with equal success. There is no point of attainment where we must stop, or beyond which effort will bring in a less valuable return.

Look at that teacher, and consider for a moment, his condition. He began to teach when he was twenty years of age, and now he is forty. Between the years of fifteen and twenty he made a vigorous effort to acquire such an education as would fit him for these duties. He succeeded, and by these efforts he raised himself from being a mere laborer, receiving, for his daily toil a mere daily subsistence, to the respectability and the comforts of an intellectual pursuit. But this change once produced, he stops short in his progress. Once seated at his desk, he is satisfied, and for twenty years he has been going through the same routine, without any effort to advance or to improve. He does not reflect that the same efforts, which so essentially altered his condition and prospects at twenty, would have carried him forward to higher and higher sources of influence and enjoyment, as long as he should continue them. His efforts ceased when he obtained a situation as teacher, at forty dollars a month, and though twenty years have glided away, he is now exactly what he was then.

There is probably no employment whatever which affords so favourable an opportunity for personal improvement—for steady intellectual and moral progress, as that of teaching. There are two reasons for this.

First, there is time for it. With an ordinary degree of health and strength, the mind can be vigorously employed at least ten hours a day. As much as this, is required of students, in many literary institutions. In fact ten hours to study, seven to sleep, and seven to food, exercise and recreation, is perhaps as good an arrangement as can be made; at any rate, very few persons will suppose that such a plan allows too little under the latter head. Now six hours is as much as is expected of teachers under ordinary circumstances, and it is as much as ought ever to be bestowed. For though he may labour four hours out of school, in some new field, his health and spirits will soon sink under the burden, if after his weary labours during the day in school, he gives up his evenings to the same perplexities and cares. And it is not necessary. No one who knows any thing of the nature of the human mind, and who will reflect a moment on the subject, can doubt that a man can make a better school, by expending six hours labour upon it, which he can go through with, with some alacrity and ardour, than he can by driving himself on to ten. Every teacher therefore, who is commencing his work, should begin with the firm determination of devoting only six hours daily to the pursuit. Make as good a school, and accomplish as much for it, as you can in six hours, and let the rest go. When you come from your school-room at night, leave all your perplexities and cares behind you. No matter what unfinished business or unsettled difficulties remain. Dismiss them all, till another sun shall rise, and the hour of duty for another day shall come. Carry no school work home with you, and do not talk of your work. You will then get refreshment and rest. Your mind during the evening will be in a different world from that in which you have moved during the day. At first this will be difficult. It will be hard for you, unless your mind is uncommonly well disciplined, to dismiss all your cares; and you will think, each evening, that some peculiar emergency demands your attention, *just at that time*, and that as soon as you have passed the crisis, you will confine yourself to what you admit are generally reasonable limits. But if you once allow school, with its perplexities and cares to get possession of the rest of the day, it will keep possession. It will intrude itself into all your waking thoughts, and trouble you in your dreams. You will lose all command of your powers, and besides cutting off from yourself all hope of general intellectual progress, you will in fact destroy your success as a teacher. Exhaustion, weariness and anxiety will be your continual portion, and in such a state, no business can be successfully prosecuted.

There need be no fear that employers will be dissatisfied, if the teacher acts upon this principle. If he is faithful, and enters with all his heart into the discharge of his duties during six hours, there will be something in the ardour, and alacrity, and spirit with which his duties will be performed, which parents and scholars will both be very glad to receive, in exchange for the languid, and dull, and heartless toil, in which the other method must sooner or later result.

If the teacher then will confine himself to such a portion of time, as is, in fact, all he can advantageously employ, there will be much left which can be devoted to his own private employment,—more than is usual in the other employments of life. In most of these other employments, there is not the same necessity for limiting the hours which a man may devote to his business. A merchant, for example, may be employed nearly all the day at his counting-house, and so may a mechanic. A physician may spend all his waking-hours in visiting patients, and feel little more than healthy fatigue. The reason is, that in all these employments, and in fact in most of the employments of life, there is so much to diversify, so many little incidents constantly occurring to animate and relieve, and so much bodily exercise, which alternates with, and suspends the fatigues of the mind, that the labours may be much longer continued, and with less cessation, and yet the health not suffer. But the teacher while engaged in his work, has his mind continually on the stretch. There is little to relieve, little respite, and he is almost entirely deprived of bodily exercise. He must, consequently, limit his hours of attending to his business, or his health will soon sink under labours which Providence never intended the human mind to bear.

There is another circumstance which facilitates the progress of the teacher. It is a fact, that all this general progress has a direct and immediate bearing upon his pursuits. A lawyer may read in an evening an interesting book of travels, and find nothing to help him with his case the next day in court—but almost every fact which the teacher thus learns, will come *at once into use*, in some of his recitations at school. We do not mean to imply by this, that the members of the legal profession have not need of a great variety and extent of knowledge: they doubtless have. It is simply in the *directness* and *certainty* with which the teacher's knowledge may be applied to his purpose, that the business of teaching has the advantage over every other pursuit.

This fact now has a very important influence in encouraging and leading forward the teacher to make constant intellectual progress, for every step brings at once a direct reward.

10. THE CHESNUT BURR. *A story for school-boys.*[1] One fine pleasant morning, in the fall of the year, the master was walking along towards school, and he saw three or four boys under a large chesnut tree, gathering chesnuts.

One of the boys was sitting upon the ground trying to open some chesnut burrs, which he had knocked off from the tree. The burrs were green, and he was trying to open them by pounding them with a stone.

He was a very impatient boy, and was scolding in a loud angry tone against the burrs. He did not see, he said, what in the world chesnuts were made to grow so for. They ought to grow right out in the open air like apples, and not have such vile porcupine skins on them, —just to plague boys. So saying, he struck with all his might a fine large burr, crushed it to pieces, and then jumped up, using at the same time profane and wicked words. As soon as he turned round, he saw the master

---

[1] Originally written for a periodical.

standing very near him. He felt very much ashamed and afraid, and hung down his head.

'Roger,' said the master, (for this boy's name was Roger,) 'can you get me a chesnut burr?'

Roger looked up for a moment to see whether the master was in earnest, and then began to look around for a burr.

A boy who was standing near the tree, with a red cap full of burrs in his hand, held out one of them. Roger took the burr and handed it to the master, who quietly put it into his pocket, and walked away without saying a word.

As soon as he was gone, the boy with the red cap said to Roger, 'I expected the master would have given you a good scolding for talking so.'

'The master never scolds,' said another boy who was sitting on a log pretty near, with a green satchel in his hand, 'but you see if he does not remember it.' Roger looked as if he did not know what to think about it.

'I wish,' said he, 'I knew what he is going to do with that burr.'

That afternoon, when the lessons had been all recited, and it was about time to dismiss the school, the boys put away their books, and the master read a few verses in the Bible, and then offered a prayer, in which he asked God to forgive all the sins which any of them had committed that day, and to take care of them during the night. After this, he asked the boys all to sit down. He then took his handkerchief out of his pocket, and laid it on the desk, and afterwards he put his hand into his pocket again, and took out the chesnut burr, and all the boys looked at it.

'Boys,' said he, 'do you know what this is?'

One of the boys in the back seat said, in a half whisper, 'It is nothing but a chesnut burr.'

'Lucy,' said the master, to a bright-eyed little girl near him, 'what is this?'

'It is a chesnut burr, sir,' said she.

'Do you know what it is for?'

'I suppose there are chesnuts in it.'

'But what is this rough prickly covering for?'

Lucy did not know.

'Does any body here know?' said the master.

One of the boys said he supposed it was to hold the chesnuts together, and keep them up on the tree.

'But I heard a boy say,' replied the master, 'that they ought not to be made to grow so. The nut itself, he thought, ought to hang alone on the branches, without any prickly covering,—just as apples do.'

'But the nuts themselves have no stems to be fastened by,' answered the same boy.

'That is true, but I suppose this boy thought that God could have made them grow with stems, and that this would have been better than to have them in burrs.'

After a little pause, the master said he would explain to them what the chesnut burr was for, and wished them all to listen attentively.

'How much of the chesnut is good to eat, William?' asked he, looking at a boy before him.

'Only the nut.'

'How long does it take the nut to grow?'

'All summer I suppose, it is growing.'

'Yes; it begins early in the summer, and gradually swells and grows until it has become of full size, and is ripe in the fall. Now, suppose there was a tree out here near the school-house, and the chesnuts should grow upon it without any shell or covering, suppose too that they should taste like good ripe chesnuts at first, when they were very small. Do you think they would be safe?'

William said, 'No! the boys would pick and eat them before they had time to grow.'

'Well, what harm would there be in that; would it not be as well to have the chesnuts early in the summer, as to have them in the fall?'

William hesitated. Another boy who sat next to him said,

'There would not be so much meat in the chesnuts, if they were eaten before they had time to grow.'

'Right,' said the master, 'but would not the boys know this, and so all agree to let the little chesnuts stay, and not eat them while they were small?'

William said he thought they would not. If the chestnuts were good, he was afraid they would pick them off and eat them, if they were small.

All the rest of the boys in the school thought so too.

'Here then,' said the master, 'is one reason for having prickles around the chesnuts when they are small. But then it is not necessary to have all chesnuts guarded from boys in this way; a great many of the trees are in the woods, which the boys do not see; what good do the burs do in these trees?'

The boys hesitated. Presently the boy who had the green satchel under the tree with Roger, who was sitting in one corner of the room, said,

'I should think they would keep the squirrels from eating them.'

'And besides,' continued he, after thinking a moment, 'I should suppose if the meat of the chesnut had no covering, the rain might wet it and make it rot, or the sun might dry and wither it.'

'Yes,' said the master, 'these are very good reasons

why the nut should be carefully guarded. First, the meats are packed away in a hard brown shell, which the water cannot get through; this keeps it dry, and away from dust, and other things which might injure it. Then several nuts thus protected, grow closely together, inside this green prickly covering, which spreads over them, and guards them from the larger animals and the boys. When the chesnut gets its full growth and is ripe, this covering you know splits open, and the nuts drop out, and then any body can get them and eat them.'

The boys were then all satisfied that it was better that chesnuts should grow in burrs.

'But why,' asked one of the boys, 'do not apples grow so?'

'Can any body answer that question,' asked the master.

The boy with the green satchel, said that apples had a smooth, tight skin, which kept out the wet, but he did not see how they were guarded from animals.

The master said it was by their taste. 'They are hard and sour before they are full grown, and so the taste is not pleasant, and nobody wants to eat them,—except sometimes a few foolish boys, and these are punished by being made ill. When the apples are full grown, then they change from sour to sweet, and become mellow; then they can be eaten. Can you tell me of any other fruits which are preserved in this way?'

One boy answered, 'strawberries and blackberries,' and another said, 'peaches and pears.'

Another boy asked why the peach-stone was not outside the peach, so as to keep it from being eaten. But the master said he would explain this another time. Then he dismissed the scholars, after asking Roger to wait until the rest had gone, as he wished to see him alone.

11. The Series of Writing Lessons. (C.[1]) Very many pupils soon become weary of the dull and monotonous business of writing, unless some plans are devised, to give interest and variety to the exercise; and on this account, this branch of education, in which improvement may be most rapid, is often the last, and most tedious to be acquired.

A teacher, by adopting the following plan, succeeded in awakening a great degree of interest in the subject, and consequently, of promoting rapid improvement. The plan was this; he prepared, on a large sheet of paper, a series of lessons in coarse hand, beginning with straight lines, and proceeding to the elementary parts of the various letters, and finally to the letters themselves. This paper was posted up in a part of the room accessible to all.

'The writing-books were made of three sheets of foolscap paper, folded into a convenient size, which was to be ruled by each pupil; for it was thought important that each one should learn this art. Every pupil in school then, being furnished with one of these writing books, was required to commence this series, and to practise each lesson until he could write it well; then, and not till then, he was permitted to pass to the next. A few brief directions were given under each lesson, on the large sheet. For example, under the line of straight marks, which constituted the first lesson, was written as follows,

Straight, equidistant, parallel, smooth, well terminated.

These directions were to call the attention of the pupil to the excellences which he must aim at, and

---

[1] The articles to which this letter is prefixed, were communicated for this work, by different teachers, at the request of the author.

when he supposed he had secured them, his book was to be presented to the teacher for examination. If approved the word *Passed*, or afterwards simply *P.* was written under the line, and he could then proceed to the next lesson. Other requisites were necessary, besides the correct formation of the letters, to enable one to pass; for example, the page must not be soiled or blotted, no paper must be wasted, and, in no case, a leaf torn out. As soon as *one line* was written in the manner required, the scholar was allowed to pass; in a majority of cases, however, not less than a page would be practised, and in many instances a sheet would be covered, before one line could be produced which would be approved.

One peculiar excellence of this method was, that although the whole school were working under a regular and systematic plan, individuals could go on independently; that is, the progress of no scholar was retarded by that of his companion; the one more advanced, might easily pass the earlier lessons in few days, while the others would require weeks of practice to acquire the same degree of skill.

During the writing hour, the scholars would practise, each at the lesson where he left off before, and at a particular time each day, the books were brought from the regular place of deposit, and laid before the teacher for examination. Without some arrangement for an examination of all the books together, the teacher would be liable to interruption at any time, from individual questions and requests, which would consume much time, and benefit only a few.

When a page of writing could not pass, a brief remark, calling the attention of the pupil to the faults which prevented it, was sometimes made in pencil at the bottom of the page. In other cases, the fault was of such a character as to require full and minute oral directions to the pupil. At last, to facilitate the criticism of the writing, a set of arbitrary marks, indicative of the various faults was devised, and applied, as occasion might require, to the writing books, by means of red ink.

These marks, which were very simple in their character, were easily remembered, for there was generally some connexion between the sign and the thing signified. For example, the mark denoting that letters were too short, was simply lengthening them in red ink. A faulty curve was denoted, by making a new curve over the old one, &c. The following are the principal criticisms and directions for which marks were contrived.

Strokes rough.	Too tall, or too short.
Curve wrong.	Stems not straight.
Bad termination.	Careless work.
Too slanting, and the reverse.	Paper wasted.
Too broad, and the reverse.	Almost well enough to pass.
Not parallel.	Bring your book to the teacher.
Form of the letter bad.	Former fault not corrected.
Large stroke made too fine, and the reverse.	

A catalogue of these marks, with an explanation, was made out and placed where it was accessible to all, and by means of them the books could be very easily and rapidly, but thoroughly criticised.

After the plan had gone on for some time, and its operation was fully understood, the teacher gave up the business of examining the books into the hands of a committee, appointed by him, from among the older and more advanced pupils. That the committee might be unbiassed in their judgment, they were required to examine, and decide upon the books, without knowing the names of the writers. Each scholar was indeed required to place her name on the right hand upper corner of every page of her writing-book, for the convenience of the distributors; but this corner was turned down when the book was brought in, that it might not be seen by the committee.

This committee were intrusted with plenary powers, and there was no appeal from their decision. In case they exercised their authority in an improper way, or failed on any account to give satisfaction, they were liable to impeachment, but while they continued in office, they were to be strictly obeyed.

This plan went on successfully for three months, and with very little diminution of interest. The whole school went regularly through the lessons in coarse hand, and afterwards through a similar series in fine hand, and improvement in this branch was thought to be greater than at any former period in the same length of time.

The same principle of arranging the several steps of an art or a study into a series of lessons, and requiring the pupil to pass regularly from one to the other, might easily be applied to other studies, and would afford a pleasant variety.

12. THE CORRESPONDENCE. A master of a district school was walking through the room, with a large rule in his hands, and as he came up behind two small boys, he observed that they were playing with some papers. He struck them once or twice, though not very severely on the head with the rule which he had in his hand. Tears started from the eyes of one. They were called forth by a mingled feeling of grief, mortification, and pain. The other who was of 'sterner stuff,' looked steadily into the master's face, and when his back

was turned, shook his fist at him, and laughed in defiance.

Another teacher seeing a similar case, did nothing. The boys when they saw him, hastily gathered up their playthings and put them away. An hour or two after, a little boy who sat near the master, brought them a note addressed to them both. They opened it and read as follows:—

To Edward and John,

I observed, when I passed you to-day, from your concerned looks, and your hurried manner of putting something into your desk, that you were doing something that you knew was wrong. When you attempt to do any thing whatever, which conscience tells you is wrong, you only make yourself uneasy and anxious while you do it, and then you are forced to resort to concealment and deception, when you see me coming. You would be a great deal happier, if you would always be doing your duty, and then you would never be afraid.

Your affectionate teacher, ———————.

As the teacher was arranging his papers in his desk at the close of school, he found a small piece of paper neatly folded up in form of a note, and addressed to him. He read as follows:—

Dear Teacher,

We are very much obliged to you for writing us a note. We were making a paper box. We know it was wrong, and are determined not to do so any more. We hope you will forgive us.

Your pupils,
EDWARD,
JOHN.

Which of these teachers understood human nature best?

13. WEEKLY REPORTS. The plan described by the following article, which was furnished by a teacher for insertion here, was originally adopted, so far as I know, in a school on the Kennebec. I have adopted it with great advantage.

(C.) A teacher had one day been speaking to her scholars of certain cases of slight disorder in the school, which, she remarked, had been gradually creeping in, and which she thought, it devolved upon the scholars, by systematic efforts, to repress. She enumerated instances of disorder in the arrangement of the rooms, leaving the benches out of their places, throwing waste papers upon the floor, having the desk in disorder inside, spilling water upon the entry floor, disorderly deportment, such as too loud talking or laughing in recess, or in the intermission at noon, or when coming to school, and making unnecessary noise in going to, or returning from recitations.

'I have a plan to propose,' said the teacher, 'which I think may be the pleasantest way of promoting a reform in things of this kind. It is this. Let several of your number be chosen a committee, to prepare, statedly—perhaps as often as once a week,—a written report of the state of the school. The report might be read before the school at the close of each week. The committee might consist in the whole, of seven or eight, or even of eleven or twelve individuals who should take the whole business into their hands. This committee might appoint individuals of their number to write in turn each week. By this arrangement, it would not be known to the school generally who are the writers of any particular report, if the individuals wish to be anonymous. Two individuals might be appointed at the beginning of the week, who should feel it their business to observe particularly the course of things from day to day with reference to the report. Individuals not members of the committee, can render assistance by any suggestions they may present to this committee. These should, however, generally be made in writing.'

'Subjects for such a report will be found to suggest themselves very abundantly, though you may not perhaps think so at first. The committee may be empowered, not only to state the particulars in which things are going wrong; but the methods by which they may be made right. Let them present us with any suggestions they please. If we do not like them, we are not obliged to adopt them. For instance, it is generally the case whenever a recitation is attended in the corner yonder, that an end of one of the benches is put against the door, so as to occasion a serious interruption to the exercises when a person wishes to come in or go out. It would come within the province of the committee to attend to such a case as this, that is, to bring it up in the report. The remedy in such a case is a very simple one. Suppose, however, that instead of the *simple* remedy, our committee should propose that the classes reciting in the said corner should be dissolved, and the studies abolished. We should know the proposal was an absurd one; but then it would do no hurt—we should have only to reject it.'

'Again, besides our faults, let our committee notice the points in which we are doing particularly well, that we may be encouraged to go on doing well, or even to do better. If they think, for example, that we are deserving of credit for the neatness with which books are kept,—for their freedom from blots or scribblings, or dogs-ears, by which school-books are so commonly defaced, let them tell us so. And the same of any other excellence.'

With the plan as thus presented, the scholars were very much pleased. It was proposed by one individual, that such a committee should be appointed immediately, and a report prepared for the ensuing week. This was done. The committee were chosen by ballot. The following may be taken as a specimen of their reports.

WEEKLY REPORT.

'The committee appointed to write the weekly report have noticed several things which they think wrong. In the first place, there have been a greater number of tardy scholars during the past week than usual. Much of this tardiness we suppose is owing to the interest felt in building the bower; but we think this business ought to be attended to only in play hours. If only one or two come in late when we are reading in the morning, or after we have composed ourselves to study at the close of the recess, every scholar must look up from her book,—we do not say they ought to do so, but only that they will do so. However, we anticipate an improvement in this respect, as we know "a word to the wise is sufficient."

'In the two back rows we are sorry to say that we have noticed whispering. We know that this fact will very much distress our teacher, as she expects assistance, and not trouble from our older scholars. It is not our business to reprove any one's misconduct, but it is our duty to mention it, however disagreeable it may be. We think the younger scholars during the past week have much improved in this respect. Only three cases of whispering among them have occurred to our knowledge.

'We remember some remarks made a few weeks ago by our teacher, on the practice of prompting each other in the classes. We wish she would repeat them, for we fear that by some they are forgotten. In the class in Geography, particularly in the questions on the map we have noticed sly whispers, which we suppose were the hints of some kind friend designed to refresh the memory of her less attentive companion. We propose that the following question be now put to vote. Shall the practice of prompting in the classes be any longer continued?

'We would propose that we have a composition exercise *this* week similar to the one on Thursday last. It was very interesting, and we think all would be willing to try their thinking powers once more. We would propose also that the readers of the Compositions should sit near the centre of the room, as last week many fine sentences escaped the ears of those seated in the remote corners.

'We were requested by a very public-spirited individual to mention once more the want of three nails for bonnets in the entry. Also, to say that the air from the broken pane of glass on the east side of the room, is very unpleasant to those who sit near.

'Proposed that the girls who exhibited so much taste and ingenuity in the arrangement of the festoons of evergreen, and tumblers of flowers around the teacher's desk, be now requested to remove the faded roses and drooping violets. We have gazed on these sad emblems long enough.

'Finally, proposed that greater care be taken by those who stay at noon, to place their dinner baskets in proper places. The contents of more than one were partly strewed upon the entry floor this morning.'

If such a measure as this is adopted, it should not be continued uninterrupted for a very long time. Every thing of this sort should be occasionally changed, or it sooner or later becomes only a form.

14. THE SHOPPING EXERCISE. (C.) I have often when going a shopping found difficulty and trouble in reckoning change. I could never calculate very readily, and in the hurry and perplexity of the moment, I was always making mistakes. I have heard others often make the same complaint, and I resolved to try the experiment of regularly teaching children to make change. I had a bright little class in arithmetic, who were always ready to engage with interest in any thing new, and to them I proposed my plan. It was to be called the Shopping Exercise. I first requested each individual to write something upon her slate which she would like to buy if she was going a shopping, stating the quantity she wished, and the price of it. To make the first lesson as simple as possible, I requested no one to go above ten, either in the quantity or price. When all were ready, I called upon some one to read what she had written. Her next neighbour was then requested to tell us how much the purchase would amount to; then the first one named a bill, which she supposed to be offered in payment; and the second showed what change was needed. A short specimen of the exercise will probably make it clearer than mere description.

MARY. Eight ounces of candy at seven cents.
SUSAN. Fifty-six cents.
MARY. One dollar.
SUSAN. Forty-four cents.

SUSAN. Nine yards of lace at eight cents.
ANNA. Seventy-two cents.
SUSAN. Two dollars.
ANNA. One dollar and twenty-eight cents.

ANNA. Three pieces of tape at five cents.
JANE. Fifteen cents.
ANNA. Three dollars.
JANE. Eighty-five cents.
SEVERAL VOICES. Wrong.
JANE. Two dollars and eighty-five cents.

JANE. Six pictures at eight cents.
SARAH. Forty-two cents.
SEVERAL VOICES. Wrong.
SARAH. Forty-eight cents.
JANE. One dollar.
SARAH. Sixty two cents.
SEVERAL VOICES. Wrong.
SARAH. Fifty-two cents.

It will be perceived that the same individual who names the article and the price, names also the bill which she would give in payment, and the one who sits next her, who calculated the amount, calculated also the change to be returned. She then proposed *her* example to the one next in the line, with whom the same course was pursued, and thus it passed down the class.

The exercise went on for some time in this way, till the pupils had become so familiar with it, that I thought it best to allow them to take higher numbers: They were always interested in it, and made great improvement in a short time, and I myself derived great advantage from listening to them.

There is one more circumstance I will add, which may contribute to the interest of this account. While the class were confined in what they purchased to the number ten, they were sometimes inclined to turn the exercise into a frolic. The variety of articles which they could find costing less than ten cents was so small, that for the sake of getting something new, they would propose examples really ludicrous, such as these. Three meeting-houses at two cents. Four pianos at nine cents. But I soon found, that if I allowed this at all, their attention was diverted from the main object, and occupied in seeking the most diverting and curious examples.

15. ARTIFICES IN RECITATIONS. (C.) The teacher of a small, newly established school, had all his scholars classed together in some of their studies. At recitations he usually sat in the middle of the room, while the scholars occupied the usual places at their desks, which were arranged around the sides. In the recitation in Rhetorick, the teacher after a time observed, that one or two of the class seldom answered appropriately the questions which came to them; but yet, were always ready with some kind of answer—generally an exact quotation of the words of the book. Upon noticing these individuals more particularly, he was convinced that their books were open before them in some concealed situation. Another practice not uncommon in the class, was that of *prompting* each other, either by whispers or writing. The teacher took no notice publicly of these practices for some time, until at the close of an uncommonly good recitation, he remarked, ' Well, I think we have had a fine recitation to-day. It is one of the pleasantest things I ever do to hear a lesson that is learned as well as this. Do you think it would be possible for us to have as good an exercise every day?' ' Yes, sir,' answered several faintly. ' Do you think it would be reasonable for me to expect of every member of the class, that she should always be able to recite all her lessons without ever missing a single question?' ' No, sir,' answered all. ' I do not expect it' said the teacher. All I wish is, that each of you should be faithful in your efforts to prepare your lessons. I wish you to study from a sense of duty, and for the sake of your

own improvement. You know I do not punish you for failures. I have no going up or down, no system of marking. Your only reward when you have made faithful preparation for a recitation, is the feeling of satisfaction which you will always experience; and when you have been negligent, your only punishment is a sort of uneasy feeling of self-reproach. I do not expect you all to be invariably prepared with every question of your lessons. Sometimes you will be unavoidably prevented from studying them, and at other times when you have studied them very carefully, you may have forgotten, or you may fail from some misapprehension of the meaning in some cases. Do not in a such a case feel troubled, because you may not have appeared as well as some individual who has not been half as faithful as yourself. If you have done your duty, that is enough. On the other hand, you ought to feel no better satisfied with yourselves when your lesson has not been studied well, because you may have happened to know the parts which came to you. Have I *done* well? should always be the question: not have I managed to *appear* well?'

'I will say a word here,' continued the teacher, 'upon a practice which I have known to be very common in some schools, and which I have been sorry to notice occasionally in this. I mean that of prompting, or helping each other along in some way at recitations. Now, where a severe punishment is the consequence of a failure, there might seem to be some reasonableness in helping your companions out of difficulty, though even then such tricks are departures from honourable dealing. But especially when there is no purpose to be served but that of appearing to know more than you do, it certainly must be considered a very mean kind of artifice. I think I have sometimes observed an individual to be prompted, where evidently the assistance was not desired, and even where it was not needed. To whisper to an individual the answer to a question, is sometimes to pay her rather a poor compliment at least; for it is the same as saying, 'I am a better scholar than you are; let me help you along a little.'

'Let us then hereafter, have only fair, open, honest dealings with each other, no attempts to appear to advantage by little artful manœuvering; no prompting, no peeping into books. Be faithful and conscientious, and then banish anxiety for your success. Do you not think you shall find this the pleasantest course? ' Yes, sir,' answered every scholar. ' Are you willing to pledge yourselves to adopt it?' ' Yes, sir.' ' Those who are, may raise their hands,' said the teacher. Every hand was raised, and the pledge, there was evidence to believe, was honourably sustained.

16. KEEPING RESOLUTIONS. The following are notes of a familiar lecture on this subject, given by a teacher at some general exercise in the school. The practice of thus reducing to writing what the teacher may say on such subjects will be attended with excellent effects.

This is a subject upon which young persons find much difficulty. The question is asked a thousand times, ' How shall I ever learn to keep my resolutions?' Perhaps the great cause of your failure is this. You are not sufficiently *definite* in forming your purposes. You will resolve to do a thing, without knowing with certainty whether it is even possible to do it. Again, you make resolutions which are to run on indefinitely, so that of course, they can never be fully kept. For instance, one of you will resolve to *rise earlier in the morning*. You fix upon no definite hour, on any definite number of mornings, only you are going to '*rise earlier*.' Morning comes and finds you sleepy and disinclined to rise. You remember your resolution of rising earlier. 'But then it is *very* early,' you say. You resolved to rise earlier, but you didn't resolve to rise just then. And this, it may be, is the last of your resolution. Or, perhaps you are, for a few mornings, a little earlier; but then at the end of a week or fortnight, you do not know exactly, whether your resolution has been broken or kept, for you had not decided whether to rise earlier for ten days, or for ten years.

In the same vague and general manner, a person will resolve to be *more studious,* or more diligent. In the case of an individual, of a mature and well-disciplined mind, of acquired firmness of character, such a resolution might have effect. The individual will really devote more time and attention to his pursuits. But, for one of you to make such a resolution, would do no sort of good. It would only be a source of trouble and disquiet. You perceive there is nothing definite, nothing fixed about it. You have not decided what amount of additional time or attention to give to your studies, or, when you will begin, or when you will end. There is no one time when you will feel that you are breaking your resolution, because there were no particular times when you were to study more. You waste one opportunity and another, and then, with a feeling of discouragement, and self-reproach, conclude to abandon your resolution. 'Oh! it does no good to make resolutions,' you say, ' I never shall keep them.'

Now, if you would have the business of making resolutions a pleasant and interesting, instead of a discouraging, disquieting one, you must proceed in a different manner. Be definite, and distinct in your plan,—decide exactly what you will do, and how you will do it—when you will begin, and when you will end. Instead of resolving to 'rise earlier,' resolve to rise at the ringing of the sun-rise bells, or at some other definite time. Resolve to try this, as an experiment for one morning, or for one week, or fortnight. Decide positively, if you decide at all, and then, rise when the time comes, sleepy or not sleepy. Do not stop to repent of your resolution, or to consider the wisdom or folly of it, when the time for acting under it has once arrived.

In all cases, little and great, make this a principle,—to consider well before you begin to act, but after you have begun to act, never stop to consider. Resolve as deliberately as you please, but be sure to keep your resolution, whether a wise one or an unwise one, after it is once made. Never allow yourself to re-consider the question of getting up, after the morning has come, except it be, for some unforeseen circumstance. Get up for that time, and be more careful how you make resolutions again.

17. TOPICS. (C.) The plan of the Topic Exercise, as we called it, is this. Six or seven topics are given out, information upon which is to be obtained from any source, and communicated verbally before the whole school, or sometimes before a class formed for this purpose, the next day. The subjects are proposed both by teacher and scholars, and if approved, adopted. The exercise is intended to be voluntary, but ought to be

managed in a way sufficiently interesting to induce all to join.

At the commencement of the exercise, the teacher calls upon all who have any information in regard to the topic assigned, suppose, for example, it is *Alabaster*, to rise. Perhaps twenty individuals out of forty rise. The teacher may, perhaps, say to those in their seats,

'Do you not know anything of this subject? Have you neither seen nor heard of alabaster, and had no means of ascertaining anything in regard to it? If you have, you ought to rise. It is not necessary that you should state a fact altogether new and unheard of, but if you tell me its colour, or some of the uses to which it is applied, you will be complying with my request.'

After these remarks, perhaps a few more rise, and possibly the whole school. Individuals are then called upon at random, each to state only one particular in regard to the topic in question. This arrangement is made so as to give all an opportunity to speak. If any scholar, after having mentioned one fact, has something still farther to communicate, she remains standing till called upon again. As soon as an individual has exhausted her stock of information, or if the facts, that she intended to mention, are stated by another, she takes her seat.

The topics at first most usually selected, are the common objects by which we are surrounded; for example, glass, iron, mahogany, &c. The list will gradually extend itself, until it will embrace a large number of subjects.

The object of this exercise is to induce pupils to seek for general information in an easy and pleasant manner, as by the perusal of books, newspapers, periodicals, and conversation with friends. It induces care and attention in reading, and discrimination in selecting the most useful and important facts from the mass of information. As individuals are called upon, also, to express their ideas *verbally*, they soon acquire by practice, the power of expressing their ideas with clearness and force, and communicating with ease and confidence, the knowledge they possess.

18. MUSIC. (C.) The girls of our school often amused themselves in recess by collecting into little groups for singing. As there seemed to be a sufficient power of voice and a respectable number who were willing to join in the performance, it was proposed one day, that singing should be introduced as a part of the devotional exercises of the school.

The first attempt nearly resulted in a failure; only a few trembling voices succeeded in singing Old Hundredth to the words, ' Be thou,' &c. On the second day, Peterborough was sung with much greater confidence on the part of the increased number of singers. The experiment was tried with greater and greater success for several days, when the teacher proposed that a systematic plan should be formed, by which there might be singing regularly at the close of school. It was then proposed that a number of singing books be obtained, and one of the scholars, who was well acquainted with common tunes, be appointed as chorister. Her duty should be, to decide what particular tune may be sung each day, inform the teacher of the metre of the hymn, and take the lead in the exercise. This plan being approved of by the scholars, was adopted, and put into immediate execution. Several brought copies of the Sabbath School Hymn Book which they had in their possession, and the plan succeeded beyond all expectation. The greatest difficulty in the way was to get some one to lead. The chorister, however, was somewhat relieved from the embarrassment which she would naturally feel in making a beginning, by the appointment of one or two individuals with herself, who were to act as her assistants. These constituted the *leading* committee, or as it was afterwards termed, Singing Committee.

Singing now became a regular and interesting exercise of the school, and the committee succeeded in managing the business themselves.

19. TABU. (C.) An article was one day read in a school relating to the 'Tabu' of the Sandwich Islanders. Tabu is a term with them, which signifies consecrated, —not to be touched—to be let alone—not to be violated. Thus according to their religious observances, a certain day will be proclaimed *Tabu*, that is, one upon which there is to be no work, or no going out.

A few days after this article was read, the scholars observed one morning, a flower stuck up in a conspicuous place against the wall, with the word TABU in large characters above it. This excited considerable curiosity. The teacher informed them, in explanation, that the flower was a very rare and beautiful specimen brought by one of the scholars, which he wished all to examine. 'You would naturally feel a disposition to examine it by the touch;' said he, 'but you will all see, that by the time it was touched by sixty individuals, it would be likely to be injured, if not destroyed. So I concluded to label it *Tabu*. And it has occurred to me that this will be a convenient mode of apprizing you generally, that any article had better not be handled. You know we sometimes have some apparatus exposed, which would be liable to injury from disturbance, where there are so many persons to touch it. I shall in such a case, just mention that an article is Tabu, and you will understand that it is not only not to be *injured*, but not even *touched*.'

A little delicate management of this sort, will often have more influence over young persons, than the most vehement scolding, or the most watchful and jealous precautions. The Tabu was always most scrupulously regarded, after this, whenever employed.

20. MENTAL ANALYSIS. Scene; a class in Arithmetic at recitation. The teacher gives them an example in addition, requesting them when they have performed it to rise. Some finish it very soon, others are very slow in accomplishing the work.

'I should like to ascertain,' says the teacher, 'how great is the difference of rapidity, with which different members of the class work in addition. I will give you another example, and then notice by my watch, the shortest and longest time required to do it.'

The result of the experiment was, that some members of the class were two or three times as long in doing it, as others.

'Perhaps you think,' said the teacher, 'that this difference is altogether owing to difference of skill, but it is not. It is mainly owing to the different methods adopted by various individuals. I am going to describe some of these, and as I describe them, I wish you would notice them carefully, and tell me which you practise.

There are then three modes of adding up a column of figures, which I shall describe.

1. 'I shall call the first *counting*. You take the first figure, and then add the next to it, by counting up regularly. There are three distinct ways of doing this.

(a.) Counting by your fingers. (' Yes, sir.') You take the first figure,—suppose it is seven, and the one above it, eight. Now you recollect that to add eight, you must count all the fingers of one hand, and all but two again. So you say seven—eight, nine, ten, eleven, twelve, thirteen, fourteen, fifteen.'

' Yes, sir.' ' Yes, sir,' said the scholars.

(b.) ' The next mode of counting is to do it mentally, without using your fingers at all, but as it is necessary for you to have some plan to secure your adding the right number, you divide the units into sets of two each. Thus you remember that eight consists of four twos and you accordingly say, when adding eight to seven, ' Seven;—eight, nine;—ten, eleven;—twelve, thirteen,' &c.

(c.) The third mode is, to add by threes, in the same way. You recollect that eight consists of two threes and a two; so you say, seven;—eight, nine, ten;—eleven, twelve, thirteen;—fourteen, fifteen.'

The teacher here stops to ascertain how many of the class are accustomed to add in either of these modes. It is a majority.

2. ' The next general method is *calculating*. That is, you do not unite one number to another by the dull and tedious method of applying the units, one by one, as in the ways described under the preceding head, but you come to a result more rapidly by some mode of calculating. These modes are several.

(a.) Doubling a number, and then adding or subtracting as the case may require. For instance in the example already specified; in order to add seven and eight, you say, ' Twice seven are fourteen and one are fifteen,' (' Yes, sir.' ' Yes, sir,') or ' Twice eight are sixteen, and taking one off, leaves fifteen. (' Yes, sir.')

(b.) Another way of calculating is to skip about the column, adding those numbers which you can do most easily, and then bringing in the rest as you best can.

Thus, if you see three eights in one column, you say three times eight are twenty four, and then you try to bring in the other numbers. Often in such cases, you forget what you have added and what you have not, and get confused: ('Yes, sir,') or you omit something in your work, and consequently it is incorrect.

(c.) If nines occur, you sometimes add ten, and then take off one, for it is very easy to add ten.

(d.) Another method of calculating, which is, however, not very common, is this. To take our old case, adding eight to seven, you take as much from the eight to add to the seven as will be sufficient to make ten, and then it will be easy to add the rest. Thus you think in a minute, that three from the eight will make the seven a ten, and then there will be five more to add, which will make fifteen. If the next number was seven, you would say five of it make twenty, and then there will be two left, which will make twenty-two. This mode, though it may seem more intricate than any of the others, is in fact more rapid than any of them, when one is a little accustomed to it.

These are the four principal modes of calculating which occur to me. Pupils do not generally practise any one of them exclusively, but occasionally resort to each, according to the circumstances of the particular case.'

The teacher here stopped to inquire how many of the class were accustomed to add by calculating in either of these ways, or in any simpler ways.

3. 'There is one more mode which I shall describe: it is by *Memory*. Before I explain this mode I wish to ask you some questions which I should like to have you answer as quick as you can.

How much is four times five?—Four *and* five?

How much is seven times nine?—Seven *and* nine?

Eight times six ?—Eight *and* six ?
Nine times seven ?—Nine *and* seven ?'

After asking a few questions of this kind, it was perceived that the pupils could tell much more readily what was the result when the numbers were to be multiplied, than when they were to be added.

'The reason is,' said the teacher, 'because you committed the multiplication table to memory, and have not learned the addition table. Now many persons have committed the addition table, so that it is perfectly familiar to them, and when they see any two numbers, the amount which is produced when they are added together, comes to mind in an instant. Adding in this way is the last of the three modes I was to describe.

Now of these three methods, the last is undoubtedly the best. If you once commit to memory the addition table thoroughly, you have it fixed for life,—whereas if you do not, you have to make the calculation over again every time, and thus lose a vast amount of labour. I have no doubt that there are some in this class, who are in the habit of *counting*, who have ascertained that seven and eight for instance, make fifteen, by counting up from seven to fifteen, *hundreds of times*. Now how much better it would be, to spend a little time in fixing the fact in the mind once for all, and then when you come to the case, seven and eight are——say at once 'Fifteen,'—instead of mumbling over and over again, hundreds of times, 'Seven, eight, nine, ten, eleven, twelve, thirteen, fourteen, fifteen.'

The reason then, that some of the class add so slowly, is not probably because they want skill and rapidity of execution, but because they work to a great disadvantage, by working in the wrong way. I have often been surprised at the dexterity and speed, with which some scholars can count with their fingers, when adding, and yet they could not get through the sum very quick—at least they would have done it in half the time, if the same effort had been made in travelling a shorter road. We will therefore study the addition table now, in the class, before we go on any farther.'

The foregoing narratives, it is hoped, may induce some of the readers of this book to keep journals of their own experiments, and of the incidents which may, from time to time come under their notice, illustrating the principles of education, or simply the characteristics and tendencies of the youthful mind. The business of teaching will excite interest and afford pleasure, just in proportion to the degree in which it is conducted by operations of mind upon mind, and the means of making it most fully so, are, careful practice, based upon, and regulated by, the results of careful observation. Every teacher then should make observations and experiments upon mind, a part of his daily duty, and nothing will more facilitate this, than keeping a record of results. There can be no opportunity for studying human nature, more favourable than the teacher enjoys. The materials are all before him; his very business, from day to day, brings him to act directly upon them; and the study of the powers and tendencies of the human mind is not only the most interesting and the noblest that can engage human attention, but every step of progress he makes in it, imparts an interest and charm, to what would otherwise be a weary toil. It at once relieves his labours, while it doubles their efficiency and success.

APPENDIX.

(A.) Page 157.

The following articles, which were really offered for such a purpose, will serve as specimens. One or two were written by teachers. I do not know the authors of the others. I do not offer them as remarkable compositions: every teacher will see that they are not so. The design of inserting them is merely to shew that the ordinary literary ability, to be found in every school, may be turned to useful account, by simply opening a channel for it, and to furnish such teachers as may be inclined to try the experiment, the means of making the plan clearly understood by their pupils.

MARKS OF A BAD SCHOLAR.

At the time when she should be ready to take her seat at school, she commences preparation for leaving home. To the extreme annoyance of those about her, all is now hurry and bustle, and ill-humour. Thorough search is to be made for every book or paper, for which she has occasion; some are found in one place, some in another, and others are forgotten altogether. Being finally equipped, she casts her eye at the clock, hopes to be in tolerable good season, (notwithstanding that the hour for opening the school has already arrived,) and sets out in the most violent hurry.

After so much haste, she is unfitted for attending properly to the duties of the school, until a considerable time after her arrival. If present at the devotional exercises, she finds it difficult to command her attention, even when desirous of so doing, and her deportment at this hour, is accordingly marked with an unbecoming listlessness and abstraction.

When called to recitations, she recollects that some task was assigned, which till that moment, she had forgotten; of others she had mistaken the extent, most commonly thinking them to be shorter than her companions suppose. In her answers to questions with which she should be familiar, she always manifests more or less of hesitation, and what she ventures to express, is very commonly in the form of a question. In these, as in all exercises, there is an inattention to general instructions. Unless what is said be addressed particularly to herself, her eyes are directed towards another part of the room; it may be, her thoughts are employed about something not at all connected with the school. If reproved by her teacher for negligence in any respects, she is generally provided with an abundance of excuses, and however mild the reproof, she receives it as a piece of extreme severity.

Throughout her whole deportment there is an air of indolence, and a want of interest in those exercises which should engage her attention. In her seat, she most commonly sits in some lazy posture—either with her elbows upon her desk, her head leaning upon her hands, or with her seat tipt forwards or backwards. When she has occasion to leave her seat, it is a sauntering, lingering gait, perhaps some trick is contrived on the way, for exciting the mirth of her companions.

About every thing in which it is possible to be so, she is untidy. Her books are carelessly used, and placed in her desk without order. If she has a piece of waste paper to dispose of, she finds it much more convenient to tear it into small pieces, and scatter it about her desk, than to put it in a proper place. Her hands and clothes are usually covered with ink. Her written exercises are blotted, and full of mistakes.'

THE CONSEQUENCES OF BEING BEHINDHAND.

' The following incident, which I witnessed on a late journey, illustrates an important principle, and I will relate it.

' When our steamboat started from the wharf, all our passengers had not come. After we had proceeded a few yards, there appeared among the crowd on the wharf a man with his trunk under his arm—out of breath—and with a most disappointed and disconsolate air. The captain determined to stop for him, but stopping an immense steamboat moving swiftly through the water, is not to be done in a moment. So we took a grand sweep, wheeling majestically around an English ship, which was at anchor in the harbour. As we came towards the wharf again, we saw the man in a small boat coming off from it. As the steam boat swept round, they barely succeeded in catching a rope from the stern, and then immediately the steam engine began its work again, and we pressed forward—the little boat following us so swiftly, that the water around her was all in a foam.

They pulled down the rope attached to the little boat,

until they drew it alongside. They then let down a rope with a hook in the end of it, from an iron crane, which projected over the side of the steamboat, and hooked it into a staple in the front of the small boat, '*Hoist away*, said the captain. The sailors hoisted, and the front part of the little boat began to rise, the stern still ploughing and foaming through the water, and the man still in it, with his trunk under his arm. They 'hoisted away,' until I began to think that the poor man would actually tumble out behind. He clung to the seat, and looked as though he was saying to himself, 'I will take care how I am tardy the next time.' However, after a while, they hoisted up the stern of the boat, and he got safely on board.

MORAL. Though coming to school a few minutes earlier or later, may not in itself be a matter of much consequence, yet the habit of being five minutes too late, if once formed, will, in actual life, be a source of great inconvenience, and sometimes of lasting injury.'

NEW SCHOLARS.

'There is, at ——, a young ladies' school, taught by Mr. ——.'

* * * * * * *

But with all these excellences, there is one fault, which I considered a great one, and which does not comport with the general character of the school for kindness and good feeling. It is the little effort made by the scholars to become acquainted with the new ones who enter. Whoever goes there,. must push herself forward, or she will never feel at home. The young ladies seem to forget, that the new comer must feel rather unpleasantly, in the midst of a hundred persons, to whom she is wholly a stranger, and with no one to speak to. Two or three will stand together, and instead of deciding upon some plan, by which the individual may be made to feel at ease, something like the following conversation takes place.

Miss X. How do you like the looks of Miss A. who entered school to-day?

Miss Y. I don't think she is very pretty, but she looks as if she might be a good scholar.

Miss X. She does not strike me very pleasantly; did you ever see such a face? and her complexion is so dark, I should think she had always lived in the open air; and what a queer voice she has!

Miss Y. I wonder if she has a taste for arithmetic?

Miss X. She does not look as if she had much taste for any thing; see, how strangely she fixes her hair.

Miss S. Whether she has much taste or not, some one of us ought to go and get acquainted with her. See how unpleasantly she feels.

Miss X. I don't want to get acquainted with her until I know whether I shall like her or not.

Thus nothing is done to relieve her. When she does become acquainted, all her first strange appearance is forgotten; but this is sometimes not the case for several weeks. It depends entirely on the character of the individual herself. If she is forward, and willing to make the necessary effort, she can find many friends: but if she is diffident, she has much to suffer. This arises principally from thoughtlessness. The young ladies do not seem to realize that there is any thing for them to do. They feel enough at home themselves, and the remembrance of the time when they entered school, does not seem to arise in their minds.'

A SATIRICAL SPIRIT.

'I witnessed a short time since, a meeting between two friends, who had had but little intercourse before for a long while. I thought a part of their conversation might be useful, and I shall, therefore, relate it, as nearly as I can recollect, leaving each individual to draw her own inferences.

'For some time, I sat silent but not uninterested, while the days of "Auld Lang Syne' came up to the remembrance of the two friends. After speaking of several individuals, who were among their former acquaintances, one asked, "Do you remember Miss W.?" "Yes," replied the former, "I remember her as the fear, terror, and abhorrence of all who knew her." *I* knew the lady by report, and asked why she was so regarded, the reply was, "Because she was so severe, so satirical in her remarks upon others. She spared neither friend or foe."

'The friends resumed their conversation, "Did you know," said the one who had first spoken of Miss W. "that she sometimes had seasons of bitter repentance for indulging in this unhappy propensity of hers? She would, at such times, resolve to be more on her guard, but after all her good resolutions, she would yield to the slightest temptations. When she was expressing, and apparently really *feeling* sorrow for having wounded the feelings of others, those who knew her, would not venture to express any sympathy, for very likely, the next moment, *that* would be turned into ridicule. No confidence could be placed in her.

'A few more facts will be stated respecting the same individual, which I believe are strictly true. Miss W.

possessed a fine and well-cultivated mind, great penetration, and a tact at discriminating character, rarely equalled. She could, if she chose, impart a charm to her conversation, that would interest, and even fascinate those who listened to it; still she was not beloved. Weaknesses and foibles met with unmerciful severity; and well-meaning intentions and kind actions did not always escape without the keen sarcasm, which it is so difficult for the best-regulated mind to bear unmoved. The mild and gentle seemed to shrink from her, and thus she, who might have been the bright and beloved ornament of the circle in which she moved, was regarded with distrust, fear, and even hatred. This dangerous habit of making satirical remarks, was evinced in childhood; it was cherished; 'it grew with her growth, and strengthened with her strength,' until she became what I have described.'

LAURA.'

Though such a satirical spirit is justly condemned, a little good-humoured raillery may sometimes be allowed, as a mode of attacking faults in school, which cannot be reached by graver methods. The teacher must not be surprised, if some things connected with his own administration, come in sometimes for a share.

VARIETY.

'I was walking out, a few days since, and not being particularly in haste, I concluded to visit a certain school for an hour or two. In a few minutes after I had seated myself on the sofa, the '*Study Card,*' was dropped, and the general noise and confusion, indicated that recess had arrived. A line of military characters, bearing the title of the 'Freedom's Band,' was soon called out, headed by one of their own number. The tune chosen to guide them was 'Kendall's March.'

" 'Please to form a regular line,' said the lady commander. 'Remember that there is to be no speaking in the ranks. Do not begin to step, until I strike the bell. Miss B. I requested you not to step until I gave the signal.'

" Presently the command was given, and the whole line *stepped*, for a few minutes, to all intents and purposes. Again the bell sounded;—' Some of you have lost the step,' said the general. Look at me, and begin again. Left! Right! Left! Right!' The line was once more in order, and I observed a new army on the opposite side of the room, performing the same manœuvres, always to the tune of 'Kendall's March.' After a time, the recess closed, and order was again restored. In about half an hour, I approached a class, which was reciting behind the railing. ' Miss A.' said a teacher, ' how many kinds of magnitude are there?' *Miss A.* (' Answer inaudible.') *Several voices.* ' We can't hear.' *Teacher.* ' Will you try to speak a little louder, Miss A.?'

' Some of the class at length seemed *to guess* the meaning of the young lady; but *I* was unable to do even that, until the answer was repeated by the teacher. Finding that I should derive little instruction from the recitation, I returned to the sofa.

' In a short time the *propositions* were read. ' Proposed that the committee be impeached, for not providing suitable pens.' ' Lost, a pencil, with a piece of India-rubber attached to it by a blue ribbon, &c. &c.

' Recess was again announced, and the lines commenced their evolutions to the tune of ' Kendall's

March.' Thought I, 'Oh! that there were a new tune under the sun.'

'Before the close of school, some compositions were read. One was entitled, 'The Magical Ring,' and commenced, ' As I was sitting alone last evening, I heard a gentle tap on the door, and immediately a beautiful fairy appeared before me. She placed a ring on my finger, and left me.' The next began, ' It is my week to write composition, but I do not know what to say. However, I must write something, so it shall be a dialogue.' Another was entitled, ' The Magical Shoe,' and contained a marvellous narration of adventures made in a pair of shoes, more valuable than the far-famed 'seven league boots.' A fourth began, ' Are you acquainted with that new scholar!' ' No; but I don't believe I shall like her.' And soon the ' Magical Thimble,' the ' Magical Eye-glass,' &c. were read, in succession, until I could not but exclaim, ' How pleasing is variety!' School was at length closed, and the young ladies again attacked the piano. ' Oh!' repeated I to myself, ' *how pleasing is variety!*' as I left the room, to the tune of Kendall's March.'

THE END.

BY THE REV. JACOB ABBOTT.

THE YOUNG CHRISTIAN; or, a Familiar Illustration of the Principles of Christian Duty. Revised, and an Introductory Essay prefixed, by the Rev. J. W. CUNNINGHAM, M.A. Vicar of Harrow. Third Edition, corrected. Price 5s. watered cloth, or 6s. embossed roan, with a Vignette by Stothard.

THE LITTLE PHILOSOPHER, for Schools and Families; designed to teach children to think and to reason about common things: and to illustrate to parents and teachers, methods of instructing and interesting children. With a COPIOUS INTRODUCTION, explaining fully the method of using the book. Price 1s. 6d. stiff covers, or 2s. half-bound.

LESSONS ON OBJECTS, as given to children between the ages of Six and Eight, in a Pestalozzian School at Cheam, Surrey. Fourth Edition. Price 3s. 6d boards.

PREPARATION FOR EUCLID as used in a Pestalozzian School, at Stanmore Middlesex. Price 3s. 6d.

LESSONS ON SHELLS, as given to children between the ages of Eight and Ten, in a Pestalozzian School at Cheam, Surrey. Illustrated by Ten Plates, drawn from Nature. Price 5s.

AIDS TO DEVELOPEMENT, or Mental or Moral Instruction exemplified, in Conversations between a Mother and her Children. Second Edition. 12mo. Price 9s.

A CHART OF ECCLESIASTICAL HISTORY, from the Christian Era to the present day. On the plan of the Stream of Time, but divided and measured by a scale of Population; showing, with all attainable correctness, the relative proportions in each age, of Christianity, both apostolic and corrupted, Romanism, Mahomedism, and Paganism; each Religion having a distinct colour. On a sheet of drawing paper. Price 7s. coloured; or mounted on rollers and varnished, 14s.

"There has lately been published a most useful Chart of Ecclesiastical History, on one large sheet, coloured. It is constructed somewhat upon the plan of the *Stream of Time*, with the difference, that the names and events inserted in it are for the most part connected with the interest of the Church of Christ; it indeed professes to comprise every fact of importance connected with Church History. We strongly recommend to our readers this ingenious and invaluable synopsis of sacred history, both for their own libraries and for the instruction and entertainment of the younger members of their families."—*Christian Observer, August* 1832.

PUBLISHED BY L. B. SEELEY AND SONS.

THE CHILD'S BOOK ON THE SOUL: with Questions adapted to the use of Sunday Schools, and of Infant Schools, By the Rev. T. H. GALLAUDET. Second Edition. 3s. 6d. half-bound.

In the first part of 'The Child's Book on the Soul,' the Author's object is to illustrate and enforce one simple truth, that the Child has a Soul, distinct from the body, which will survive it, and live for ever.

In the second part, the inquiry of the child, whither his soul will go, after his body is dead, and who will take care of it, is attempted to be answered.

"In composing this excellent series of lessons on the Soul, Mr. Gallaudet has paid the strictest attention to the admirable principles laid down in his preface. * * * The work consists of a number of conversations, between an intelligent mother and her little son, aged five years. Beginning with sensible objects, such as a pebble, a rose, a watch, an animal, and lastly, a human being: and calling in the aid of simple reason, the young learner is led in a most engaging manner, step by step, up this intellectual Jacob's ladder, to compare the qualities of different objects, until he arrives at the consideration of the highest matters and things incorporeal. After this natural and easy method, the child's mind is familiarized with some of the sublimest truths; becoming satisfied that he himself, in common with every human being, is gifted with a 'something within him, which thinks, and feels, and knows what is right and what is wrong,' and which in one word is called the SOUL. The dialogues are written in an admirably simple and luminous style; and the overwhelming idea of Eternity is impressed upon the mind by one of the happiest and most striking expedients we ever remember.........It was certainly a bold endeavour to reduce such a lofty subject as that of the Soul, to a level with the capacity of an infant. But Mr. Gallaudet has succeeded: and his work may be ranked as the first of a class of its own."
—SUNDAY SCHOOL TEACHER'S MAGAZINE. *October*.

MANNA LAID UP FOR THE SABBATH: or a Series of Religious Instructions for Sunday Schools, and a detailed method of conducting them. With a Preface by the Author of "the Last Day of the Week." 18mo. Third Edition. In Two Parts, 1s. 6d. each, sewed; or in one volume, 3s. 6d. half bound.
Part III. 1s. 3d. sewed.

A DICTIONARY of the most important Names, Objects, and Terms found in the Holy Scriptures; intended principally for Sabbath School Teachers and Bible Classes. By HOWARD MALCOM, M.A. 18mo. 3s. 6d. half-bound.

MISSIONARY STORIES, or Sketches of the most interesting portions of the labours of the United Brethren. 2s. 6d.

THE CHILD AT HOME. By the Rev. J. C. ABBOTT, Author of 'The Mother at Home.'
Part II. uniform with the above, in the Press.

THE HISTORY OF JONAH, for Children and Youth, designed also as an aid to Familiar Biblical Exposition, in Families, Sunday Schools, and Bible Classes. By the Rev. T. H. GALLAUDET, late Principal of the American Asylum for the Deaf and Dumb. With Engravings. Price 2s. 6d.

PUBLISHED BY L. B. SEELEY AND SONS.

The Christian Lady's Magazine.

Edited by CHARLOTTE ELIZABETH. Published Monthly. Price 1s.

THE COLLECTS of the Church of England explained, in the Form of a Catechism, chiefly for the Use of Children and Sunday Schools. By the Author of "Hymns for every Sunday in the Year." Price 6d.

THE 39 ARTICLES OF THE CHURCH OF ENGLAND. With Scripture Proofs. 6d. sewed: or on writing paper, with a large margin. 12mo. 1s. 6d.

WATTS' DIVINE and MORAL SONGS for the Use of Children. Price 2d.

MEMOIRS OF REFORMERS, British and Foreign. By the Rev. J. W. MIDDELTON, A. M. formerly of Trinity College, Oxford. Three Volumes. 18mo. 12s.

SERMONS prêchés dans l'Eglise Francois de Londres. Par CHARLES SCHOLL. 8vo. 8s.

THE CHURCH CATECHISM; Divided into Short Questions and Answers, with Scripture Proofs and Explanatory Notes. By the Rev. CHARLES BIRCH, Vicar of Happisburg, Norfolk. Price Eightpence sewed.

LITTLE MARY; or God in every thing. 3rd Edition. Price 6d.

AN HISTORICAL ATLAS; being a series of Maps of the World as known at different periods; constructed on the same scale, and coloured so as to exhibit the successive changes of empire. With a connected Narrative accompanying each Map, so as to afford a complete view of Universal History. By E. QUIN, M. A. of Magdalen Hall, Oxford. Imperial 4to. £3. 10s. half-bound. The maps by SIDNEY HALL.

MOTHER'S FRIEND. By the Editor of the WEEKLY VISITOR. Price 6s.

TWO ADDRESSES TO YOUNG PERSONS—one *before*, the other *after*, Confirmation. By the Rev. CHARLES BRIDGES, M.A. Vicar of Old Newton, Suffolk. Price 3d. each.

THE BREAD OF DECEIT; illustrated in the History of Maurice Chalmers. 2nd Edition. 18mo. Price 2s. 6d. half-bound.

PUBLISHED BY L. B. SEELEY AND SONS.

THE NURSERY MAGAZINE. Edited by Mrs. CAMERON. With Woodcuts. 4 Vols. price 3s. 6d. each, half-bound.

INFANT EMANCIPATION; or reading made easy. Second Edition. Price 9d.

A TREATISE ON LANGUAGES; their Origin, Structure, and Connexion; and on the best method of Learning and Teaching them. By the Rev. A. JENOUR. 12mo. 3s. 6d.

THE SCRIPTURE DIRECTORY; or, an Attempt to assist the Unlearned Reader to understand the General History and Leading Subjects of the Bible. By the Rev. THOMAS JONES, Vicar of Creaton. Seventh Edition. 12mo. 5s.

HYMNS ON THE COLLECTS; designed for the Use of Children and Sunday Schools. By the Author of " the Catechism on the Collects. Price 6d. sewed.

THE CHILDREN'S WEEKLY VISITOR; with Woodcuts. Three Volumes, 6s. each, cloth.